PETER SUTCLIFFE

This book is dedicated to all of the victims, and families of the victims of Peter Sutcliffe, whether they have been officially acknowledged or not. Bit by bit, the truth will come out.

PETER SUTCLIFFE

THE FULL CRIMES OF THE YORKSHIRE RIPPER

CHRIS COOK

First published in Great Britain in 2024 by
PEN AND SWORD TRUE CRIME
An imprint of
Pen & Sword Books Ltd
Yorkshire – Philadelphia

Copyright © Chris Cook, 2024

ISBN 978 1 03610 103 9

The right of Chris Cook to be identified as Author of this work has been asserted by her in accordance with the Copyright, Designs and Patents Act 1988.

A CIP catalogue record for this book is available from the British Library.

All rights reserved. No part of this book may be reproduced or transmitted in any form or by any means, electronic or mechanical including photocopying, recording or by any information storage and retrieval system, without permission from the Publisher in writing.

Typeset in Times New Roman 10/12 by SJmagic DESIGN SERVICES, India.
Printed and bound in the UK by CPI Group (UK) Ltd, Croydon, CR0 4YY.

Pen & Sword Books Limited incorporates the imprints of Atlas, Archaeology, Aviation, Discovery, Family History, Fiction, History, Maritime, Military, Military Classics, Politics, Select, Transport, True Crime, Air World, Frontline Publishing, Leo Cooper, Remember When, Seaforth Publishing, The Praetorian Press, Wharncliffe Local History, Wharncliffe Transport, Wharncliffe True Crime and White Owl.

For a complete list of Pen & Sword titles please contact
PEN & SWORD BOOKS LIMITED
George House, Units 12 & 13, Beevor Street, Off Pontefract Road,
Barnsley, South Yorkshire, S71 1HN, England
E-mail: enquiries@pen-and-sword.co.uk
Website: www.pen-and-sword.co.uk

or
PEN AND SWORD BOOKS
1950 Lawrence Rd, Havertown, PA 19083, USA
E-mail: uspen-and-sword@casematepublishers.com
Website: www.penandswordbooks.com

Contents

Foreword vii
Introduction viii
Acknowledgements ix

Chapter 1   Peter William Sutcliffe 1
Chapter 2   Sonia Szurma 10
Chapter 3   Gloria Wood 18
Chapter 4   Anna Rogulskyj 20
Chapter 5   Olive Smelt 23
Chapter 6   Tracy Browne 26
Chapter 7   Wilma McCann 31
Chapter 8   Rosemary Stead 38
Chapter 9   Emily Jackson 40
Chapter 10   Marcella Claxton 46
Chapter 11   Maureen Hogan 49
Chapter 12   Irene Richardson 50
Chapter 13   Debra Schlesinger 57
Chapter 14   Patricia Atkinson 59
Chapter 15   Jayne MacDonald 65
Chapter 16   Maureen Long 72
Chapter 17   Jean Jordan 78
Chapter 18   Carol Wilkinson 89
Chapter 19   Marilyn Moore 92
Chapter 20   Yvonne Pearson 98
Chapter 21   Helen Rytka 102
Chapter 22   The Letters 110
Chapter 23   Vera Millward 114

Chapter 24	The Students	122
Chapter 25	Ann Rooney	124
Chapter 26	Joan Harrison	127
Chapter 27	Josephine Whitaker	130
Chapter 28	The Tape	137
Chapter 29	Barbara Leach	147
Chapter 30	The Campaign	152
Chapter 31	Yvonne Mysliwiec	155
Chapter 32	Marguerite Walls	166
Chapter 33	Uphadya Bandara	170
Chapter 34	Mo Lea	173
Chapter 35	Theresa Sykes	176
Chapter 36	Jacqueline Hill	179
Chapter 37	Arrest	197
Chapter 38	Interviews	213

Epilogue 243
Bibliography 244

Foreword

This book is a very valuable contribution, knocking all the other books out there about Sutcliffe well off the shelf!

This is a very thorough and incredibly well researched account of the murders and attacks of Peter Sutcliffe. Chris has produced a comprehensive report that is the best reference book on Peter Sutcliffe's killing spree. Aspects of the consequences of the investigation are laid bare, clearly underlining where procedures went wrong, especially relating to how the police took John Humble's hoax seriously.

Chris provides insight with an intelligent overview of the Byford and Sampson Reports, whose findings show how the West Yorkshire Police mishandled the investigation.

Compact, concise and a valuable read to anyone interested in Sutcliffe's crimes.

– Mo Lea, survivor of an attack by Peter Sutcliffe

Introduction

For the first time ever, this book tells the full story of the serial killer Peter Sutcliffe, also known as the Yorkshire Ripper. We take into account his confessions in 1981, and his later confession in 1992 to two further attacks, as well as attacks on women which the police later felt they had enough evidence to charge him with – should the need arise. We also delve deep into the police investigation and highlight the many failings of the West Yorkshire Police Force and the many times Peter Sutcliffe should have been caught.

Using expert witness testimony, both from survivors of attacks by Peter Sutcliffe and those carrying out the investigation, we see how those who survived did so, and get a true idea not only of how difficult it was to run an investigation of this size without computers (it was Britain's biggest murder investigation), but also how easy it was for just one mistake to potentially cost a person their life. Many times, the investigation drew a blank and the investigating officers later admitted that the only way they thought they could catch him was if he continued to strike until he made a mistake.

We will also explore how the misguided belief of the former Chief Constable of West Yorkshire Police, Ronald Gregory, cost three women their lives.

As the crimes and investigation unfold in this book, we will take comment from Sir Lawrence Byford. On Tuesday 26 May 1981, William Whitelaw, the Home Secretary, had asked Her Majesty's Inspectorate of Constabulary to undertake an inquiry into the handling of the Yorkshire Ripper case by West Yorkshire Police and Lawrence Byford, local Inspector for the North East, was tasked with the job. His report enables us to look closely at all the wrong turns taken by the investigation.

We will also finally debunk one of the biggest myths of this case – the Yorkshire Ripper did not go out to attack prostitutes. Of the thirty-two attacks I have linked him with, only nine were on prostitutes, and only twelve women were attacked or murdered in an area known for prostitution. The rest were women walking home from work, women who had been out with friends for the evening – and seven of them were university students.

Using Home Office files that the author had released under the FOI Act at the National Archives, this is the true story of the Yorkshire Ripper – and the women whose lives he either ended, or affected forever.

Acknowledgements

This book wouldn't have been possible without the close support and encouragement of my friends and family. Jon Wright, Harriet Fielding, Karyn Burnham and Charlotte Mitchell at Pen and Sword publishers also have my gratitude and a big 'Thank You' must also go to Mo Lea, Georgi Black (georgi_lvs_books) and Adam Walsh.

Women are not attacked with hammers with any regularity for no apparent reason. There was a failure during the investigation to link incidents with the series, even as possibly connected. The criteria used as to whether to include, or not to include, were too narrowly drawn. An open mind should have been kept on other cases and the information, particularly the physical description, regularly assessed...

It is difficult to understand, even recognising that the benefit of hindsight exists, why certain cases were excluded from being possibly connected and ... had this been done ... the investigation might have been resolved much earlier.

– Sir Lawrence Byford

Chapter 1

Peter William Sutcliffe

Peter William Sutcliffe was born just after 22.00 on Sunday 2 June 1946 at Bingley and Shipley Maternity Hospital in Bingley, West Riding of Yorkshire. He was the first child born to Kathleen Sutcliffe (née Coonan) and her husband John, who had met while working at a bullet factory; they became engaged in 1941, before John left to join the Merchant Navy. It was while John was on leave in 1945 that he learned Kathleen was pregnant and so they quickly decided to marry.

John left the Merchant Navy in April 1946 and got work in a local bakery, but he developed some sort of intolerance to the conditions and lost over four stone in weight. This led him to quit the job, and around the same time Kathleen fell pregnant again. John quickly regained his weight and strength and their second child, Thomas Arthur Sutcliffe, was born in September 1947; three days after he was born, disaster struck when he suddenly stopped feeding. John Sutcliffe rushed him to the local hospital, but Thomas passed away just a few hours later. He was later buried without ceremony.

In what was clearly a troubling time for the family, Peter was sent to live with his Catholic maternal grandmother, Lottie, who would often take him to Mass. Peter would later go on to become an altar boy, but when he finally returned home to his parents, he discovered that his mother was already four months pregnant. She gave birth to a daughter called Anne in 1948.

Peter was a small boy for his age and suffered from weak joints. He began to walk when he was 18 months old, but he would always hold on to his mother's skirts and dresses and follow her wherever she went, which his father, John, found unsettling. This lasted for a couple of years.

Peter attended St Joseph's every Sunday morning, at first with his grandmother, and later with the rest of his siblings. When he was 4 years old, he began attending Cottingley Primary School, where it was noted that he was a shy, obedient, yet otherwise unremarkable boy.

Kathleen Sutcliffe then gave birth to another son, Michael John Sutcliffe, who was born on 6 September 1950, shortly before the family moved to a new three-bedroom semi-detached council house on Manor Road, Cottingley, in 1951. Peter now began to attend St Joseph's Roman Catholic School.

By now, John Sutcliffe was working the night shift as a weaver in a mill near Bingley and the move meant he had further to travel. He also had many outside interests which he would go to both before and after his shift, which meant Kathleen was left alone at home more and more with just the children for company.

John started body building for a while, when two of his colleagues started to bring weights into work and he soon found out that they had a home gym in a garden shed behind one of their houses. The weights would come out every break and lunch, and soon John was keeping up with the pair.

He was also a keen sportsman and played many sports, including cricket for three different teams, playing when his night shift allowed. He was such a talented goalkeeper for Bingley Town Football Club that many thought he could have played professionally.

Peter Sutcliffe was clearly affected by not having his father around the house much. He struggled to make friends with other boys and his father recalled an incident when he once watched Peter at playtime at school just standing alone in the playground not talking to, or playing with, anyone. In John's mind, this confirmed to him that Peter would always be a 'mummy's boy'.

John still tried with Peter though, and when he was home, he would force Peter out onto the street to find friends he could hang around with, instead of following his mother everywhere; when he was 6 years old Peter became part of the 'Bus Shelter Gang'. They would play various games out on the street, but when it came to any rough play, or a fight broke out, Peter would not join in – preferring just to stand and watch.

John also spent time helping out at the Idle and Thackley Amateur Dramatic Society on the nights when he wasn't working. Before the outbreak of the Second World War, he had been part of an all-male choir and while stationed in Gibraltar he would often put on shows to entertain his fellow troops.

It seems as though John wasn't too interested in being supportive of his wife, or actively helping to raise their children. They all later recalled that their father often came home late from the pub on the evenings he wasn't working, having been out after a show or after a sports match, and drinking even more alcohol before venting his anger on them. Peter later recalled that he and his father didn't get on that well because he didn't have an interest in sport and so they had little in common, meaning his father never much bothered with him.

As was the way back then, Kathleen had to tolerate either an absent, or a drunk husband. In 1954 they had another daughter, Maureen.

Aged 10, Kathleen's 'little angel' was a Wolf pack cub leader, known as a 'sixer', with two yellow stripes on the arm of his green pullover and badges on his chest and arms. He also wore the cub uniform of green cap with yellow cord stripes on it, and a woggle and yellow neckerchief.

By 1957, Peter was being bullied relentlessly at Cottingley Manor Secondary School, so he took matters into his own hands and played truant. He would say goodbye to his mother as normal in the morning and close the front door, pretending he had left the house, before sneaking upstairs to the loft where her would read comics and fall asleep. This went on for two weeks until the school contacted John and Kathleen to ask why Peter hadn't been attending. They immediately confronted Peter and he confessed to them that he was being bullied, so John went up to the school to get the situation sorted. Peter never truanted again.

By now Peter had developed a bit of a reputation as a sleeper and possibly even 'dozy', as he was always the last one to get up in the mornings for school or church, and would often fall asleep when reading his comics at home. This carried on into adulthood where Peter would eventually be sacked from several jobs for poor timekeeping and was often late for appointments.

In 1959, the growing Sutcliffe family moved to another council house at 57 Cornwall Road, Bingley, where Peter was forced to share a bedroom with his younger brother Mick. The house was closer to Kathleen's mother, Lottie, and she often helped her daughter cope with the four young children. By the following year, Kathleen had given birth to a third son, Carl.

Colleen Hawkes, a friend of Sutcliffe's sister who lived in Cornwall Road, recalled that he was 'weird' and 'he used to frighten me'. She said:

> When I was about 10 or 11 and he was a teenager, I was at his house visiting his sister, Jane, my friend. I was at the top of the stairs and he just picked me up and threw me to the bottom. There was no reason for it, except that he didn't like me in front of him and didn't much like kids around.

She then recalled an incident when she stayed over one night:

> He seemed to come to life at midnight. He was always walking around when everyone else was in bed. I once woke up to find him in the bedroom. I shouted at him and asked him what he was doing. I would only be about 10 at the time. He just turned and walked out again without saying a word. He frightened me to death.

Doreen, Colleen's sister, recalled: 'He was weird. He always had a far away expression on his face and a strange grin. Local girls wouldn't bother with him, he was so deep and close.'

Peter Sutcliffe left school in summer 1961 at the age of 15 without any qualifications, and on 17 August started a job as an apprentice engineer with a local engineering company called Fairbanks and Brearley Limited. In his spare time, he began playing around with motorbikes and at one point even had an old motorbike engine stored under his bed that he would pull out to take apart and reassemble. The apprenticeship only lasted for seven months before Sutcliffe quit, claiming he was being 'exploited'. It is more likely that Sutcliffe was being bullied and quit because he couldn't take any more. He was still a shy, quiet and reserved boy; his sister Maureen recalled:

> I've walked into the house many a time and he's been just sat quiet in the kitchen without me realising for ages. Not reading or anything; just sort of sat there staring at space. Pete were one of these who could sit for hours on his own without getting restless, like some blokes can't; they've got to be either watching television or talking to somebody or going out for drinks with their mates. Pete were quite happy in his own company. He didn't get bored.

Peter then began working with his father as a weaver at the Angora Mill near Bingley because he was told he had to start bringing some money home; before long he was introduced to the colleagues his father worked out with. To John's surprise, Peter began working out with them too and bought himself a chest-expander; he was known to beat others in repetitions in competitions at work. He soon left that job too, claiming the work was affecting his hearing. For the next eighteen months he worked at Fibre Products at Castlefield Industrial Estate, Crossflats, in Bingley.

John Sutcliffe wasn't averse to making money on the side, and on Christmas Day 1961 he was arrested and charged with burglary. The *Bingley Guardian* stated:

> He was on his way home from a Christmas Eve party which lasted until 4.30 a.m. on Christmas Day. Some young people in another room were having a party which was just about breaking up. On hearing a light switch in the kitchen they went to investigate, just in time to see Sutcliffe, whom they recognised, making a dash for the door. Some youths chased him down the road, caught him and sent for the police. As he ran, Sutcliffe left a trail of packets of raisins, sweets etc behind him, which he had stuffed into his pockets.
>
> He was genuinely sorry for the theft because the complainants were distant relatives of his and hitherto, he had had a perfectly clean record.

John Sutcliffe was conditionally discharged for twelve months on payment of costs at the magistrates' hearing.

In June 1962, Peter Sutcliffe began work as a general labourer at Parkland Manufacturing Company Limited, a textile firm, where he remained until 1964. He left the job because of his poor prospects and bad working conditions.

In 1963, he had his first brush with the law. The now 17-year-old was arrested by Keighley Police for driving a car unaccompanied while being a provisional licence holder and for failing to display 'L' plates. He was fined £3 for each offence. Interestingly, he was arrested on the exact same charge again in May 1964, but this time for also driving the vehicle with no lights and driving without due care and attention. Could Sutcliffe have been on the prowl for lone women even at this early stage? He appeared before Bradford City Magistrates' Court, where he was given the first of what would be eleven motoring convictions, and was fined a total of £35.

In July 1964 Sutcliffe took employment with the Bingley District Parks Department as a grave digger at Bingley Cemetery. He later stated that he took the job as he had friends already working there.

At home, Kathleen had been struggling with the housework and looking after the children and now her own health was beginning to fail, so her mother Lottie moved in – despite her own ill health and failing eyesight.

Peter later recalled an incident that happened one day while he was at home, and that scarred him for life. He told of his grandmother walking down the stairs when he noticed their new kitten sitting on the bottom step. He called out to his grandmother to alert her of the kitten's presence, but she didn't hear him and didn't see the kitten. She accidentally trod on its head, and he recalled hearing the kittens head crunch and seeing blood coming from its nose and mouth. The kitten had died instantly, and he recalled shouting at his grandmother and calling her 'stupid & clumsy'.

Less than a week later, Peter's grandmother passed away from an embolism. He recalled being with her when she died and seeing her in her open coffin before she was buried. Lottie Coonan was laid to rest at Bingley Cemetery, where Peter was then working.

Peter Sutcliffe got on well with his colleagues and his macabre sense of humour was allowed to develop. Laurie Ashton, one of those colleagues, recalled at Peter Sutcliffe's trial in 1981 a couple of instances that had stuck with him:

> One time, while we were reopening an old grave, Pete brought out a skull and chased some girls from Bingley Grammar School close by with it. He seemed to find it a great joke. Another day he wanted to return to the mortuary adjoining the cemetery to examine a couple of bodies. He thought that was funny too.

Another of his colleagues, Eric Robinson, recalled Sutcliffe stealing rings from the fingers of corpses: 'He told his sister she could have one for her wedding, but when he said where it came from she jumped back in horror. He thought that was a big laugh.'

Eric told how Peter Sutcliffe wasn't at all phased by seeing dead bodies and would happily dig through bones left in the old graves. He told the court that when Peter was after a bit more money he would work as a mortuary attendant, where he would wash bodies and prepare and clean instruments used during a post-mortem. He told the court: 'One night after we'd been out drinking together, he brought out a key for the mortuary and suggested we went and looked at the bodies. I didn't fancy the idea at all.'

Peter would go out after work most nights for drinks with his colleagues and he bought himself a motorbike, having been put off driving by his convictions. They would travel to pubs and cafes in the local area, but no one wanted to ride as Peter's passenger because he was known to drive his motorbike recklessly.

His poor driving came to the fore in 1965 when he was involved in an accident and suffered a head injury when he came off his motorbike and collided with a lamp post. Donald Summer, who was riding pillion behind Peter and would later become a distant relation by marriage, recalled: 'We had a puncture while we were going along and came off the bike. Peter went into a lamp post, and I went sliding down the road. Peter hit his head and was bleeding. There was damage to his crash helmet. He looked a right clown.'

At his trial, Peter Sutcliffe stated that the accident was as a result of having had one of his tyres purposefully let down 'after some trouble with a coach-load of engineers' and explained the story:

> Five of us on our bikes went out to Dick Hudson's pub on the moors above Gilstead. A coachload of about fifty lads came in the bar and later this fight broke out in the gents' toilets. Us lot decided to leave. But one of this lot came up to me in the car park. I was sitting on my bike. It was a BSA 250 that night. I knew he wanted trouble because he felt safe like, there were so many of them. I put my head down quick just as he was aiming a punch, and his fist smashed into my crash helmet. He reeled backwards, swearing. I jumped off my bike, had him down and gave him a kicking, a right good

kicking. My mates were putting the boot into some of the others in the car park. But then loads more of them came streaming out of the pub, so we decided to call it a day.

We rode off on our bikes. I suppose I went too fast down the steep hill we used to call the Woolpack. One of my tyres was a bit flat and as I turned sharp right the bike skidded, and I flew over the handlebars. My mates picked me up and took me to a house nearby. I was out, unconscious. When I came round, I saw my helmet. It was smashed, eggshell. The woman in the house told me I'd been unconscious for ages. But I soon felt better so we never called an ambulance. Now I wish I'd gone to casualty, or at least seen a doctor. I had headaches for a long time after, really bad ones.

He was back in trouble with the authorities again in March 1965 when he was caught not far from his house in Old Main Street, Bingley, attempting to steal from an unattended motor vehicle with his friend Eric Robinson. They were seen trying the door handles of a locked car that had property left on the rear seat. They were disturbed by two people who saw them, and the police were called. Constable Thornley quickly arrested the pair and when they appeared before Bingley West Riding Magistrates' Court Peter Sutcliffe was fined £5 with £2 7s. 6d costs.

He was in court three days later for more motoring offences. Clearly, he was accessing cars illegally. This time he faced two charges of failing to notify the authorities about the change of ownership of his vehicle, one charge of having no vehicle excise licence, one charge of using an uninsured motor vehicle and having no driving license. He was fined a total of £20.

It was around this time that his fellow gravediggers first recalled seeing him go into a trance-like state. They were in a pub one evening after work when they noticed Peter sitting at a table. He was sat bolt upright and, for no apparent reason, he smashed a beer glass onto the table in front of him, breaking it into splinters and pieces of glass. He remained seated and just stared dead ahead. He made no attempt to apologise or explain why he had done it, and this angered others who were in the pub. One drinker was so annoyed that he walked up to Peter and poured a whole pint of beer over his head, but there was no response – he just sat there staring ahead.

Peter's friend, Eric Robinson, recalled on another occasion:

> Pete was walking behind this right big fat 'un who was on her way to the toilet, followin' on with that stiff walk of his, when suddenly he just went boomph! Kicked her up the arse and sent her reelin'. And he got a right laugh out of that, did Pete. He found it rather funny.

Sutcliffe was dismissed from his post as a gravedigger in November 1965 for bad timekeeping. This was followed by a period of employment as a labourer with the textile firm of Charles Sowden Limited in Cottingley. He quit this job in May 1966.

His motoring offences continued and he appeared before Keighley Borough Magistrate's Court, again charged with having no driving licence and fined a further £15 and disqualified for driving for six months. That was no deterrent for him and he appeared before the same court six months later, on 22 March 1966, for driving while disqualified and using an uninsured motor vehicle. He was fined £30 and disqualified for driving for three years. Still, this wasn't enough and, exactly three months later, he was back in court charged with obstructing a police constable in the execution of his duty, failing to produce a driving licence, failing to give his name and address and driving a motor vehicle with no lights. He was fined just £10 in total. Was he again looking for women to attack?

It was around this time that a 20-year-old Peter Sutcliffe met 18-year-old Trevor Birdsall and his unhealthy interest in prostitutes came to the fore. The two young men became best friends and would go out for a few drinks together before heading for the red-light areas of Leeds' Chapeltown and Bradford's Manningham Lane. Initially they would go in Birdsall's Robin Reliant and Mini saloon before later going in one of Sutcliffe's cars, where they would sit and watch prostitutes going about their business on the streets.

It is also highly probable that the men were using the services of these prostitutes, as a short time later Keith Sugden bumped into Sutcliffe one evening while out drinking in the Ferrands Arms in the centre of Bingley. As the men were talking Peter asked Keith to go with him to the toilets and when they were alone Peter asked Keith to look at his penis. Keith recalled:

> It looked a mess and it certainly seemed as though he had contracted venereal disease. I told him the best thing he could do was to go to St Luke's Hospital in Bradford and get it sorted out. I was staggered really because I had never seen Peter Sutcliffe bother with girls.

Trevor Birdsall also later claimed that Sutcliffe would only really comment on women 'If he saw a particular young woman with big knockers on', and claimed that Sutcliffe had told him that he had been with prostitutes more than once and that sometimes he didn't even pay.

In June 1966, Sutcliffe again obtained employment as a grave digger/labourer with the Bingley District Parks Department, where he remained until November 1967. He was again dismissed for bad timekeeping. It was during this period that Sutcliffe was also using the services of prostitutes alongside his brother, Mick, who later recalled:

> I suppose we were a little wild, but Peter never got into any trouble with the police. It is true when we were younger we had picked up prostitutes, but it was all for fun. We might have been drinking and just fancied a bit of what the lads call 'rough'.

On 14 February 1967, Peter Sutcliffe went to the Royal Standard pub in Manningham Lane (in the heart of Bradford's red-light district) where he met a young 16-year-old girl called Sonia Szurma.

Sonia, who was still a student at Grange Grammar School, had snuck out of home in order to attend the Valentine's Day disco that evening and Sutcliffe took an instant liking to her. He later recalled: 'Trying to get to know her was like trying to climb Mount Everest. She was remote and unattainable. I was fascinated by her from the start.'

Sonia Szurma was the daughter of Eastern European refugees from Czechoslovakia. She had an older sister called Marianne and they lived with their parents at 44 Tanton Crescent, Bradford. Their father, Bohdan, had been a PE Teacher in his native Czechoslovakia and when he moved to England he worked as a wool comb box mender in a local mill, before he had to give up work in the late 1950s due to ill health. Sonia's mother, Maria, worked as a nursing auxiliary in a local private hospital.

Sonia and Marianne had spent almost all of their lives at home. They were not allowed to watch TV or to play out with other children. They literally went to school and then continued learning when they got home, where their father taught them about the importance of literature, classical music and educational games like chess. They also spoke only in their native Ukrainian and Czech at home which left Sonia with a strange accent. On the night she met Peter at the disco she had lied to her parents and told them that she was going to a local opera performance.

Peter and Sonia began seeing each other at the weekends, where Peter would mainly take her to the local pub. He recalled: 'I did not go to her home for the first few months. I used to see her on Saturday and spent half the day and the evening with her.' He was quick to show her off to his family, but Sonia took an almost instant disliking to most of them, later telling journalist Barbara Jones: 'Pete and his sister, Anne, were so like their mother. The rest of the family is riff-raff. I completely disassociated myself from them, always. Pete came into my world.'

It's believed that Sonia felt this way because Peter's younger brother Mick had a reputation locally as a thief and hard man with a criminal record, and their father was a wife beater who had turned into a violent drunk. Peter's youngest brother, Carl, recalled:

> We were all frightened to death of me dad. He were like a monster. He were never in house, but when he was, he ruled the roost. When he came in drunk we'd all sit there in fear; you didn't move. Whatever was on television, no matter how many were watching, was straight off and switched over to what he wanted to see, which were usually sport.
>
> Oh Christ, he had a foul temper. I seen Maureen get a beating off him when she was about fifteen, an' he once beat me black and blue when I were a kid.

It didn't take long for a feeling of resentment to form between Sonia and the rest of the Sutcliffe family. Whenever Sonia visited Peter's home, she always remained almost silent, and when she did speak it was in an almost whisper. At first, the family put this down to shyness, but after a while they began to feel that she was being arrogant and judgemental. Mick never liked Sonia and later described her as looking 'like a fucking horse'.

It took Sonia a while to take Peter home to meet her parents, but when she did, they immediately took to him and were impressed with his manner and his respect for them.

Peter and Sonia had no privacy at either of their homes so they sometimes went for a drive up onto the moors. On one of these trips, a morbid joke of his backfired on him. He was telling Sonia all about his work and jumped over a wall – intending to jump out and scare her by pretending to be a ghost – but he misjudged the drop on the other side of the wall and fell 20ft and broke his ankle.

After five months of dating, Sonia left school and decided to attend Bradford Technical College for her A-level studies. Sonia and Peter were still only seeing each other for a few hours every Saturday and that left Peter plenty of time to visit and watch the local prostitutes with his friend Trevor Birdsall. It was during one of these visits that they saw a woman staggering around the road in a drunken state. Peter, who was driving on this occasion, stopped the car and went with her, leaving Birdsall in the car for ten to twenty minutes. This wasn't the first, or last, time that Peter Sutcliffe would use a prostitute in the presence of Trevor Birdsall.

In 1968 he began work as a labourer with the Water Board at Bingley. It was at this time that Trevor Birdsall again later stated that he and Sutcliffe were out one evening in his Robin Reliant when they parked up on Barkerend Road, Bradford. He recalled that Sutcliffe left the vehicle and went over to speak to a woman before the two of them disappeared. When he returned to the car, he told Birdsall that he had been 'comforting her'. Birdsall later stated that he did not know whether Sutcliffe had attacked the woman or used her for sex.

Chapter 2

Sonia Szurma

In 1969, while digging trenches at the side of a main road in Bingley, Peter's brother Mick spotted Sonia out with an Italian ice-cream van driver. He saw a white sports car drive past and recalled: 'There were a scarf blowing off a bird in passenger seat, a sort of silk job blowing over top, and I just fucking realised who it were when she got level. It were her.'

The following day Mick told his brother what he had seen and so Peter decided to confront Sonia, but she refused to answer any of his questions. Sutcliffe recalled that at the time he was working at the Water Board and had an assistant with him who 'did not understand very much about the workings of the job. I had arranged to leave early that day to catch Sonia coming out of the tech.' He felt that the Italian had taken advantage of the fact that he only saw Sonia once a week and recalled:

> I wanted to catch her before she got home and before she got into his company again. I left early and unfortunately there was a disaster at the waterworks which nearly drowned several men through the assistant. I was blamed for that, although they said I could leave at the time suggested. I caught Sonia going down the road. I approached her but she walked the other way as if shocked to see me, so I knew what I had heard was true.

The near 'disaster' that he tried to blame on his assistant was entirely his fault. Stanley Wesley, one of the men nearly killed, recalled:

> It was a stupid and dangerous thing that he did. A gang of men were working in a 48-inch pipeline trying to release a scouring brush which had become jammed. This sort of thing happens from time to time, and it means that valves have to be closed and sluice gates shut to make sure there can be no danger to the men working on the line. Sutcliffe's job at the time was looking after the pumping station on the moors above the filter plant at Gilstead, near Bingley ... On this particular day he wanted to be off at 4 pm ... so he opened the sluice gate without making a safety check. And he just left.

What happened then is described by another official:

> The men inside the pipeline were about 20 yards away from the escape hatch when they first heard the water rushing down towards them. You can

imagine the panic. It is a terrifying sound. Just like a train going through a tunnel. They knew that they did not have long to get out before the pipeline was filled with water. There were four men scrambling together in the 48-inch pipeline trying to get to the hatch. One of them told me later it seemed to be a mile away and they could hear the water getting closer.

The men were lucky to get out alive. Sutcliffe was sacked the next day for a gross breach of discipline. A full report was made and it is still on file. And it is still talked about today.

Sutcliffe was actually dismissed from his job at the Water Board for twice being late (for which he had received official warnings) and on the third occasion he failed to turn up for work following this incident. He then took up a job as a wire polisher at T. Lund Limited in Bingley.

On the day of the incident, Sutcliffe walked Sonia home, but she coldly refused to answer any of the questions he asked her regarding both their own relationship and hers with the Italian. When they reached Sonia's home she went indoors, and he knew that he was not allowed to follow. He later recalled at his trial: 'It was resolved eventually when she gave me her word that she was not going to see this chap anymore.' However, this was roughly six months after he had confronted her.

Sonia refusing to answer Sutcliffe's questions left him feeling angry and upset, and he did not know whether Sonia was sleeping with the Italian. He decided to get his revenge by sleeping with a prostitute.

He has always stated that this was his first experience with a prostitute but, as has been proved already, he had been using them for a while by this time. He simply stated this to the police during his confessions because it fitted in with the story being told by the West Yorkshire Police that the Yorkshire Ripper was fascinated by prostitutes and was only looking to attack them.

The following is his account of what took place that night and over the next couple of weeks, as told to the police during his confession. He gave this as the reason why he attacked prostitutes.

He stated that he drove, alone, up to the Manningham Lane red light area of Bradford, where he saw a prostitute touting for business at a petrol station. They agreed on a price of £5 and he recalled:

> I thought I would have intercourse with the prostitute, but I changed my mind when it got to the stage where we had got to do it. We were on the way to her place and were talking and I realised what a coarse and vulgar person she was. We were practically there, and I realised I didn't want anything to do with her. Before getting out of the car I was trying to wriggle out of the situation, but I felt stupid as well.

He said that the men who worked at the petrol station must have been her 'protectors'.

> I'd given her a £10 note and she said she'd give me my change later. We got to her house and went inside. There was a huge Alsatian dog on a mat

in front of the fire downstairs. She started going upstairs and I realised I just didn't want to go through with it. The whole thing was awful. I felt disgusted with her and myself. I went upstairs behind her into the bedroom. I even unzipped her dress, but I told her straight out I didn't want to do anything with her. She could keep the money, just give me my change.

She said she'd have to go back to the garage where I'd picked her up, to get some change, so I drove her there. I just wanted to get away. I felt worse than ever about Sonia and everything. We went back to the garage by car, and she went inside and there were two chaps in there. I don't know whether she did this regularly, but she wouldn't come back out. One of the men came banging on the car roof when I refused to go away. He said: 'If I were you, I wouldn't get out of that car. You'd better be going.' I would have had a go at him, but he was holding the wrench in a menacing sort of way. Then I saw the girl come out with another big-built bloke. They walked off together, having a laugh. I just felt stupid, I drove home more angry than ever. I felt outraged and humiliated and embarrassed. I felt a hatred for [the prostitute] and her kind.

Still feeling angry, humiliated, embarrassed and upset he saw the same prostitute again three weeks later in a pub on Lumb Lane:

I went and approached the one I had been with three weeks previously and told her that I hadn't forgotten about the incident and that she could put things right and give back the payment I had made to her. She thought this was a huge joke and, as luck would have it, she knew everybody else in the place and went round telling them ... before I knew what was happening, most of the people were having a good laugh.

Being publicly humiliated was the final straw for Sutcliffe. He recalled being left 'in a turmoil', and he developed 'a general loathing for any prostitute'. He said he found himself being pushed 'over the brink'. Less than a month following this showdown, Peter Sutcliffe attacked his first victim.

It was early September 1969 and Peter Sutcliffe had spent many nights looking for the prostitute who he felt had tricked him out of his money and humiliated him. With his rage ever increasing following this incident, and with Sonia still seeing the Italian, he went out with his best friend Trevor Birdsall to tour the local pubs in the hope of finding the prostitute.

Having had no luck in finding her, Sutcliffe and Birdsall were sat in Birdsall's Mini saloon eating a supper of fish and chips and commenting on the behaviour of the girls they were watching. Sutcliffe suddenly jumped out of the vehicle and walked up St Paul's Road until he was out of Birdsall's sight. He returned to the vehicle around ten minutes later and Birdsall recalled at the trial: 'He looked a bit excited and was not breathing normally. It looked as if he had possibly been running.'

As they were driving off towards Bingley, Birdsall asked him what had happened, and Sutcliffe claimed he had followed an 'old cow' to a garage and had hit her on the back of the head with a stone in a sock. He then took a sock from his pocket and threw it, and the contents, out of the window.

Following his arrest in 1981, Sutcliffe recalled that: 'I got out of the car and asked her the time and hit her with a sock with a stone in it. I had got depressed. I had trouble with violent headaches.'

He also stated: 'I was out of my mind with the obsession of finding this prostitute. I had been out with Trevor, looking out for this particular one and it was getting late. I just gave vent to my anger on the first one I saw.' He claimed to know that the woman was a prostitute, 'because she was walking slowly along the kerb, looking at cars across the road.'

The following day he got a shock when the police turned up at his home in Cornwall Road asking to speak to him. The woman he had attacked had managed to note down the registration plate of Birdsall's Mini saloon and the police had paid him a visit. Birdsall had admitted to them that his car was in the area at the time and that he was with Sutcliffe, who had disappeared for a short time. Birdsall then gave the police Sutcliffe's address.

He admitted to the police that he had hit the woman, but claimed it was with his hand and that no weapon was used. The police warned him and said he was 'very lucky' as the lady did not want to press charges because she was a known prostitute and her husband was serving a jail sentence for assault, implying that the lady did not want her husband to find out that she was 'on the game'.

The spark of thrill and excitement experienced by Sutcliffe that night lit a fire in him; he went out alone on 29 September with one objective in mind: to attack and kill a woman. He was spotted in the red-light district of Manningham Lane, Bradford, in his car with the engine running quietly but the lights switched off. The locals thought the car and occupant were suspicious, so they reported the vehicle to the police and PC Bland was dispatched to investigate. He quickly found Sutcliffe's vehicle but, as he approached it, Sutcliffe noticed him coming towards him and drove off at speed.

An immediate search for the vehicle commenced and it was found a short time later a few streets away – minus the occupant. The car still had its engine running and lights off so a search for the driver quickly began. Nearby gardens were searched, and PC Bland found Sutcliffe hiding behind a privet hedge. He was immediately searched and was found to be in possession of a hammer. Asked to explain himself, Sutcliffe claimed that he was looking for a hubcap that had come off his car and he had the hammer because he was going to use it to reattach the hubcap.

He later claimed that when he was put into the police vehicle, he managed to hide a knife that he had concealed in his jacket near the mudguard cover and that it was never discovered by the police.

Two weeks later, at Bradford Magistrates' Court, Sutcliffe denied the charge of 'going equipped to steal', but was found guilty and fined £25, to be paid at £2 a week. Nine days later, Sutcliffe appeared at Bingley West Riding Magistrates' Court for using an uninsured motor vehicle and was fined a further £5.

It wasn't until 1970 that Sonia finally stopped seeing the Italian ice cream salesman and her relationship with Sutcliffe got back on track. Whatever happiness Sutcliffe might have felt, however, was short lived. The couple were invited by Sutcliffe's father to meet him at 'The Bankfield', a local hotel. Both Sutcliffe and Sonia found this strange as this had never happened before; when they arrived, they saw Sutcliffe's sister Maureen sitting there too. All three were as confused as the other as to what was going on.

John Sutcliffe had discovered that Kathleen had been having an affair with a policeman named Albert and had arranged for Kathleen to meet who she thought was Albert at the hotel. When she arrived, she immediately saw John sitting there with Peter, Sonia and Maureen, and knew she'd been found out. In front of them (and guests at the hotel), John made Kathleen admit that she had been having an affair, and even made her show them the lingerie she had bought especially for the occasion.

This left Peter feeling torn. He had just re-embraced the love of his girlfriend and begun to think things might be OK, but then discovered that his mother, whom he still doted on, was a cheat. His feelings were confused. On the one hand, he loved his mother and felt sorry for the way she had been embarrassed, but on the other hand was upset that she had been sexually promiscuous.

Sutcliffe was then involved in a motor accident. He appeared at Bingley Magistrates' Court on 20 April 1970 on charges of driving a motor vehicle without due care and attention, failing to stop after an accident, failing to report an accident, failing to display 'L' plates and being a provisional license holder driving unaccompanied. He was fined £26 and disqualified from driving for six months.

Sutcliffe eventually passed his driving test and one of his friends, Keith Sugden, recalled an incident when they met for a drink in a local pub. He said that Peter was always shy with women and would be OK talking to them initially but would then run out of conversation and go quiet. On this particular occasion, Keith had a new girlfriend, Doreen, and Peter felt put out by her. He turned up to collect Keith and Doreen for a night out and oddly had two women in the car with him, saying he had met them in a pub in Keighley. They arrived at a pub and when the two women went off to the toilet, Peter made it very clear to the couple that the two women were prostitutes. Keith's girlfriend immediately felt uncomfortable, and she asked Keith to take her home, which he did. Peter then took the two prostitutes back to Keighley and Keith saw very little of him after this.

Keith recalled: 'It was a deliberate plot to split us up. He didn't like it a bit when Doreen and I got serious.' He said that when Sutcliffe arrived with the prostitutes, 'he told me there was a "bird for each of us" and this was to make Doreen think that I went with these women when I wasn't with her.'

Doreen had been a neighbour of the Sutcliffe family when they lived in Cornwall Road, and Keith had met Sutcliffe through one of his old school friends; the two men would spend time tinkering with cars.

Things weren't helped when later in the year Sonia moved to London in order to attend the Rachel MacMillan Teacher's Training College at Deptford, where she planned to specialise in Art. It was at this juncture that Peter Sutcliffe bought his first motorcar – a green Ford Capri (EUA 831K).

Sutcliffe's mother had ended the affair with the policeman and stayed with John, but things were very strained at home and so Peter spent as much time visiting Sonia as he could. He began by leaving work on Friday evenings and driving straight down to meet her, returning to Bradford very early on Monday mornings in time for work. As Sonia's halls of residence were female only, Sutcliffe found himself sleeping alone in his car.

He quit his job as a wire polisher in May 1971 and tried to move to London permanently, but struggled to find anywhere to live. At first, he stayed in a bedsit close to Sonia's halls of residence and earned money by doing bits of car maintenance and became self-employed doing property repair work, before Sonia's future brother-in-law, Haleem, offered him room in a house he was renting to Indian immigrants in Wembley.

However, there were no rooms available, and he found himself sleeping on the sofa. On top of this, the drive from Wembley to Deptford wasn't convenient and by November 1971 he had returned to Bradford and got himself a job at Baird Television and Radio Manufacturers in Lidgett Green as an assembler, working alongside his best friend Trevor Birdsall and Trevor's future wife, Melissa.

With Sutcliffe back in Bradford, Sonia became more and more isolated and wasn't enjoying her course. She had a falling-out with her course tutor but found some solace by learning Flamenco dancing in the evenings in Swiss Cottage, North London.

Sonia very rarely socialised otherwise, and her only interests were Sutcliffe and her sister Marianne, who would visit her occasionally. In her classes she would sit in silence and didn't seem interested. In her halls of residence, it was noted that she was constantly agitated and would shout and scream and lash out for no apparent reason. Sutcliffe had witnessed this for himself on a couple of occasions while visiting and had been forced to restrain her by pinning her arms to her side to stop her lashing out. She had become violent, aggressive, restless and often dressed and undressed at inappropriate times. Visibly, Sonia had lost over a stone in weight.

The reason soon became clear. Sutcliffe recalled:

> I got a telegram from Sonia saying: 'Meet me at King's Cross Station'. That was all, no time, no date, nothing. I thought there was something strange about it, so I took it to her parents. She was still their responsibility. Her father dashed off to London and found she had had a nervous breakdown and had been taken to Bexley [a mental hospital].

Bohdan Szurma rushed down to London as quickly as he could and soon discovered that the police and ambulance services had been called to his daughter's halls of residence because she had been out in the streets in the middle of the night in her nightclothes, hallucinating. Sonia had believed she was the second coming of Christ, that she had stigmata on her palms, that all machinery was about to stop, and that the end of the world was coming. She also told people that she wanted to be a teddy bear.

Bohdan managed to get Sonia transferred to Linfield Mount Hospital in Bradford where she was diagnosed with Schizophrenia. On admission she was said to be erratic, aggressive and deeply disturbed. She complained of hearing voices and had to be held down by two nurses.

Her parents visited her every day, but they told Sutcliffe not to see her until she was better. Once her medication had kicked in, Sonia's parents relented and allowed Peter to visit. He recalled: 'She just looked grey. She looked terrible.'

Sonia stayed at Linfield Mount for three weeks, and the medication made her put on so much weight that Sutcliffe hardly recognised her. She continued to receive treatment as an outpatient over the next three months but was deemed well enough to attend Trevor

Birdsall's wedding some time in 1972. She would also occasionally go out for drinks with Sutcliffe, Birdsall and his new wife but then, only a couple of weeks after attending the wedding, Sonia suffered a relapse.

She began to tear her clothes off at completely random moments, both indoors and out, and she refused to be separated from an annual about pop music that her father had taken away from her as a child. Her odd behaviour was also noticed by Sutcliffe's family. His sister, Jane, recalled:

> One night she came round, and Pete went straight off to the bathroom as usual and left her with me. I were just sitting quiet, reading, when Sonia stood up and did a little twirl in front of the settee. 'Guess who I am today?' she asked. She were just wearing a little summer cotton frock, a shawl and these silver sandals. 'Cinderella' she said. I thought 'Oh, bloody hell'.

With an adjustment of her medication, Sonia was able to stay at home. But this meant that Sutcliffe now had far more time on his hands, and he and Trevor Birdsall continued to watch and torment the prostitutes around Manningham Lane. Sutcliffe would wind down his car window, agree on a price with a prostitute, and then suddenly drive off at speed while laughing his head off.

He also changed jobs again in June 1972, when he resigned from his job at Baird Television due to the distance involved in travelling to work. He found employment as a furnaceman at the Britannia Works of Anderton International in Bingley, working the night shift from 20.30–07.30, and it was here that his colleagues told him about 'a plague of prostitutes' in nearby Keighley. He soon opted to check this area out for himself.

Meanwhile, the tension between his parents was still palpable – made worse when John started an affair with a deaf woman called Wendy Broughton, who lived on the same estate. When Kathleen found out she went berserk. Their daughter Maureen, who had left home by then, visited one day and recalled: 'I were just on me way up to bed when me mother, who was usually the most placid person, came out of the kitchen screaming and belled me dad one. She pinned him up against piano and belled him. I were just speechless.'

John Sutcliffe left and moved in with Wendy Broughton for three months, before moving back home and arrogantly insisting that he had taken his revenge. He later claimed:

> Although I were paying her money every week, she was getting into so much debt in one way or another during that traumatic time that it was obvious to me she'd been taught her lesson. So, I went back and all her financial difficulties were straightened up within a fortnight.

Peter Sutcliffe hated the atmosphere at home and decided that he wanted to marry Sonia. Her parents agreed that he could marry their daughter as they were impressed by the way he had stood by her during her schizophrenia. Peter and Sonia married on 10 August 1974 at Clayton Baptist Chapel; Sonia's 24th birthday.

Ronnie Wilson was a surprise choice for Sutcliffe's best man. This was because Sonia had already vetoed Trevor Birdsall and Sutcliffe's brother Mick, whom she didn't like.

Ronnie Wilson was as surprised as anyone to be asked, as he hadn't seen Sutcliffe for quite some time and never saw him again after the wedding. He recalled: 'I hadn't seen much of him for a long time since we used to tinker with cars together ... He asked me to do it as a favour a few days before the wedding. He said he was stuck.'

Following the reception at the Quarry Arms pub on Bradford Road, Clayton, the newlyweds went to Paris for their honeymoon. Sutcliffe later told psychiatrists, just before his trial, that while in Paris a prostitute had come up to them while they were holding hands and that he hadn't reacted, but later on while they were leaving a train station, Sonia was dragged away by a man who had thought she was a prostitute. He recalled: 'I must have thought that the man thought Sonia was a prostitute rather than Sonia saying something to him. From that time we stayed glued together.'

When they returned from the honeymoon, Sutcliffe moved in with Sonia at her parents' home at 44 Tanton Crescent, and the couple began saving as much money as possible in order to buy their first home together.

Living with Sonia and her parents was no different than living with his own family insofar as his late night excursions were concerned. Over the next three months he would often use his nightshift as an excuse, so that his wife and in-laws were unable to keep track of his movements. He would leave earlier in the evenings than he needed to and cruise around the red light area of Manningham Lane in his Ford Capri. He would also check out Keighley, following the tip-off from his fellow workers about there being prostitutes there, but he was also following and watching *any* woman who seemed to be walking alone. He was also able to renew his friendship with Trevor Birdsall now that they lived closer to each other, and the two of them again spent their Saturday evenings watching prostitutes and lone women following a pub crawl. It was at this time that Sutcliffe also made friends with the next-door neighbours at his new home, David and Ronnie Barker. Ronnie Barker always kept a diary and it was to prove a good piece of evidence for the prosecution at Sutcliffe's later trial.

Chapter 3

Gloria Wood

At between 19.30 and 20.00 on Monday 11 November 1974, 28-year-old student teacher Gloria Wood was on her way home to her new council flat at 13 Telscombe Drive in Holme Wood, Bradford, having recently separated from her husband. She recalled:

> As I was coming through the school grounds this man approached me. He came up to me and said, 'Can I carry your bag love?' I replied, 'No thanks, I haven't got far to go.' He seemed a right big man with staring eyes. Dark brown eyes and he was olive skin coloured. Not black, not white, but Mediterranean looking. Greek or Italian. He had a black beard, black hair.

Gloria then turned away from the man and was struck four times as she did so, with what was later thought to have been a walling hammer.

> I didn't feel a hammer blow. I didn't even feel it hit me. There were some youths playing at the end of the snicket. It must have interrupted him.
> A little girl found me. She went into her mother and said: 'There's a lady on the grass with red paint all over her.' That must have saved my life really.
> I remember waking up at the hospital with my mother and my father at the end of the bed and I wondered why the police were there. It just didn't register with me that I'd been attacked. They said the cause of the injuries was a hammer blow. They had to cut a hole in my skull to get at the splints of bone that had gone into my brain.
> The police thought I knew who'd attacked me and I couldn't tell them because I didn't know. I couldn't think of anyone who'd want to attack me.
> I told them my attacker was a man with olive skin, quite tall [5ft 8in in her statement], a beard, black hair and they wrote it all down and went away. I didn't hear from them for ages after that.

She also later described the hair and beard as 'curly', and that her attacker was smartly dressed in a dark suit. The description was a perfect match for Peter Sutcliffe.
Gloria had suffered four deep scalp lacerations – each leaving a crescent shaped indentation on her skull and typical of injuries sustained by later victims of Sutcliffe. There is little doubt that the children had disturbed her attacker and this had saved Gloria's life.

Gloria Wood

While Gloria had been preparing her new home following her divorce, her two children had been taken into care. She recalled: '

> The worst thing for me was I'd been on the verge of getting my children home. It was all arranged. They were coming home, but in the event the children were sent to their father because I was in no condition to look after them – I couldn't even look after myself.

Soon after the attack, Gloria suffered a nervous breakdown and was still receiving psychiatric treatment twenty-two years later.

> Nobody knows what that man put me through, he robbed me of my family.
> I don't like being associated with the Ripper because in the public eye he only went for prostitutes. But there's a lot more to the Ripper than that. He went for anybody. Any woman who was on their own. It wasn't just prostitutes.

An hour after the attack, Sutcliffe clocked in for his nightshift at the engineering plant – just a fifteen-minute drive away along the A650, which would have given him plenty of time to escape and clean himself up.

Although he never admitted to this attack, he was known to be in the vicinity; Gloria's description matched him and she was attacked from behind with a hammer while walking alone. Her attacker had also tried to engage her in conversation. The attack fits Sutcliffe's Modus Operandi perfectly. It is a shame the police thought she must have known her attacker and probably believed it was her ex-husband. They never linked this case with the rest and Peter Sutcliffe was never charged.

Four months later, in February 1975, Sutcliffe took voluntary redundancy from Britannia Works of Anderton International and used half of his £400 redundancy money to train as a HGV driver. He passed his test at Steeton in June 1975, which meant that he was no longer working nights. However, to get to Steeton, Sutcliffe had to skirt the centre of Keighley, where he had spent some time watching women. And one woman in particular.

Chapter 4

Anna Rogulskyj

At around 01.30 on Saturday 5 July 1975, 34-year-old Anna Rogulskyj was attacked in Keighley, West Yorkshire.

She had been born Anna Patricia Brosnan in March 1941 in Tralee, County Kerry, Ireland, as one of twelve Catholic children. She left school at 15, moved to Keighley with her eldest sister, Helen, and worked as a shop assistant in Woolworths, where she met her future husband. Roman Rogulskyj was of Ukrainian descent and the couple married in February 1957. They didn't have any children and divorced in July 1973.

Anna then went out with a man called Geoffrey Hughes, but it was a very volatile relationship. He was controlling and abusive to her; on one occasion he plunged her head into a bucket of cold water for no apparent reason, and on the night she was attacked he had decided to hide all her shoes because he didn't want her to go out. She learned much later, once the relationship had finished, that when they first met he had just been discharged from a psychiatric hospital with a recommendation that he 'keep away from women for five years'.

Sutcliffe had been keeping an eye on Keighley ever since a former colleague mentioned to him that there were prostitutes there. He would pass it on his way to and from Steeton, and a few weeks before he attacked Anna he had actually spoken to her in the Town Hall Square, telling her he would like to go home with her for a cup of tea. Anna had said no at this suggestion and walked away, only to then realise that he was following her. Concerned, she quickened her pace and was lucky enough on that occasion to escape.

Sutcliffe returned alone to Keighley a couple of weeks later and again spotted Anna in the town centre. He followed her a short distance and when she entered Wild's Coffee Shop he offered to buy her a drink. She said no and it quickly became obvious to him that she was about to make a fuss about his unwanted attention, so he left the shop feeling embarrassed and annoyed. He then returned to Keighley for a third time on the evening of Friday 4 July 1975.

That night, Anna had left home at 62 Highfield Lane, Keighley, and called on her sister to tell her what Geoffrey Hughes had done with her shoes; her sister wasn't in. She then caught a bus to Bradford and went to The Great Victoria Hotel to meet her friends for a drink and they then went to the Capricorn Club, more commonly known as 'Bibby's'. As she was leaving the bar later that evening, 'Irish Annie' (as she was known to her friends) met two Jamaican friends she knew and they gave her a lift back home to Keighley.

When Anna entered her flat she quickly realised that her boyfriend had taken his belongings and must have gone back to his own flat. She put on a record and it was only then that she realised that he must have taken her cat with him. Angered by this, Anna stormed round to his flat in North Queen Street, which was a mainly boarded-up and vacated area. She walked down Highfield Lane, crossed North Street and walked to Lord Street where she turned down an alleyway that ran beside the Ritz cinema and came out on North Queen Street. As she got near the end of the alleyway she heard a man's voice from the shadows ask her if she 'fancied it'. She told him 'Not on your life!' and carried on quickly towards her boyfriend's flat without looking at the man.

When she reached the flat there were no lights on and so she tried to wake him by banging on the door and shouting but he did not reply. Angry, and feeling as though he was ignoring her on purpose, Anna took off one of her shoes and smashed his ground-floor window. Little did she know that Sutcliffe, the voice from the shadow, was watching all of this.

Anna walked off and headed back the way she had come towards her home on Highfield Lane. She went back down the same alleyway, which was just 50 yards from her boyfriends home, and again the voice asked her if she 'fancied it'. She was in no mood for games and lashed out.

Sutcliffe later recalled: 'I tapped her up again and she elbowed me. I followed her and hit her with the hammer and she fell down. I intended to kill her but I was disturbed.'

He had allowed her to walk just a couple of steps before positioning himself behind her and striking her three times on the head with a ball pein hammer. When she was on the ground Sutcliffe raised her blouse and slashed at her abdomen. As he was about to stab her, a neighbour, living at 10 Lord Street, heard the commotion and shouted out of his window, asking what was going on. At that, Sutcliffe ran back to the car park of the Eastwood Tavern pub, where he had left his car.

Anna Rogulskyj was found unconscious forty minutes later by a passer-by at 02.20. When the person who found her asked her who was responsible, she muttered something like the name, 'Geoffrey Shilton'. She was immediately rushed to Airedale General Hospital and then transferred to Leeds General Infirmary where she underwent a twelve-hour operation to remove splinters of bone from her brain. At one point she was barely clinging to life and was given the last rites.

The three hammer blows had all left crescent-shaped lacerations on her head, as they had on Gloria Wood, and each one left a depressed fracture on her skull. She also had bruising across her hands and right forearm where she had clearly tried to defend herself from the blows and fallen. She had a 7-inch slash on her abdomen, possibly from a Stanley knife or similar tool, which ran horizontally below the naval, and above this were seven small but deeper scratches.

A forensic examination of the scene and of her clothing indicated the presence of semen. It was clear that at some point during the attack, when Anna Rogulskyj was unconscious, Peter Sutcliffe had masturbated over her. A vaginal swab also indicated the presence of semen, but it was thought that this was due to sexual activity some time prior to the attack. She had no recollection of being attacked.

The attack was investigated by Detective Superintendent Peter Perry of West Yorkshire's Western Crime Area, and an incident room was immediately established. Despite the similarities, this attack was not linked to the attack on Gloria Wood.

Anna Rogulskyj survived the attack but was left psychologically traumatised. She broke off her relationship with her violent boyfriend when the police disclosed to her his past in a psychiatric hospital (they believed for a short time that he could have been responsible), and she even had to learn to cut her own hair after a hairdresser was unable to hide her shock at the dents in Anna's skull the first time she went for a hair cut following the attack.

Shockingly (and unforgivably), a police dossier on Anna stated:

> She is a very heavy drinker and has cohabited with a number of men. She has a history of mental instability. In July 1975 she was associating with a local man who had moved into her home. She was apparently unhappy with her sexual relationship and left her home on the night of Friday, 4 July 1975 saying she was going to Bradford to see her Jamaican boyfriend. She visited Bradford that night and had some drink. About midnight she left Bibby's Club and got a lift in a car with two Jamaicans who took her back to Keighley and dropped her off home.

There was absolutely no evidence to support the claims that Anna was either a heavy drinker or mentally unstable. Her boyfriend was not living with her (although he did have possessions at her home for when he stayed over) and the constant referral to her having Jamaican boyfriends and friends does make you wonder if there was a racist undertone to the investigation.

Years later, Anna herself refuted the claims: 'I don't go round the pubs. I never have done in my life. I'm not a gallivanting woman: I choose my men carefully, and they're few and far between.'

She said that Anna died that day and she changed her name to Joanna in order to live the rest of her life without the stigma of the 'Yorkshire Ripper' being attached to her.

Anna lived out the rest of her life behind a barricade of alarms, wires and bars at her home. While in London for the trial in 1981 she took an overdose of her brothers blood-pressure tablets and had to be rushed to Edgware General Hospital to have her stomach pumped. It was one of a number of attempts she made on her own life following the attack.

She passed away in Airedale General Hospital in April 2008, aged 67. She had been suffering from both breast cancer and pneumonia.

Relevant Statistics

Incident Room set up	5 July 1975
House to House Enquiries	116
Actions	225
Statements	70
Vehicle Enquiries	N/A
Officers Engaged	N/A
Hours Worked (Not inc. Overtime)	N/A
Incident Room Closed	N/A

Chapter 5

Olive Smelt

At 23.45 on Friday, 15 August 1975, 46-year-old Olive Smelt was attacked in Halifax, West Yorkshire – five weeks and six days after the attack on Anna Rogulskyj.

Olive was born in 1929 and raised by her mother and grandmother in Halifax. When she was 19 years old she married her boyfriend, 21-year-old Harry Smelt. The newlywed couple lived briefly with Olive's mother in Boothtown, Halifax, before they moved to the Ovenden area and started a family. They then moved to 16, Woodside Mount, Halifax.

In the mid-1970s Olive worked as an office cleaner for three separate firms. She worked only in the evenings from Monday – Friday. After work on Friday evenings Olive would regularly go out for a few drinks in the town centre with her close friend, Muriel Falkingham.

On the evening she was attacked, Olive and Muriel went to four different pubs before moving on to the White Horse Inn; at 22.20, Muriel left to catch the last bus home. Olive then went on alone to the Royal Oak, 3 Clare Road, as she had done many times before. Unfortunately for Olive, Sutcliffe was out that night on a pub crawl with his best friend, Trevor Birdsall. Birdsall later recalled: 'We went out to Halifax in Peter's car and went to a few pubs. We probably saw about half a dozen unattached women. I remember Peter leaning across to them and talking to them. I think he said he thought it was a prostitutes' pub.'

While there, Sutcliffe pointed out Olive Smelt to Birdsall and said: 'I bet she's on the game.' Sutcliffe then said something similar to her face as she passed him on her way to the toilet. Olive quickly put him in his place, leaving Sutcliffe feeling angry and embarrassed.

Just before closing time, Olive met up with two men she knew and they offered to give her a lift home. Olive asked to be dropped off just before they reached her home so that she could pick up a fish & chip supper for her and her husband, Harry, who had been at home looking after the children. The men dropped her off in a lay-by in Boothtown Road, roughly 400-yards from her home. The time was roughly 23.30.

Sutcliffe and Birdsall also left the pub around the same time and Birdsall recalled:

> On the way home we passed through the Boothtown area of Halifax, which is not a red-light area. Peter stopped the car and got out and said he was going to speak to somebody. I didn't take any notice if he had anything with him but he seemed to put his hand down the side of the seat.

According to Sutcliffe: 'I kept a hammer down by the side of the driving seat. I stuffed it into my jacket pocket.'

Birdsall recalled, 'There was a couple of people walking past, and I remember seeing a woman. She was walking quickly and Peter went round the back of the car and disappeared. He didn't seem to go in the same direction as the woman but was away ten to twenty minutes.'

Sutcliffe later said: '[I] ran down the alley parallel to where she were walking. I caught up wi' her and said summat about the weather ... She didn't answer.'

He went on to say he had told Birdsall that the woman was 'a prostitute we saw in the public house'. Are we really to believe that Birdsall and Sutcliffe just happened to 'bump into' the same woman who had humiliated Sutcliffe in the pub previously that evening? Or is it likely that they followed her from the pub?

It was around 23.45 that Sutcliffe finally caught up with Olive, who was near to her home after finding the fish & chip shop closed. As he passed her he mentioned something about the 'weather letting us down', as it had been raining, and he then struck Olive twice on the head with a ball pein hammer.

Sutcliffe recalled: 'I hit her on the head and scratched her buttocks with a piece of hacksaw blade or maybe a knife. My intention was to kill her but I was disturbed by a car coming down the road ... I didn't have time to finish her off.'

He had made two slash marks, one 12-in long and the other 4-in long (in a Y shape), just at the top of her buttocks but, before he could kill her, a car turned into the far end of the alley and Sutcliffe ran back to his car and the awaiting Birdsall, who recalled: 'When he came back he said he had been talking to a woman, but he was quiet, unusually quiet.'

Olive was found in the alleyway barely conscious by a neighbour who took her to his home. Another neighbour ran to get her husband Harry, and told him that she had been involved in some kind of accident. When he got to Olive she was being attended to by paramedics; she was rushed to Halifax Infirmary and then on to Leeds Infirmary where, after brain surgery, she spent the next ten days. She had suffered two depressed fractures of her skull from the hammer blows, one on the top and the other at the back. She also had lacerations above her left eyebrow and right eyelid, possibly from where she had fallen face first to the cobbled floor.

When Olive awoke from the operation, Detective Chief Inspector Dick Holland (who would later be involved in the Ripper Squad) was at her bedside and questioned her about her movements and what had happened to her.

Olive was able to describe her attacker as aged about 30, 5ft 10in tall, slightly built, with dark hair and some beard, or growth, on his face.

Unfortunately, the police did not believe her account of what had happened. She told them that the first blow she felt had happened immediately after the attacker had spoken to her, but police said she was found several yards away, and there were no signs that her attacker had dragged her there. They couldn't find a motive for anyone to attack her either, as she was well-liked and nothing had been stolen from her, so robbery was ruled out as a motive. Despite the strange scratches just above her buttocks they also ruled out a sexual motive. They soon convinced themselves that she had been attacked by her husband, Harry. Olive recalled: 'For weeks they accused Harry. One detective in particular would shout at me, "You know who attacked you, Olive. Tell us before he does it again and succeeds".'

The evening following the attack, Trevor Birdsall recalled reading about it in the *Bradford Telegraph & Argus*. 'It crossed my mind that Peter might be connected with it', he was to say at the eventual trial. However, he did nothing about it at the time, possibly because he knew that he could be implicated in the attack as he and Sutcliffe had followed her from the pub. To him, violence against women was just a part of life. He was violent towards his wife, and Melissa had even complained to their neighbours that Birdsall would hit her – on one occasion even showing them her bruises.

Olive's physical injuries healed remarkably quickly and the doctors were amazed at her speed of recovery, but her mental health never fully recovered. She suffered from clinical depression following the attack and was scared to go out of the house. It wasn't helped by the attitudes of the police. A dossier wrongfully described her as 'of loose morals' on the grounds that she was a married woman whose 'usual custom several nights a week [was] to visit public houses in Halifax on her own'. Even in the notes given to the prosecution at Sutcliffe's trial in 1981 it was written:

> Olive Smelt has no convictions for prostitution, nor has she been cautioned for such offences. Nevertheless, it seems that in the past she could have been euphemistically described as an 'enthusiastic amateur'. In a more benign fashion she could be described prior to the attack upon her, as a woman with an extrovert personality who, in pursuing an independent social life on Friday nights, enjoyed a fondness of company to break the routine of an otherwise mundane existence. In 1972, Mrs Smelt was barred from the Shakespeare Hotel due to behaviour towards men.
>
> Mrs Smelt's regular 'Friday night on the town', consisted, primarily of visiting a number of low class public houses situated in the Halifax town centre with her friend of many years, Muriel Falkingham. It is pertinent to mention that from time to time the accused, Peter William Sutcliffe, frequented some of the same establishments accompanied by Trevor Birdsall. Sometimes, Sutcliffe and Birdsall were also accompanied by their respective spouses.

To make matters even worse, in 1986 Chief Constable Ronald Gregory – by then retired, but demonstrating that he didn't know much about the biggest murder investigation, not only of his own police force, but also in Britain – wrongly described Olive as a prostitute in his memoirs. Olive recalled:

> Of all the things which have happened since Sutcliffe ruined my life, this was without doubt the worst. I was horrified and Harry said he just couldn't take anymore, while Linda [their daughter] became very ill with her nerves. All my family just felt as if they couldn't face their friends and workmates while I just wanted to hide. They'll never know how much harm they caused by that libel. Money could never make up for the pain inflicted on us. It just about broke us and I'll never forgive them for it – if anything was guaranteed to make the Ripper stigma stick to me for good, that was it.

Olive passed away from pneumonia in April 2011 after a short illness, aged 82. She had survived three strokes in 2004 and suffered from a serious pancreatic condition.

Chapter 6

Tracy Browne

On Wednesday 27 August 1975, 14-year-old Tracy Browne was attacked at around 23.00 in Silsden, near Keighley – twelve days on from the attack on Olive Smelt, and just 4.5 miles from the scene of the attack on Anna Rogulskyj. It's highly possible that Sutcliffe attacked her as she was an easy target and, having failed to kill Olive Smelt, he felt he had unfinished business.

Tracy Browne was born along with her twin sister Mandy in 1961. She also had two other sisters. Tracy was actually christened Caroline Tracy Browne but preferred to be called Tracy. Her mother, Nora, bred dogs at Upper Hayhills Farm, near Silsden, and it was to here that she was walking when she was attacked.

Tracy and Mandy had been at a friend's house in Weatherhead Place, roughly a mile-and-a-half away, and they left to walk home together. Tracy recalled that because it was the school holidays:

> We were allowed half an hour later to get home. Normally, it was about quarter past ten and we were allowed to be home for quarter to eleven. They were still fairly light nights as well. We started walking back, took a short cut through the park, which took about five or ten minutes off the journey. But I hung back to chat to my friends, whereas my sister, she carried on.

When she realised Mandy was out of sight, Tracy reluctantly left the park and her friends and headed up the steep country lane towards home.

> As I was walking up my feet were hurting – I was wearing those platform shoes that were in fashion, so I decided to sit down on these bricks and take my shoes off.
>
> I just happened to look up and I was aware of this man walking towards me and he just stood there, looked at me for a couple of seconds and then started walking up the road.

She later stated:

> He was about two feet away but directly in front of me. I looked at him, but he just stared intensely down at me for a few seconds and then walked on without saying a word.

Sutcliffe was walking very slowly, and Tracy soon caught up with him and they began a conversation.

It was now around 23.00 and Tracy recalled: 'I started walking up and he asked me my name and I told him. He said, "Have you a boyfriend?" He seemed a really nice, charming man. I had no reason to think that I was in a dangerous situation.'

Sutcliffe told her that his name was 'Tony Jennis'. Tracy found this funny as she had spent a lot of her holidays with a Tony Jennison. Sutcliffe also said to her that there was 'nothing doing in Silsden'.

Tracy continued:

> I felt quite comfortable with him because he seemed such an unassuming, charming sort of guy. I said, 'I've never seen you walking up here before. Where do you live?' He told me, 'Up at Hole Farm', which is at the top of Bradley Road, about half a mile from my home. [Again, Sutcliffe seemed to know the area well.] …
>
> Our conversation tailed off into complete silence for a time but then he said, 'My pal normally gives me a lift home but he's in the nick for drink-driving.'

Sutcliffe stopped twice to blow his nose, saying he had a summer cold, and stopped again to tie his shoelace. 'Other than that, he never took his hands out of his pockets. We had walked together for almost a mile – for about thirty minutes – and I never once felt intimidated or in danger.'

When they reached the gateway to Tracy's farm, Sutcliffe had hung back a little and as she turned to thank him for accompanying her, she recalled:

> He hit me five times on the head. I heard him grunt like Jimmy Connors serving, each time he struck. But amazingly I never lost consciousness throughout it all …
>
> I was shouting, 'Please don't, please don't', and at the same time I could hear his grunts with the sheer impacts of the blows.

The first blow had knocked her down to her knees and as she scrambled around on the road on her knees she fell into the verge on the other side of the road. 'Then the headlights of a car disturbed him. He picked me up and threw me over the fence to get me out of the way as quickly as possible.' She never forgot the sound of his shoes on the tarmac as he began to walk away.

As the car neared, Sutcliffe walked back the way he had come, downhill, towards Silsden. When the car had passed him, he began to run downhill towards his car, which he had left parked on Skipton Road.

Tracy recalled:

> I remember scrambling around the fields, and I remember feeling really weak, although I wasn't aware I was nearly bleeding to death.
>
> My vision had gone because I was so stunned from the attack and my eyes had filled with blood. I pulled myself up and slowly managed to stand

up. I was very shaky and began staggering around the field disorientated and still unable to see anything. I fell down several times but forced myself back up. I told myself I had to get home in case he came back to finish me off. That fear drove me on. I knocked on the door of a farmhouse, but no one answered. I staggered around for another hundred yards, by which time I was covered from head to waist in blood.

Tracy managed to fumble her way to a caravan in one of the fields, where farmhand Fred Hargreaves helped her. 'He cleaned me up and then drove me back to the farm.'

When she got home her mother, Nora, recalled: 'When she came through the door her jumper was squelching with blood.' Tracy was immediately taken to Chapel Allerton Hospital in Leeds for emergency lifesaving surgery. Neurosurgeons operated on Tracy for four hours in order to remove a sliver of bone from her brain. She had sustained five blows to her head from a ball pein hammer which had fractured her skull.

Tracy survived and was able to give one of the best descriptions of the Yorkshire Ripper. After all, it had just been her and Sutcliffe walking and talking for over thirty minutes. She described her attacker as having staring, almost black eyes, and:

I remembered his taupe-coloured V-neck jumper over a light blue open-necked shirt and dark trousers, which had slit pockets at the front, rather than the side. I told the policemen he was 5ft 8in, had very dark, almost black Afro-type wrinkly hair and a full beard. I even mentioned the gap between his teeth and his insipid voice – a little man with a high-pitched voice. His accent I recognised as being local even though it wasn't strong.

Her description was confirmed by a witness who came forward later and provided a photofit of a dark-haired, bearded man, who had been seen in the neighbourhood that night, and had been seen standing near what was described as a white Ford car.

Found near the scene of the attack was a distinctive bracelet of wooden beads and a paper handkerchief, both believed to have belonged to Sutcliffe.

Tracy recalled: 'The police asked me if I could do an identikit picture, which I did. To me, you couldn't have got a picture more perfect than that. It was pinned up on shop windows and shop doors for a few weeks after that.'

Detective Chief Superintendent Jim Hobson, who was later in charge of the Ripper Squad, was put in charge of the investigation and 200 officers were involved in the hunt for Tracy's attacker, but without success.

Just two weeks on from the attack, Tracy donned a wig and, while accompanied by a policewoman, toured the local pubs and discos around Silsden and Streeton looking for the man who had attacked her, but without success.

This may have been partly because following the attack Sutcliffe, his wife and her parents, had left immediately for a holiday to Prague, stopping off in Rome on the way.

When initially arrested in 1981, Peter Sutcliffe didn't mention anything regarding Tracy Browne in his confession, as this would've left his defence of 'God' instructing him to attack and kill prostitutes in tatters. After his trial, the Assistant Chief Constable, Colin Sampson, was asked to write a report regarding the police investigation into the

Ripper crimes. He came up with a list of other possible attacks that could have been carried out by Peter Sutcliffe and it was then that the attack on Tracy was looked at again.

In 1992 Sutcliffe was questioned by Cleveland Police's Chief Constable Keith Hellawell about these possible attacks but he refused to accept responsibility and said the police had no evidence. He then told the Chief Constable, who had been Assistant Chief Constable with West Yorkshire Police at the time of the Ripper crimes: 'You're right; it sounds as if I've done them. The description is of me. It's in the right timescale. The way that the person killed or attempted to kill is the way that I operated. Therefore, it must be me.' Eventually, Sutcliffe caved in and admitted to the attack on Tracy, telling Keith Hellawell that he remembered seeing a photofit of himself in the local newspaper following the attack and had commented to his mother-in-law: 'Look, this could be me', and they both laughed and joked about it. Keith Hellawell recalled:

> He related, all those years on, detailed circumstances of those attempted murders that only the criminal would know. He also remembered he put her [Tracy Browne] over a fence, being careful that he didn't scratch her on the barbed wire. That hadn't been disclosed. We hadn't made that public at all. So only he would know that.

The Criminal Prosecution Service decided that it was not in the public interest to prosecute Sutcliffe for the attack.

After six weeks of rest, Tracy returned to school wearing a wig. She recalled:

> I had regular brain scans and was on drugs for two years to monitor any possible damage and prevent me suffering seizures. But I made a full recovery and I refused to dwell on things. I think I was helped because I had such a clear recall of my attacker that I knew I would recognise him straight away.

In his memoirs, Chief Constable Ronald Gregory gave a nonsensical explanation for why Tracy was never considered a Ripper victim throughout the original investigation. 'Tracy was not a prostitute; we thought at the time she was hit with a piece of wood and all the other attacks were in city areas.'

Here, then, were four attacks carried out by Peter Sutcliffe, the Yorkshire Ripper, that should have been linked yet were not. The attack on Tracy Browne was never linked to the previous ones on Gloria Wood, Anna Rogulskyj or Olive Smelt, despite the obvious similarities. All victims attacked were women; all attacked at night; a blunt instrument had been used to inflict the initial injuries; all described the attacker as a bearded, dark-haired man. Olive and Tracy even recalled him having a Yorkshire accent, and all attacks had taken place within a matter of weeks in a relatively local area.

There was also evidence to suggest that their attacker had stalked them. Anna Rogulskyj stated that the man who had attacked her had previously approached her more than once; Olive Smelt had seen her attacker earlier in the pub and he had probably followed her from there to where she was attacked; and Tracy Browne's attacker said his name was one extremely similar to that of one of her friends. Also, the area where

Tracy was attacked was so remote that any chance of Sutcliffe accidentally bumping into a single woman walking alone there was extremely remote. At this juncture, a large-scale police operation should've been launched.

On his return from holiday, Sutcliffe got a job as a tyre fitter and driver at T. Waite & Sons, Common Road Tyres, Cleckheaton, which entailed travelling throughout Yorkshire and occasionally to Manchester and the Midlands but, within three weeks, his employers had reported him to the police for the alleged theft of second-hand tyres. On 15 October 1975, he was arrested by PC Sutcliffe (no relation) and he immediately admitted the offence and produced the stolen tyres from the boot of his car. They were worth 50p each. Amazingly, Sutcliffe held on to his job.

The compulsion within Sutcliffe soon rose to the fore again and he set out to vent his frustrations – and this time his victim would not live to tell the tale.

Chapter 7

Wilma McCann

On Thursday 30 October 1975, 28-year-old Wilma McCann was murdered at around 01.30 in Chapeltown, Leeds – two months after the attack on Tracy Browne. She is the first known victim murdered by the Yorkshire Ripper and, despite not having any convictions for prostitution, it is believed she may have been working as one. The police certainly treated her murder as one of a prostitute.

Willemena Mary Newlands was born on 1 July 1947 to George and Betsy Newlands in Dalreich, Dumbarton, Scotland, where she spent her early years, before the family moved to the Shetland Isles. Things didn't work out there, so the family moved to Inverness. She was one of eleven children (seven boys and four girls). Her father was a farm worker, lorry driver and plumber, and her mother, Betsy, stayed at home to look after the children.

Wilma, known to be quite an emotional girl, went to Inverness High School and left aged 15 without gaining any academic qualifications. She quickly found a job as a counter assistant with a local department store before getting a job at the Gleneagles Hotel near Perth, where she worked for two years before she moved to Leeds aged 18, where five of her brothers lived.

She met a man called Gerald McCann who was from Londonderry, Northern Ireland, and they had a daughter called Sonje (pronounced Sonia) two months before they married on 7 December 1968.

The newlyweds moved to 65 Scott Hall Avenue, Chapeltown, Leeds, where they had another three children in quick succession – Richard (1969), Donna (1970) and Angela (1972), but the marriage was over by 1974. Wilma enjoyed nights out, drinking and having fun, and struggled to adapt to motherhood and marriage. In March 1970 she was fined £2 at Leeds Magistrates' Court for being 'drunk & incapable'. It is believed she had cheated on her husband multiple times. Gerald was also unfaithful during the marriage and was often violent towards Wilma. Their son Richard would recall many years later that Wilma twice had to receive psychiatric care for nervous breakdowns caused by Gerald's emotional and physical abuse.

Gerald left Wilma and moved in with another woman, with whom he quickly fathered another child. He continued to visit the four children he had with Wilma after school, and still bought them birthday and Christmas presents, but Wilma never asked him for any maintenance money and never claimed any benefits. Instead, she began to go out, and occasionally charged men for her sexual services when money became tight. She appeared four times at Leeds Magistrates' Court on theft charges and once on a charge of 'Abstract Electricity' (dishonestly using, wasting, or diverting electricity).

Gerald and Wilma decided to divorce and it was Gerald who brought the proceedings against Wilma due to her adultery. Wilma did not contest it. Court proceedings were imminent when she was murdered.

Wilma didn't see why having four young children at home should stop her going out at night and having fun. She would often leave her eldest child, Sonje, in charge of the other three young children. At first it was just at weekends, but it quickly became every Thursday, Friday, Saturday and even sometimes Sunday too. The house was often left unclean as Wilma was too busy sleeping off a hangover and the children were left to fend for themselves.

After Gerald had moved out Wilma had a number of different boyfriends – mostly drunks only hanging around for the sex.

In 1974, when Sonje was just 6 years old, one of Wilma's boyfriends raped her before quickly disappearing off the scene. Sonje never told her mother what had happened to her and kept it to herself until she reached adulthood.

Another of Wilma's boyfriends was extremely violent and would snap without warning. He often beat Wilma and even once threatened Gerald with a hammer when he called round to see his children.

Shortly before her death, Wilma began to see a Scottish long-distance lorry driver called Tommy. He and Wilma had an argument on the 12 October 1975 and it ended with Wilma's neighbours finding her in her back garden, agitated and severely beaten from where Tommy had hit her and threatened her with a knife.

Social Services quickly became involved and all four children were put on the 'At Risk' register. Wilma was certain that it was her neighbours who had reported her for leaving the children alone when she went out in the evenings and so, instead of leaving by the front door, she started to leave via the back door. She would go out of the gate at the back garden and onto a grassy area known as the Prince Phillip Playing Fields, where she would walk along the edge and come out further down Scott Hall Lane, away from any prying eyes.

Wilma had four convictions for drunkenness, theft and disorderly conduct, and at the trial of Peter Sutcliffe the Attorney General described her as someone who, 'drank too much, was noisy and sexually promiscuous – she distributed her favours widely'.

A confidential police report stated: 'McCann was neglectful of her home and children, her house was filthy and in a deplorable condition.'

At 19.30 on the evening of Wednesday 29 October, Wilma headed out as usual, leaving her eldest daughter Sonje in charge of the other children. She went out of the back door, past the Prince Phillip Playing Fields and headed for the pubs and clubs.

She was spotted in a number of pubs that night, including 'The Regent', 'The Scotsman', 'The White Swan' and 'The Royal Oak', where she drank whisky and beer. Later samples taken from her body showed that she had consumed 12–14 measures of spirits. On weeknights the pubs closed at 22.30, so when it reached closing time she went to the 'Room At The Top' club, which played mostly Reggae, Soul, Motown and Disco, and she stayed until just before 01.00. She was then spotted by two policemen on nearby Meanwood Road between 01.00–01.30, where they noticed that she was drunk and was carrying a container of curry and chips.

Wilma wasn't very far from home at all, but she decided to try and thumb a lift, possibly in the hope of being able to charge a man for sex in order to fund her next night out. She was seen by multiple motorists stumbling around the pavements and trying to flag down vehicles. One lorry driver pulled over, but when Wilma began swearing and telling him what to do, he quickly drove off.

Peter Sutcliffe had spent the day delivering items around the Skipton and Barnoldswick areas and when he clocked off he went for a few drinks alone around the pubs in his Ford Capri.

He recalled in his confession statement:

> I'd gone under the underpass and taken the A58 Wetherby turn-off and followed this round ... she was at the bottom of a road where it straightened out, on the left side walking on the grass. She was obviously hoping to get a lift. I stopped and asked her how far she was going. She said, 'Not far, thanks for stopping' and was cheerful and friendly, so I set off and carried on driving and instead of carrying on round to the right, she suggested I carried straight on. She remarked something about it being a nice car.
>
> I just stopped on impulse to give her a lift, as I'd just come round the bend. I'd gone there for the purpose of picking up a prostitute with the intention to kill her. I realised shortly after she had got into the car that she was a prostitute because she asked me if I 'wanted business', and the evil chain of events went on from there.
>
> To me, I didn't know what she meant by this. I asked her to explain and straight away a scornful tone came into her voice, which took me by surprise because she had been so pleasant. She said, 'Bloody hell! Do I have to spell it out for you?' She said it as though it was a challenge. My reaction was to agree to go with her.

This was a clear lie as he knew the phrases prostitutes used because he had been picking them up for a while. He continued:

> She told me where to park. It was just off this road, we turned left, we came to this field which sloped up. I parked near the field. We sat there for a minute talking then all of a sudden her tone changed and she said, 'Well? What are we waiting for? Let's get on with it!' Before we stopped she had said it would cost a fiver.
>
> I was a bit surprised, I was expecting it to be a bit romantic. I think she had been drinking because she was being irrational. I couldn't have intercourse in a split second, I had to be aroused.

This wouldn't be the last time Sutcliffe would suffer from erectile dysfunction. Did he need Wilma to be motionless and silent for him to become aroused, as happened with Anna Rogulskyj when he masturbated at the scene of the attack, and as he would do so to others later on?

'At this point she opened the car door and got out. She slammed the door and shouted, 'I'm going, it's going to take you all fucking day!' She shouted something like, 'You're fucking useless!'

Clearly this never happened, as the caretaker and his wife who lived just yards from where Sutcliffe parked the car said they hadn't heard a thing that night despite leaving the window open, and their dog had stayed silent all night, too.

> I suddenly felt myself seething with rage. I got out of the car wanting to hit her to pay her back for the insult. I went to her and said, 'Hang on a minute, don't go off like that.'
>
> She was only 3 or 4 strides away, she turned and came back to me. She said something like, 'Oh, you can fucking manage it now, can you?' She sounded as though she was taunting me.
>
> I said: 'There's not much room in the car, can we do it on the grass?' This was with my idea of hitting her. She said, 'I'm not going to do it bloody well next to the car.' With that, she stormed up the hill into the field.
>
> I had a tool box on the back seat of the car and I took a hammer out of the tool box. I followed her into the field. I took my car coat off and carried it over my arm, I had the hammer in my right hand. I put my coat on the grass. She sat down on the coat. She unfastened her trousers. She said: 'Come on then, get it over with'. I said: 'Don't worry, I will'.

This must also be a lie. First of all, why would Wilma suddenly change her mind? And secondly, Wilma was found on a small slope that led from the car park up onto the fields. Clearly she had not walked onto the field.

> I then hit her with the hammer on her head. I was stood up at the time behind her. I think I hit her on the top of the head. I hit her once or twice on the head. She fell down flat on her back and started making a horrible noise like a moaning gurgling noise.

How could she fall down if she was sat on his coat undressing? Sutcliffe then tried to show how he was torn between going through with the killing or not:

> I thought, 'God, what have I done?' I knew I had gone too far. I ran to the car intending to drive off. I sat in the car for a while, I could see her arm moving. I was in a numb panic. I still had the hammer in my hand. I put it back in my tool box.
>
> I half expected her to get up, and realised I would be in serious trouble. I thought the best way out of the mess was to make sure she couldn't tell anybody. I took a knife out of the toolbox. It had a wood handle with one sharp side. The blade was about 7in long.
>
> I went to her. She was still lying on her back. I thought that to make certain she was dead I would stab her in places like the lungs and the throat. I stabbed her at least four times, once in the throat. Before I stabbed her in the body, I pulled up her blouse or whatever it was and her bra, so I could see where I was stabbing her. I was in a blind panic when I was stabbing her, just to make sure she wouldn't tell anyone.

Unbelievably, Sutcliffe then stated:

> What a damn stupid thing to do just to keep somebody quiet. If I was thinking logical at the time, I would have stopped and told someone I'd hit her with the hammer. That was the turning point. I realise I over reacted at the time, nothing I have done since then affected me like this.
>
> After I stabbed her I went back to the car. I remember that I'd taken my coat off the ground after I'd hit her with the hammer and I'd taken my coat back to the car. I started the car and shot off backwards along the narrow road leading to the road, swung the car round, and drove away towards Leeds. I drove home as soon as possible.
>
> I was then living at my mother-in-law's house … I was very frightened and don't even remember driving there. I thought I was bound to get caught. I parked my car outside her house … I looked over my clothing before I went in the house. I went straight to the bathroom and washed my hands and went to bed.

Sutcliffe later corrected aspects of his original confession:

> I may have given the impression by what I've said to her and what she replied, that the intent was to have sex, but this was not the case. This kind of talk was just a preamble leading up to the true purpose of my killing her. It was my idea to get her to go up a distance up the field. To accomplish this I had to put up with all kinds of language and abuse because she couldn't see the point. I had the tackle [a hammer and a kitchen knife] with me in my pocket and, in fact, I didn't go back to the car and return to it. I hit her with the hammer, she still made loud noises and I hit her with it again, and the noises still didn't stop. I then took the knife out of my pocket and stabbed her about four times, as I've previously described.

There was absolutely no mention of Wilma's purse with the word 'MUMIY' written on it (a gift from her daughter Sonje) that was missing from the scene and never found, which would suggest that he had taken it as a trophy.

Wilma's two eldest children, Sonje and Richard, woke early to find that their mother wasn't home. They left the other two children at home and went out of the back door and onto the Prince Phillip Playing Fields and planned to head to the bus stop, as that was the route their mum would take if she was just late getting home and they were hoping to bump into her. It was still pitch black and a thick fog had formed, but Sonje recalled years later that she saw 'a bundle, about twenty-five yards away', and thought that it was just a Guy Fawkes that had been left on the field. It was actually their mother's dead body.

Sonje and Richard carried on past the bundle and waited at the bus stop. By now it was 06.00 and an 11-year-old neighbour, Tracy Attram, saw the two of them waiting for their mum. When Wilma didn't get off the first two buses that morning, Sonje and Richard went home to get breakfast ready for the other two children.

Wilma McCann's body was found at 07.41 by milkman Alan Routledge and his 10-year-old brother Paul. At first Alan thought it was a bundle of rags but when Paul looked closer he shouted, 'It's a body!'

Wilma's body was just yards away from the caretaker's house; as mentioned, both he and his wife had heard nothing throughout the night, despite their bedroom window being open. More surprisingly to them, their dog hadn't barked – which was unusual because it normally did at the slightest of noises from outside.

The caretaker, Mr John Bould, recalled how the milkman had banged on his door telling him about the body and to phone the police. John Bould looked over his garden fence and recalled: 'Both my wife and I knew her because she used to bring her kids to the nursery school. It was a terrible sight – she was lying on her back with her eyes staring, her clothes open, her body covered in blood. I told the milkman to get on the phone and dial 999.'

When the police arrived they discovered Wilma McCann lying on her back. Her trousers were down by her knees and her bra had been lifted to expose her breasts. Her strawberry blonde hair was matted with blood and there were clear stab wounds to her body – one in the neck, two below her right breast, three below her left breast and nine to her lower abdomen.

Blood from her stab wounds had leaked over to the right side of her body which had dried and soiled the right side of her blouse and more blood from the stab wounds on the left side of her chest had trickled down to the edge of her knickers.

The stab wound to the throat had led to heavy soiling of the skin at the front and right side of the neck, and blood had stained the grass behind Wilma's head.

Forensic Pathologist Mike Green later recalled: 'The unusual thing about the stab wounds was that whoever has done it [had] taken time to push that instrument around and then time to stand back.'

Other spots of dried blood could also be seen on the front of both Wilma's thighs, on the upper surface of her trousers and the upper part of her right hand.

Wilma was still holding the strap from her handbag in one of her hands, showing how sudden the attack had been, and again goes against Sutcliffe's version of events.

Her knickers were still in the normal position. A small button lay by her head and some coins were in the grass nearby. Vaginal swabs at the post-mortem indicated no presence of semen, but there was a positive reaction on the back of her trousers and knickers. It was not possible to get a blood group from the semen and this was because the person did not secrete blood cells in his bodily fluids. Clearly, Sutcliffe had masturbated over Wilma as she lay either dead or dying.

The Pathologist's opinion was that Wilma had been struck with the hammer while in a standing position and that the subsequent injuries were inflicted as she lay unconscious on the ground.

The murder was investigated by Detective Chief Superintendent Dennis Hoban of West Yorkshire's Eastern Crime Area and an incident room was set up at the former Leeds City Police HQ in Brotherton House. The murder was treated as an independent case and none of the previous attacks on Gloria Wood, Anna Rogulskyj, Olive Smelt or Tracy Browne were linked to it.

At a press conference, Detective Chief Superintendent Hoban described the murder as:

> particularly savage and sadistic. The body was found less than a hundred and fifty yards from Mrs McCann's council house. We would like to speak to any person who might have seen her last night or yesterday afternoon. It is common knowledge she frequented local public houses and city centre public houses. We would like to see any relatives – we believe she has brothers living in the Leeds area.

He asked that Wilma's 'many boyfriends' came forward, and concluded that 'She was a quiet woman and had very little contact with neighbours.'

Regarding items missing from the scene, Hoban stated: 'This purse is now missing and we would urgently like to speak to anyone who feels they know anything about such a purse. It would now seem that, as well as the sexual assault, robbery may have been an additional motive for her death.'

As information came in to the incident room, the first lead pointed towards a red Hillman Avenger, driven by a black male aged around 35, with a moustache which was rounded to the corners of his mouth, which had been seen by multiple witnesses in the area at the time the murder was committed. A description of both the car and the driver were circulated but they were never traced. The same informant also saw an articulated lorry which had been parked nearby, but despite enquiries at 483 haulage companies the police drew a blank.

The details of injuries sustained by Wilma McCann were kept from the press by the police and they were only told that she had died from head injuries. Details of all stabbing injuries were kept from them in all of the cases in order to stop any copy-cat killer.

A week after Wilma was murdered, a late-night road-block was set up along the route Wilma had taken when she left the 'Room at The Top' club. As a result, the lorry driver who stopped to talk to her but didn't pick her up was traced.

Wilma's children were first taken into care, and then went to live with their father, who was violent towards them. Sadly, Sonje McCann committed suicide in December 2007, reportedly after suffering years of depression and alcoholism related to her mother's death.

Relevant Statistics

Incident Room set up	30 October 1975
House to House Enquiries	5,058
Actions	2,880
Statements	538
Vehicle Enquiries	3,490
Officers Engaged	137
Hours Worked (Not inc. Overtime)	53,399
Incident Room Closed	20 January 1976

Chapter 8

Rosemary Stead

On Tuesday, 6 January 1976, 18-year-old Rosemary Stead was attacked at around 18.30 in Queensbury, Bradford, – just over two months after the murder of Wilma McCann.

Rosemary, who had become engaged on her 18th birthday to boyfriend Alan Elsey, worked as a shop assistant at Sandmartin Supermarket on Wakefield Road, Bradford; on the evening of 6 January she finished work later than usual, which meant that she missed her usual bus home to 27 Hainsworth Moor Grove, Queensbury, a small village on the moors outside the city. She decided to walk home and by the time she reached the outskirts of the village it was dark.

As she was walking along Halifax Road she became aware of a man walking behind her. As she walked down a dark, muddy snicket she was suddenly and viciously attacked from behind with a blunt object. She was hit on the back of her head and it knocked her unconscious.

Both the cars driving by and other pedestrians disturbed her attacker and he ran off. They were able to describe him as 25–30 years old, 5ft 9in, slim build, dark hair, a moustache and beard, wearing a green jacket and dark jeans. A perfect description of Peter Sutcliffe.

When she came round, blood soaked, Rosemary staggered the few yards to her home and fell into the arms of her brother, Peter. Another brother, Allan, said: "We got her in the chair and got her some water. It was dark in the kitchen and at first we didn't see how badly hurt she was. When we got her in the light we could see that her nose and lips were all swollen and bleeding and there was a big gash in the back of her head. Her collar was soaked in blood.

"It was a while before she could tell us what happened. Her glasses had been smashed and she had lost the bag she was carrying. She told us that after getting off the bus she heard someone behind her. She started to walk faster but the footsteps were still there so she turned round. After that she can't remember anything."

Detective Superintendent Len Shakeshaft described the attack as "vicious and apparently motiveless." He added: "Rosemary was wearing a checked overcoat, red polo-necked jumper, a white skirt and navy-blue platform shoes."

Her case was not linked with the murder of Wilma McCann, or the attacks on Gloria Wood, Anna Rogulskyj or Olive Smelt, but neither was it linked with that of Tracy Browne, who had also been attacked from behind with a blunt instrument in a rural area four months previously.

Peter Sutcliffe never admitted to this attack and it was never linked with the Ripper series of crimes, but it was on the list of possible further crimes he may have committed that was compiled by Assistant Chief Constable Colin Sampson following Sutcliffe's trial. He was questioned about it later by West Yorkshire's Chief Constable Keith Hellawell.

Going by the witness descriptions, location and MO of the attack it is highly likely that this attack was carried out by Peter Sutcliffe.

Annoyed that he had failed to kill having been disturbed, Sutcliffe went back to the easier hunting grounds of the red light areas.

Chapter 9

Emily Jackson

On Tuesday 20 January 1976, 42-year-old Emily Jackson was murdered at around 19.30 near Chapeltown, Leeds – exactly two weeks after the failed attempt to murder Rosemary Stead.

Born Emily Monica Wood on 30 March 1934, she was the sixth eldest of twelve children. They lived in Fitzwilliam, near Wakefield, until Emily was 10 years old, when they moved to Armley, Leeds.

Emily got a job in a local weaving factory upon leaving school, and married Sydney Jackson on 2 January 1953 when she was 19 years old and he was 21. The early part of the marriage was spent moving around and living at different addresses in the Leeds area and in 1955 they had their first son, Derek. Three years later Neil arrived.

The marriage was a violent one at times, with Sydney breaking Emily's collarbone when he hit her with a poker – which he claimed he had done after finding out that his wife had been cheating with another man.

Emily left him in 1959 to live with another man, but was back with Sydney two years later and they moved with the children to Northcote Crescent in Morley. They soon had a third son, Chris, but it wasn't long before Sydney was beating Emily again.

She quickly moved out and took up home with a labourer called Mick, and this time she began divorce proceedings against her husband; things didn't work out with Mick and in the autumn of 1968 she moved back in with Sydney. It wasn't long before tragedy struck – in 1969, 14-year-old Derek had an accident at home and was killed. His death sparked a change in the married couple, bringing a halt to the affairs and the violence; they moved to 18 Back Green, Churwell.

Emily then gave birth to their fourth child, and first daughter, Angela. They began their own roofing company (S. & E. Jackson, Roofing Contractors) and Emily ran the business side of things due to Sydney's illiteracy. She quickly learned how to drive (as Sydney couldn't) and would drop Sydney and his tools off at the jobs, leaving the Commer van with him before she got a bus home. She would then do the return journey in order to bring him home every day too.

Since the death of Derek, Sydney recalled:

> We decided life was too short; we would live for today and not bother about the future. Sometimes she would go out alone, and I would meet up with her for a drink later on. But I do know that she never went in pubs on her own. She's been in the Gaiety five times at the most, and always with me. We got on together as well as most. We both believed in having a

good time – after all, why stop in every night? We believed in having fun while we could.

The Gaiety pub that Sydney mentioned was a notorious pub on the Roundhay Road, where many local prostitutes used to hang out in the Chapeltown red light district of Leeds. The reason he mentioned this was because by Christmas 1975 the roofing business had got into some financial difficulty. According to Sydney, he couldn't keep up with his wife's sexual appetite and it was she who volunteered to sell sex to ease the financial strain. This came as a complete shock to her friends and neighbours.

Emily would go out in the evenings to pubs and bars and if she met a man she would offer her services to him; they would use the back of the van if the man didn't have his own vehicle.

On some occasions Sydney would go with her and they would park the van in the Gaiety pub car park. They would go into the pub and he would drink until closing time, while Emily would go off looking for punters either in the pub or, if business was slow, she would go out onto the street corners and pick them up from there, making sure she was back at the Gaiety for closing time at 22.30 to take Sydney home.

At 18.00 on 20 January 1976, Emily and Sydney drove to the Gaiety, arriving approximately fifteen-minutes later. As Sydney sat down and ordered his first drink, Emily left the pub and went looking for business out on the streets as the van was too full with building material to be used that night. That was the last time Sydney saw his wife alive.

In the car park outside, Emily bumped into 19-year-old prostitute Maria Sellars, and the two exchanged pleasantries before Emily continued her journey to look for business. The time was now 18.55.

Peter Sutcliffe was on his way home from work and later recalled:

> This time I drove to Leeds looking for a prostitute because I felt I could not justify what I had done previously, and I felt an inner compulsion to kill a prostitute…
>
> I drove to Leeds in my Capri … I saw a woman dressed in an overcoat trying to stop drivers from the pavement on the road that leads to Wetherby Road. It was near some phone boxes. I stopped and wound the window down. I said, 'How much?' She said, 'Five pounds'. She got in the car. I remember when she got in there was an overpowering smell of cheap perfume and sweat, this served all the more for me to hate this woman even though I didn't know her. Looking back I can see how the first murder had unhinged me completely.
>
> She had an overcoat on and she was heavily built and had brown hair. She said she knew where we could go. I knew from the outset I didn't want intercourse with her. I just wanted to get rid of her. At that time I think I was dressed in my working clothes, at that time I used to wear wellington boots at work.
>
> At her direction, I turned the car round and drove back the way I'd come. We had just gone about 400 yards and she told me to turn left.

> I turned in and then left again and drove behind some old buildings, it was a cul-de-sac. I couldn't bear even to go through the motions of having sex with this woman. On the journey she told me that she could drive.

They had parked in the Manor Industrial Estate on Manor Street, just across the road from where Wilma McCann was last seen at the 'Room at the Top club'.

Sutcliffe continued:

> I wanted to do what I'd got in mind as soon as possible. I remember turning on the ignition again so that the red warning light came on, and pretended that the car would not start. I said I would have to lift up the bonnet to sort it out. I asked her if she would give me a hand. We both got out of the car. I lifted up the bonnet of the car. I had picked up a hammer which I had put near my seat for that purpose. I told her I could not see properly without a torch. She offered to use her cigarette lighter to shine under the bonnet.
>
> She was holding her lighter like this [demonstrating], I took a couple of steps back and I hit her over the head with the hammer. I think I hit her twice. She fell down onto the road. I took hold of her hands or wrists and pulled her into a yard which had rubbish in. I then made sure she was dead by taking a screwdriver and stabbing her repeatedly. I pulled her dress up and her bra before I stabbed her to make it easier. To be truthful, I pulled her clothes up in order to satisfy some sort of sexual revenge on her as on reflection I had done on McCann.
>
> I stabbed her frenziedly without thought with a Phillips screwdriver all over her body. I had taken the screwdriver with the hammer in the well of the driving seat. I was seething with hate for her. I remember picking up a piece of wood from the yard, about 2–3ft long and 3in x 1in, and pushing up against her vagina with it as she lay on her back. I cannot recall taking her knickers down. I threw the wood away in the yard.
>
> I left her lying on her back, I never took anything from her. Just as I was about to get in my car, a car came round with its lights on and stopped a few yards from where my car was. I didn't know what make of car it was, but it scared me. I put the hammer and the screwdriver on the car floor and drove away. I went straight home to my mother-in-law's house.
>
> At that time I had a feeling of satisfaction and justification for what I'd done. I found that I didn't have any blood on my clothes which I could see, so I had no need to dispose of them. I am still unable to recall if it was the same hammer I used on Jackson as I did on McCann, but I do recall buying a new hammer from a hardware shop near the roundabout in Clayton. It had a flat head on one side and a nail extractor on the other, which I later used on women. The hammer I used on the first two [Rogulskyj and Smelt] had a flat head on one end and a ball on the other.

As closing time approached at the Gaiety pub, Sydney left and went into the car park where he saw the Commer van but no sign of his wife. He waited for a short while but when she did not turn up he decided to take a taxi home and just thought that she was late finishing up with a punter.

At 08.10 the following morning, a workman was walking past the end of a short cul-de-sac between two derelict buildings when he saw something which caught his eye. He saw a bulky object that appeared to be partially covered by a coat. He had found Emily Jackson's body, 15ft inside the alley.

He immediately called the police and when they arrived Police Inspector Bateson saw Emily's body lying on its back under an archway with her legs just outside a doorway. She was still wearing her red, blue and green checked overcoat and her fawn-coloured handbag was lying nearby, but nothing appeared to have been taken. Her right arm was lying at right angles from her body and her right leg was bent upwards and outwards, flexed at the knee and hip. Her tights were laddered and they bore a six-inch hole above her knee. Her black knickers were still in place, but the left side of the upper edge of her tights was slightly displaced downwards, exposing the knickers. On her right thigh was an impression from the sole of a boot which was later identified as being from a heavily ribbed Dunlop Warwick wellington boot. The boot size was probably a size 7 and certainly no larger than an 8. A similar print was found in sand nearby. Her feet were bare, with one white sling-back shoe lying on the ground beside her right foot and the other a short distance away. The front of her body was soiled by dirt in various areas, especially the front and outer sides of the thighs. Her face was also heavily soiled with mud and blood, with blood staining on the front of her dress, her right arm and right hand. There were also bruises and abrasions on her face and throat, and all these injuries made it obvious that she had been dragged on her face along the ground.

The ground beneath and above her head was soiled by small pools and trickles of coagulated blood and there were also small areas of blood on the surface of the cobbles and concrete on the ground. There were clear marks on the ground which showed how Sutcliffe had dragged her body to the spot where it was found.

The post-mortem showed evidence of semen in her vagina that was believed to have come from an earlier punter. It also showed that Emily Jackson had been hit over the head with a hammer and that a sharpened screwdriver had been used in a frenzied attack to stab her fifty-two times. She had wounds to her throat, chest and abdomen, and thirty-eight of the stab wounds to her back were in an area 6in x 8in. One of the wounds to her chest was so deep that it had passed through the sternum and left a cruciform shape in the bone. There were also twelve stab wounds on the trunk that were very close together and which made it impossible to assign individual tracts to most of them. One of the wounds was to the left hip.

From the injuries received, and the fact that her body was found just 400 yards from where Wilma McCann was seen thumbing for a lift, the police linked the two murders.

As with the Wilma McCann case, Detective Chief Superintendent Hoban was put in charge of the investigation, and he established an incident room in the newly opened Millgarth Police Station.

Local prostitutes were spoken to and asked to give descriptions of any client who had acted violently towards them. A month after the murder it was established that Emily Jackson was last seen at about 19.00 getting into a green Land Rover near the Gaiety pub by a woman called Maria Sellars, who had stopped to talk to Emily. As they were chatting, the green Land Rover pulled up nearby and Emily went over to talk to him. She then got in and they drove off along Gledhow Road.

Maria Sellars described the driver as white, aged around 50, fattish build, mousey-coloured ear-length hair, a full beard and bushy ginger/blonde sideburns. He had an obvious scar which ran from the knuckles on his left hand to the wrist. This was probably the man who left the semen in Emily. An artist's impression of the driver was compiled, the most distinctive feature being his bushy ginger beard.

The description of this man was given to local prostitutes and some of them knew of a punter who matched the description, and they were able to add that he had an Irish accent. The description also matched that of a man who had attacked another prostitute in March 1975 called Barbara Miller and the police were eager to trace him, although they never did.

The police created a line of enquiry to trace and eliminate all persons with Land Rovers, and extended it to certain vans and Moskovitch cars which had a similar square appearance. Although 1,294 Land Rovers were traced and the drivers eliminated, posters of the artist's impression displayed, beyond the meagre information described, there was nothing for the police to act on.

Police tried to engage the public in helping to find the killer, and at one press conference Detective Chief Superintendent Hoban said:

> We are quite certain the man we are looking for hates prostitution. I am quite certain this stretches to women of rather loose morals who go into public houses and clubs, who are not necessarily prostitutes. The frenzied attack he had carried out on these women indicates this.
>
> I believe the man we are looking for is the type who could kill again. He is a sadistic killer and may well be a sexual pervert ... I cannot stress strongly enough that it is vital we catch this brutal killer before he brings tragedy to another family.

The details of the stab wounds were again kept from the press.

So far, the police had only linked the murders of Wilma McCann and Emily Jackson, and believed that they were both prostitutes, so the murderer was out to target prostitutes only. The police had failed to link the attacks on Gloria Wood, Anna Rogulskyj, Olive Smelt, Tracy Browne and Rosemary Stead. Those who had seen their attacker had all provided similar descriptions of him, and those who had heard him speak all noted that he spoke with a local accent.

Almost three weeks later, on the 9 February 1976, Peter Sutcliffe appeared at Dewsbury Magistrates Court on the charge of theft of the second-hand tyres from his workplace during the previous October. He was found guilty and fined £25. A week later he was fired for poor time keeping.

It was around this time that Sonia began some part-time work with her mother at the Sherrington Private Nursing Home. They needed money to pay off Peter's fine and also needed money coming into the house now that he was out of a job. Sonia worked mostly Friday, Saturday or Wednesday nights with her mother, not getting home until breakfast time. As will be seen, most of Peter Sutcliffe's subsequent attacks would take place when Sonia was working.

Sutcliffe disposed of his Ford Capri around 1 March 1976 and subsequently bought a white Ford Corsair saloon registered number KWT 721D, having seen it advertised in the *Telegraph and Argus* newspaper dated 29 April. Having taken it for a test drive, Sutcliffe agreed to pay £170 for it and took full ownership of it on 3 May.

By May, Sonia was deemed by her doctor to have made a good recovery from her schizophrenic illness and recommended that she was well enough to restart her teacher training, so she began that summer at the Margaret MacMillan Teachers Training College in Bradford. She also continued her evening shifts at the nursing home.

Relevant Statistics

Incident Room set up	20 January 1976
House to House Enquiries	3,720
Actions	5,226
Statements	830
Vehicle Enquiries	3,509
Officers Engaged	102
Hours Worked (Not inc. Overtime)	64,009
Incident Room Closed	6 February 1977

Chapter 10

Marcella Claxton

On Sunday 9 May 1976, unemployed 20-year-old Marcella Claxton was attacked on Soldiers' Field, Roundhay Park, Leeds at 04.00 – 3½ months on from the murder of Emily Jackson.

Marcella moved to the UK from the Caribbean island of St Kitts with her parents when she was 10 years old and lived in a house just off Roundhay Road in Leeds. Roundhay was considered one of the best areas of Leeds to live in – its only problem being that it backed on to the red light area of Chapeltown. By the time of her attack, Marcella had two children who were in care, and was pregnant with her third.

On Saturday 8 May, Marcella had been out at a late-night party in Chapeltown; as the clock ticked into Sunday she set off for home in a drunken state. Unfortunately for her, Sutcliffe, who had earlier taken his wife and mother-in-law to work at the nursing home, was cruising through the streets of Chapeltown in his new car.

Sutcliffe stopped his car next to her on Spencer Place and asked her if she wanted a lift. He recalled: 'She asked me if I was the police, I said, "No, do I really look like a policeman?" She decided to get into the car.' Marcella told him where she was going but as he pulled away he went in a different direction and they ended up at Soldiers' Field in Roundhay Park. He then drove a short way onto the field, (which is actually a large park) and stopped the car before offering her £5 to get out of the car, take her clothes off and have sex on the grass. It's at this point that the accounts of Marcella and Sutcliffe differ.

Marcella claims she told Sutcliffe that she did not want to have sex with him and then went behind a tree to urinate.

Sutcliffe, on the other hand, claims that Marcella was a prostitute and that when he picked her up, they agreed a price of £5 for sex. Once at Roundhay Park, which was sometimes used by Chapeltown prostitutes and their clients, Marcella 'went behind some trees to urinate and suggested that we "start the ball rolling on the grass".'

As he got out of the car while Marcella was urinating, Sutcliffe dropped his hammer and the noise alerted her. She asked what the noise was and he told her that he had just dropped his wallet. He then snuck up behind Marcella and hit her eight times over the head with his ball pein hammer.

Remarkably, Marcella remained conscious throughout and vividly recalled Sutcliffe undoing his trousers and masturbating while she lay on the grass moaning. Sutcliffe then walked back to his car before returning with some tissues and wiping himself down, before throwing the tissues on the ground and shoving a £5 note into her hand and telling her not to call the police.

Sutcliffe vehemently denied masturbating at the scene. When Marcella's version of events was put to him after his eventual arrest, he stated: 'I didn't want sex with any of them. And certainly not that one. Even the police said she were like a gorilla.' This was a reference to an outrageously offensive and racist remark made privately by the police that Marcella – who is on record as having a low IQ – was regarded by them as 'just this side of a gorilla'.

The truth of how Marcella Claxton and Peter Sutcliffe ended up on Soldiers' Field is probably a mix of both their stories. The police certainly believed that Marcella was working as a prostitute and in their report written in 1983 titled: 'Report into the Investigation of the Series of Murders and Assaults on Women in the North of England between 1975 and 1980', it is written that Marcella:

> went with a man to Roundhay Park in Leeds. Having been given money, on a pretext, she ran away and hid in nearby bushes. Thinking the man had gone, she returned ten minutes later to retrieve her shoes which had come off, when suddenly she was knocked to the ground and feigned unconsciousness.

Covered in blood and using her knickers to try and stem the blood flow from her headwounds, Marcella half-crawled and half-staggered all the way to a phone box on the junction of Roundhay Road and Princes Avenue, and managed to call for an ambulance. She recalled:

> After I had dialled 999 and was sat on the floor of the telephone box, a man in a white car kept driving past. He seemed to be staring and looking for me. It was the man that hurt me ... He got out and began searching the spot where he had left me. He must have come back to finish me off.

Marcella required extensive brain surgery and fifty-two stitches to close the wounds caused by the eight hammer blows she had received. She also miscarried her baby. Despite her injuries, on 10 May she was able to describe her attacker as a 30-year-old white male with crinkly black hair and beard, a Yorkshire accent (but not from Leeds) and drove a white car with red upholstery. She also recalled that he was wearing a gold ring. She said: 'He was like a salesman type, but at the same time the most terrifying person you can imagine. His eyes were glazed and he didn't seem to have any control of himself.' She compiled a photofit of her assailant, and on the same day details of the assault were published in 'Police Reports'.

In spite of the description, the attack on Marcella would not be conclusively linked to the Yorkshire Ripper case until he confessed to it following his arrest almost five years later. Following a murder in the exact same spot nine-months later at the hands of the Ripper, Detective Chief Superintendent Jim Hobson told the press that 'We have an open mind on this girl's story.'

This could be because – despite her insistence that her attacker was white – in yet another show of the police force's racism they were telling her he was black! She recalled that when this was put to her, 'I said no black man would have done this to me'.

The attack was investigated by Detective Chief Inspector Bradley and was thought of as a standalone case of serious assault and not linked with any previous murders or assaults.

Shortly after being discharged from hospital, Marcella went out with friends to the Gaiety pub, where Emily Jackson had been and was a local hangout for prostitutes. She was convinced that her attacker had then come into the pub, looked around, and walked out. She became upset and told her friends, but when they went outside the man had disappeared.

The 1983 'Report into the Investigation of the Series of Murders and Assaults on Women in the North of England between 1975 and 1980' concludes that this attack 'ought to have been included as a "possible" and had this been done the information available, particularly the description of the offender and vehicle, linked with similar information to be forthcoming from later attacks, would have assisted the enquiry.'

The same report states that: 'It is considered that the senior investigating officer on the Jackson investigation should have recognised the possibility that this was another attack in the series.'

Chapter 11

Maureen Hogan

At 01.30 on Sunday 29 August 1976, 39-year-old mother of four Maureen Hogan was attacked in Listerhills, the student area of the University of Bradford – 3½ months on from the attack on Marcella Claxton.

Maureen had spent the night out with friends having a few drinks and they had visited the Europa Club before they moved on to the Pentagon nightclub in the city centre for a dance. She left there around 01.30 and began walking home but was attacked from behind shortly afterwards.

Around five hours later, a milkman out on his rounds stumbled across her in a shop doorway; she was still unconscious. She was taken to Bradford Royal Infirmary and the surgeons were able to identify that she had severe head injuries and stab wounds to the abdomen. Her wounds were strikingly similar to those inflicted on Wilma McCann and Emily Jackson.

The attack was investigated by Detective Superintendent Dick Holland, who had investigated the attack on Olive Smelt, but as Maureen had been attacked from behind and knocked unconscious almost straight away, she was unable to provide any description of her attacker.

Sutcliffe never confessed to this attack, but he surely has to be the prime suspect. Although questioned about it by Keith Hellawell following a review of other possible attacks Sutcliffe might have carried out, he remained tight lipped. How many other men in that area and at that time would have been attacking women late at night by hitting them over the head with a hammer and slashing/stabbing at their abdomens?

In October 1976, Peter Sutcliffe found himself a job as an HGV driver at T. &W.H. Clark (Holdings) Ltd on the Canal Road Industrial Estate in Bradford – right next to Bradford's Manningham Lane red light district. It entailed the delivery of engine parts throughout the north of England, the Midlands and Scotland. The job took him further afield than he had been before and sometimes it included overnight stays. This, along with Sonia's studying and part-time evening work, created the perfect climate for Sutcliffe and would lead to 1977 being his most active year.

Chapter 12

Irene Richardson

On Saturday 5 February 1977, 28-year-old Irene Richardson was murdered on Soldiers' Field, Roundhay Park, Leeds, in the same spot where Sutcliffe had attacked Marcella Claxton nine months previously – five months and one week on from the attack on Maureen Hogan. The length of time between the last attack and this one can be explained away; Sutcliffe knew the police were keeping an eye on the red light areas because they believed the Ripper was out to kill prostitutes. This made an attack on a woman who was not a sex worker much more likely, but also much harder for Sutcliffe because a sex worker would likely take him somewhere quiet and away from prying eyes – the perfect killing ground.

Irene was born into the Osborne family on the 28 March 1948 in Possilpark, Glasgow, Scotland and had six sisters and three brothers. She had a fairly unremarkable childhood, but was remembered as a shy and sensitive young girl at her primary school.

However, this all changed when she went to Springburn Secondary School where she began smoking and skipping school. Her older brothers and sisters had begun to leave home and had moved to various parts of England; when Irene was 15 she ran off to London, subsequently appearing before the South East London Crown Juvenile Court on 18 October 1963 because she was found to be a 'young person in need of care'. She was given a two year supervision order and moved back to Glasgow, taking a job in a tea factory. Here, on 8 April 1964, she appeared before Glasgow Central Police Court on two charges of theft, to which she pleaded not guilty. The case was adjourned *sine die*. She then ran away to Bolton, but trouble followed her here too. She appeared before Bolton Juvenile Court on 19 August 1964, where she was made the subject of another Supervision Order. She was sentenced to residence in a Probation Hostel for one year and put under a Supervision Order for two years. Aged 17, Irene was back in London and had cut all ties with her family. She had a succession of jobs in the hotel industry, mainly as a chambermaid and waitress. By the time she was 19, she had given birth to two children.

Her first child, a daughter called Lorraine, was fathered by a man called John Henry Wade who Irene had been seeing, but her second child – a son called Alan – may have been fathered by a friend of John Wade's, known only as Dennis, or a mechanic named Jim Brown, neither of whom the police managed to track down.

Irene was not a natural at motherhood and needed to work to earn money, so she fostered Lorraine out in 1968 when she was 18 months old to George and Mary Dwyer from Croydon in Surrey. Two-and-a-half years later, when Lorraine was 4, the couple officially adopted her. Irene's son, Alan, was also fostered out.

Needing a change of scenery, Irene then moved to Blackpool to be near her sister, Helen, who had work there. Irene took work as a chambermaid at a local hotel. It is listed in the prosecution files that 'during this period it became evident that the deceased had a fondness for male company and she has been described as "man-mad" at this time'.

In November 1970 she met a man called George Richardson. He was working as a barman-turned-plasterer, but he was also an alcoholic; the couple married in June 1971. They had two daughters; the first, also called Irene, was born in 1973, and their second, Amanda, was born two years later.

In the summer of 1975, Irene secured employment as a cleaner at Pontins holiday camp in Blackpool. Not long after giving birth to Amanda, Irene left her husband and two young daughters without saying a word and headed back to London; the reason for this is not known, though it could have been a result of post-natal depression.

George reported her as 'missing' to the police but they were unable to find her. A few months later, totally out of the blue, she got in touch with George and he went with their two young daughters to London to talk to her. They found her working in the Grosvenor Hotel, South Kensington, and George and the children rented a flat nearby while he and Irene attempted a reconciliation. However, in April 1976, Irene again deserted them and George had no choice but to return to Blackpool with the two children, who were subsequently fostered out.

Irene had actually stayed in London and began living with a man called Steven Bray, who was on the run from Lancaster Prison and had a cash-in-hand job as a chef. She didn't tell him she was married, and it appears that it was at this point that she became involved in sex work.

Irene and Steven then moved to Leeds in October 1976 and lived in a few boarding houses around the red light district of Chapeltown. He soon found a job as a doorman at 'Tiffany's Club', while Irene found employment in the local hotels as a chambermaid. She then took a second job as a cleaner at a YMCA hostel, the Residential Boys Club, in Chapel Allerton.

Irene had been using Steven Bray's surname while in Leeds and the couple arranged to get married at Leeds Registry Office on 22 January 1977, but neither of them turned up. Steven Bray was also already married but hadn't told Irene; they both got cold feet on the big day as neither wanted to commit bigamy.

Irene was now in a desperate financial state and just ten days before her death, she failed to turn up for work at the YMCA hostel. She had spoken to the warden, Mrs Nellie Morrison, and asked for an advance on her wages as she said she had a large bill to pay, but Mrs Morrison was only able to give her £1. Irene then disappeared, reappearing a few days later and apologising for her behaviour, saying she had to get away from the man she was living with. She then put her shoes and her overalls into her bag, and left again.

Shortly afterwards a man appeared at the YMCA and collected her wages, but Irene never saw the money. This was probably Steven Bray. Not long after that, Bray left Irene and moved back to London for a short while before catching a ferry to Ireland.

A woman who lived in a rooming house in Cowper Street, Leeds, later told detectives that Irene and Steven Bray had twice rented a room in the house (number 1), but shortly before Irene was murdered the landlord had let her stay in a ground-floor room rent-free until he found a paying guest.

When a guest turned up, Irene was out on the streets. She was severely depressed and now living rough, sleeping in a public lavatory and selling her body on the street corners of Chapeltown. A few of her fellow prostitutes allowed her to take an occasional bath in their flats, but they were not allowed to let her move in.

On the 5 February Irene told her friend Pam Barker, that she was going to 'Tiffany's Club' to find Steven Bray, possibly to find out what he'd done with her wages. She didn't know that he had left and gone back to London. She was nicely dressed, wearing a matching yellow skirt and jacket and calf-length boots. At 23.15 she went to visit another friend, Marcella Walsh on Sholebrook Avenue, and left there around 23.30. Marcella was the last person to see Irene Richardson alive.

Sutcliffe recalled to detectives:

> The next one I did was Irene Richardson ... I drove to Leeds after the pubs shut. It was my intention to find a prostitute to make it one more less. I saw this girl walking in some cross streets in the middle of the vice estate near a big club. I stopped my car and she got in without me saying a word. I told her I might not have wanted her. She said, 'I'll show you a good time. You are not going to send me away, are you?'
>
> She told me to drive to the park. At this time you knew where I was picking them up. She told me where to drive and we came to this big field which was on my left. I drove off the road onto the field and stopped near some toilets. She wanted to use the toilets, so she got out and went over to them. She came back and said they were locked. Before she went to the toilet she took off her coat and placed it on the ground.

They were not, in fact, toilets but changing rooms for the football and lacrosse players who used the fields at weekends. Irene had probably gone there so she could remove her tampon in private.

Sutcliffe continued:

> When she came back she said she would have a wee on the ground. She took her boots off and placed them on the ground, then she crouched down to have a pee. By this time I was out of the car and I had my hammer in my hand.
>
> As she was crouching down, I hit her on the head from behind, at least twice, maybe three times. She fell down. I then lifted up her clothes and slashed her in the lower abdomen and also slashed her throat. I left her lying face down and I covered her up with the coat. I put her knee boots on top of her before I covered her up. I then got in my car and drove off the field. I cannot remember whether I drove off or backed off. When I got to the road, I saw a couple sitting on a bench near the toilets. I did not see a car.

He later told detectives that he left the scene because he had heard a car being driven away from the entrance to a house, and he later discovered that the house was owned by the disgraced former DJ, Jimmy Savile.

Sutcliffe went into a little more detail later on:

> I drove straight home. I looked at my clothes before I went in. I did not see any blood stains. I was wearing jeans and I believe I had some boots on. I don't remember throwing any of my clothes away.
>
> I kept the Stanley knife, but I haven't seen it for a long time, I think I may have lent it to someone...
>
> By this time, after the Richardson killing, prostitutes became an obsession with me and I couldn't stop myself, it was like some sort of drug.

He was then asked why it had been over a year since he had killed Emily Jackson. (The police failed to link him to the attempted murders of Marcella Claxton and Maureen Hogan in between). Sutcliffe responded: 'I was having a battle in my mind. My mind was in turmoil whether I should kill people.'

At 07.30 the following morning, a 47-year-old man called John Bolton was jogging across Soldiers' Field when he spotted a body lying on the ground near the rear of the changing rooms. As he approached, he asked 'What's the matter?' Getting no response, he brushed the hair aside from her face and saw 'blood on her neck and her eyes were glazed and staring'. He ran to a nearby house and raised the alarm.

When the police arrived, they immediately set up a cordon around the body. They found Irene was lying face down, with her hands under her stomach and her head turned to the left. Her long hair was matted with blood and it was hiding the stab wounds to her neck and throat, which was gaping. She was still wearing her long brown cardigan with a zip and her imitation suede fur-trimmed coat had been placed over her buttocks and legs, leaving just her bare feet visible.

Irene's calf-length boots had been placed carefully over her thighs. Unlike the other murders, her bra was found to still be in position, but her skirt had been pulled up and her tights had been pulled off her right leg and pulled down. Besides the neck and throat wounds, Irene had been stabbed three times in the stomach and the wound furthest to the left was almost 7in long. The knife had sliced straight through the abdominal wall and it left a number of coils of her intestine protruding. The coils were soiled with blood and had pieces of leaves and twig attached. It was established that all of the stab wounds were severe downward strokes.

The blood which had soiled her head and hair had also soiled some leaves which lay beside her head, and police also discovered her used tampon not far from her body.

There was a trail of blood roughly 4ft long which ran from where her body lay to where her handbag was found lying on some leaves, which indicated she had been moved after the initial strikes with the hammer. The flap of the handbag was open and next to it was a small cosmetics bag and a lipstick. Found beneath the handbag was a mortice key and a 1p coin, while inside the handbag was a letter from a family in Roundhay; it appeared that Irene had been trying to turn her bad luck around and had applied for a job as a nanny with a local family.

The post-mortem indicated that Irene Richardson had had sex with someone in the twenty-four hours before she died, and on the inside of her coat, and outside of her tights and knickers there was an area of seminal staining found. This would again point to the probability that Sutcliffe had masturbated over her dead or dying body.

Perhaps the most shocking aspect of her death though were the head injuries she had sustained – and one in particular. The pathology report states:

> This was an almost circular, punched-out depressed fracture of the central disc of the bone driven deeply into the underlying brain. The bevelling up of one edge of the fracture of the skull clearly showed where the hammer had got stuck by the force of the blow into the skull and had to be levered out to get it clear of the bone.

The murder was investigated by Detective Chief Superintendent Jim Hobson and an incident room was set up at Millgarth Police Station. It was quickly learned that at 23.35 on the night of the murder (shortly before Sutcliffe picked up Irene Richardson), a man in a white vehicle had, on several occasions, propositioned a woman near Nassau Place, Chapeltown. This was clearly Sutcliffe.

Detectives quickly discovered an important clue at the scene of the crime. Because it was February the ground underfoot was soft, so the tyre tracks on the grass and mud left by Sutcliffe's car were clearly visible; they took a plaster cast of each tyre mark. They were able to determine that these tyre marks had been left by a car with two India Autoway tyres, a Pneumant tyre and an Esso 110 tyre.

The rear track width also indicated that only twenty-six vehicle makes could have left the tyre marks – Sutcliffe's Ford Corsair being one of them. This did, however, mean that in West Yorkshire alone they would need to check 100,000 cars before the killer had an opportunity to change his tyres. 80,000 of these cars were checked within the first nine months of the investigation by officers in the streets, at scrapyards, vehicle dismantlers and car auctions.

Detectives immediately began a 'Tracking Inquiry' to trace the owner of the car, and officers on nightshift duty were asked to examine any car they happened to stop in the course of their usual patrol and make a note of the make, the registration number, and details of the tyres. They were then asked to pass on these details to Millgarth Police Station, where a card was made out to indicate that the car had been checked and could be eliminated from the inquiry.

Due to the size of this task and the manpower needed to complete it, a more refined selection system was soon brought in by a Tyre Company expert, and enquiries to trace registered owners of the relevant twenty-six vehicle makes was carried out by local Vehicle Licensing Offices and the Police National Computer. This produced 53,000 registered owners of fifty-one different vehicle models living in the West Yorkshire Metropolitan areas, and the Harrogate area of North Yorkshire. Sutcliffe and his white Ford Corsair were among those 53,000.

Detective Chief Superintendent Jim Hobson told the gathered press:

> One hundred and twenty men are working on the murders. We are still interviewing prostitutes in the Chapeltown area and asking them about any man who may have been violent towards them. If we can get a number

of descriptions we can put them together and get some sort of an idea of the man we're looking for. We are also following up a possible link with another similar type of murder in Preston in November 1975 [Joan Harrison – more of which later] when a prostitute was found stabbed to death in the town centre. The fact that all three women – McCann, Jackson, Richardson – were picked up in the same area, the fact that two of them were found dead on playing fields, and the fact that the injuries are very similar, makes a link between them.

He then stated: 'Mrs Richardson was not a known prostitute but we know she was depressed. She could have gone in a car with a man as a "punter" after she had visited "Tiffanys". We are still trying to trace her movements that night.'

Detective Chief Superintendent Jim Hobson then made what was, in hindsight, an extremely dangerous move. He put policewomen on the streets posing as sex workers at night. The policewomen were watched at all times by other officers and they never got into any vehicles. The officers watching them were there simply to observe and take details of any car that stopped and attempted to pick them up.

This not only put the lives of the policewomen in danger, but because they would not get into any vehicles, the sex workers were able to pick them out straight away. All this did was drive both punters and sex workers into areas where the police were not operating.

A couple of days later, on 10 February 1977, investigating officers went to see Marcella Claxton to discuss the statement she had given when she was attacked in the same area. She recalled to reporters:

> I am still in fear of my life. I think I can identify him, and he must know that. I had been to a party and I was drunk. I was on my way home when a man in a white car stopped to give me a lift. He was well spoken and smartly dressed and said he did not live in Leeds. He took me to the fields and ordered me to strip. I said 'No' and then he started to beat me. I don't know what he hit me with. I was in hospital for several days and I needed fifty stitches in the head. Since then I have seen the police several times and tried to help them find this man.

Despite her claims, however, Detective Chief Superintendent Hobson then told the press: 'At the time of the savage attack last year, Marcella Claxton was working as a prostitute in the Chapeltown Road area. It now seems that West Avenue, Roundhay, the spot where Mrs Richardson's body was found, was a favourite spot for prostitutes to take clients.'

The police were, wrongly, still convinced that Marcella Claxton was a prostitute, despite her protestations, and because she and Irene Richardson had been attacked in the same area, were now suggesting that Irene Richardson was a prostitute too.

Jim Hobson went further still, completely dismissing the photofit compiled by Marcella Claxton of her attacker, saying it was 'not necessarily a description of the murderer'. It was not released to the press or the public, although Hobson described it to the waiting press – failing to mention anything about the beard and moustache. That photofit only ever appeared in a confidential police report and a separate police circular.

The 1983 'Report into the Investigation of the Series of Murders and Assaults on Women in the North of England between 1975 and 1980' states that 'When the murder of Irene Richardson occurred in February 1977, also in Soldiers' Field, Leeds, it should have strengthened the links between this and the Claxton attack.'

Not every detective was convinced that the murder of Irene Richardson was linked with those of Emily Jackson and Wilma McCann, and it wasn't until a 'Special Notice' to all forces included this case on the 9 May – three months later, that it was officially linked.

Steven Bray was found and arrested in London on 15 March 1977 and taken to Leeds Prison for questioning regarding Irene Richardson's murder. When it became clear that he was not connected he was returned to Lancaster Prison.

Relevant Statistics

Incident Room set up	6 February 1977
House to House Enquiries	4,385
Actions	4,400
Statements	1,611
Vehicle Enquiries	99,502
Officers Engaged	108
Hours Worked (Not inc. Overtime)	94,783
Incident Room Closed	23 April 1977

Chapter 13

Debra Schlesinger

On Thursday 21 April 1977, 18-year-old Debra Marie Schlesinger was murdered on Craigside Walk, Hawksworth, Leeds.

Debra had spent the evening with her friends Pat and Anne in a Leeds city centre pub before they caught the bus home. Her friend, Pat Power, recalled:

> We all walked home together – Anne going into her home first and then my home was next [on Craigside Walk] and Debbie had to walk around the block.
>
> As I got in I was talking to my father and I heard a scream – a really bad scream. My dad opened the front door and said it sounded like Debbie.

Within yards of her front door, Debra was stabbed through the heart and chased across the road to the local Conservative Club by a man who witnesses described as being a white male, with dark hair and a beard, aged around 30 and 5ft 6in in height.

Pat Power recalled: 'I came running over and found her slumped in the club doorway. There was no movement. I never thought she was dead at the time, I just thought she'd fainted or something.'

Debra's sister, Karen, recalled:

> Police or ambulance men, I can't remember which, were just sort of all crowding and you didn't know what had happened and no one was telling you anything. Just sort of like, 'get back home.' I said, 'Well, what's up?' I was just told that a terrible thing has happened and I said, 'No, she's not dead?' and they said, 'I'm afraid she is.'
>
> Until I heard it myself I just would not believe that anyone could've killed her.

Sutcliffe had been going to the Kirkstall Forge engineering plant in Hawksworth on a frequent basis with his job. It was just 100 yards from Debra Schlesinger's home and his work records show that he was collecting from the Forge on the day Debbie was killed. The bus stop was also right opposite Kirkstall Forge and as has already been shown, Sutcliffe liked to stalk his victims.

Had he seen her that night while he was loading the lorry, followed the girls and then attacked Debra when she was on her own? His aim always was to kill, and as she was on her garden path just yards from her front door had he chosen to stab her, as a blow to the head may make her scream for help? Or did he drop the hammer? Or did he choose a different method of killing because he was trying to throw the police off his scent? As will be seen, he later committed, and admitted to, two attacks where he changed his MO in order to throw the police off his scent. He then only had to run 100 yards back to the safety of his vehicle.

Detective Chief Superintendent Jim Hobson was also put in charge of this investigation. The following morning, he was interviewed by a local television news crew and was asked if he had any idea what the motive could be for the murder. He replied: 'No, not at this stage. She hadn't been sexually assaulted and robbery doesn't seem to be the motive at this stage.'

The police did not link it to any of the other previous attacks. Pat Power recalled: 'The police said from the start that it was somebody local and that it would be sorted by the weekend and they would have this person, no problem.'

Leads quickly dried up and no one was ever charged with the murder of Debra Schlesinger. However, when Patricia Atkinson was murdered just two days later, Pat Power asked detectives if the same man could be responsible:

> It was a Ripper case and I asked if he could be responsible for Debbie's murder, because there was no motive to kill her. But they said it wasn't the red-light area where he usually worked so there was no way that it could have been him. And I just had to accept what they said – but I always had in the back of my mind that it could have been him. Always.

It is more understandable how this attack was not linked at the time to those of the Yorkshire Ripper. For a start, there were no hammer blows to the head, she had simply been stabbed once through the heart. The police obviously believed that it definitely wasn't the Ripper because Debra wasn't a sex worker either. But, as with other attacks carried out later on, Sutcliffe didn't always stick to the same methods.

In 2002, the Law Lords found against the Home Secretary being able to increase the minimum life sentencing tariff recommended by the judiciary (after which the murderer would have to face a parole board before being considered for release). Sutcliffe had been sentenced to life with the recommendation he serve a minimum of thirty years, meaning he would be eligible for parole in 2011. This was later increased by the Home Secretary to a whole life sentence, meaning he would never be eligible for parole. The police were then instructed to gather further evidence against Sutcliffe in order to lay new charges against him should the need arise to keep him in prison.

The police were confident that they could bring new charges against Sutcliffe for the murder of Debra Schlesinger and the later attempted murder of Mo Lea. So confident, in fact, that they had enough evidence to pass a file to the Criminal Prosecution Service. Sutcliffe never acknowledged his guilt for this murder.

Annoyed at being disturbed, not gaining his sexual gratification from this murder, and not liking the different method he'd chosen (as he would admit later), Sutcliffe went back to the easier hunting grounds of the red light areas.

Chapter 14

Patricia Atkinson

On Saturday 23 April 1977, 32-year-old Patricia Atkinson was murdered at around 23.15 in her flat in Bradford – just two days after the murder of Debra Schlesinger. She was the first of Sutcliffe's victims known to be a full-time sex worker, and was the only one to be killed indoors.

Patricia was born on 9 May 1944 to James and Gladys Atkinson and had two brothers called Barry and Anthony. They lived first at 459 Langdale Road and later at 39 Orchard Grove in Thorpe Edge, Bradford. When she reached 15 years of age she left school and worked at Parkland Mills, Greengates, Bradford, as a 'burler and mender'. A year later she met her husband at a dance hall in the town, Ramen (Ray) Mitra, a man of Pakistani origin. They married on 1 April 1961, when Patricia was still only 17, and lived with her parents for a short while before finding themselves a house in Girlington, an area of Bradford next to Manningham, Bradford's red light district.

Just five months into their marriage, tragedy struck when Patricia's father, James, passed away aged just 50 and the following year her mother, Gladys, also died, aged just 43.

Patricia and Ramen went on to have three daughters, Judy, Jill and Liza; by the age of 22 Patricia had been in the same relationship for six years and had three children. She decided that she wanted to live a little while she was young and began going on nights out, leaving Ramen at home with the children. Patricia knew that she was attractive and she cheated on Ramen many times. Due to this, she and Ramen separated on several occasions, but always got back together for the sake of the children.

Patricia then left home for the final time in 1975 and drifted into prostitution. She was convicted for soliciting in the same year and received a £10 fine. Following her conviction, Patricia gave up sex work for a while and met a man called Robert Henderson; unfortunately, her drinking soon became a problem. She was convicted on the same charge of soliciting on 3 February 1976, when she was fined £25, and again on 5 August, when she was fined £12. Ramen divorced her on 25 September 1976 and, due to her lifestyle, was awarded full custody of their three children.

Ten days before she was murdered, she rented flat 3 at 9 Oak Avenue, Manningham, and began using the alias 'Tina Magee'. The flat was described at Sutcliffe's eventual trial as 'a room only capable of use for prostitution; there were no cooking facilities or any domestic furniture.'

On the night of her murder, Patricia went to the 'perseverance' pub in Lumb Lane and she wore her usual blue jeans, short leather jacket and blue shirt, which was mainly unbuttoned. She got very drunk and then went to 'The Carlisle', which was close to her flat.

Patricia had been drinking throughout most of the day and by now was almost paralytic. When she realised that the stripper who had been booked at the pub had failed to turn up she jumped up on the stage and stripped until she was completely naked. Things quickly became rowdy and Patricia was thrown out. It was now around 22.20 and she headed in the direction of 'The International Club'. She was last seen staggering around the streets at 23.10 by a number of sex workers who knew her.

Having failed to gain any sexual gratification from the murder of Debra Schlesinger, Sutcliffe decided to return to a practice he knew was safer for him – picking up a prostitute. He also knew that he had been seen at the scene of Debra's murder and so he needed to act quickly.

He recalled:

> I drove off Lumb Lane into Church Street, I knew this was a prostitute area. I was in my Corsair ... I saw this woman in St Paul's Road at a junction with another road. She appeared drunk and was banging on the roof of a white Mini and was shouting and bawling, 'Fuck Off!' and such things to the driver, who then drove off at speed. I pulled up to her and stopped and without asking she jumped in the car. She said, 'I fucking told him where to get off!' She said, 'I've got a flat, we can go there.' She told me where to go. We turned right at the junction with Manningham Lane, turned left down Queens Road, left into Oak Avenue, and turned 2 left and stopped at her flat.

Flat 3 could only be reached via the main front entrance of the block, then down the staircase directly opposite the entrance to the ground floor and then left along a wide corridor into the side wing of the building. Turning left once more, Number 3 was on the right-hand side.

Sutcliffe continued:

> She told me she lived alone. I parked up outside her flat and she got out and went in. I picked up a hammer as I got out of the car. I remember this was a claw hammer that I had bought at the Clayton hardware shop.
>
> I followed her into the flat, she closed the curtains, and I hung my coat on the hook on the back of the door. She took her coat off and sat on the bed, her back was slightly towards me. I went up to her and hit her on the back of the head with the hammer. She fell off the bed onto the floor. I picked her up and put her back on the bed. That was the first time I had noticed the red blood, before it had always been dark, but this time in the light I saw lots of blood on the bed and on the floor. When she was on the floor I hit her another twice, or three times, before I put her on the bed. I pulled the bedclothes back before I put her on the bed.
>
> She had already pulled her jeans down before I hit her. I pulled her clothes up and I hit her several times on her stomach and back with the claw part of the hammer and I saw that I was making marks on her body doing this. I then covered her up in the bedclothes. I think she was lying face down or on her side when I left her.

When I first hit her she was making a horrible gurgling sound, and she carried on making this noise even though I'd hit her a few times. She was still making a gurgling noise when I left, but I knew she would not be in a state to tell anybody.

I drove home and put my car in the garage. I looked at my clothes in the garage. I saw that I had some blood on the bottom of my jeans. I went in the house, my wife was in bed. I took my jeans off and rinsed them under the cold tap and hung them up. I also saw some blood on one of my shoes or they may have been boots, I rinsed this under the tap and wiped it with a sponge. I believe I was wearing a pair of brown Doc Martins boots at that time. I'm trying to think what I did with the claw hammer, I think I used it again on a woman. I have thrown it away over a wall near Sharps Printers at Cottingley, I can't remember when it was exactly.

At that time I carried on as though nothing had happened. I was then working at Clarks in Bradford.

What needs to be noted here is that there was no garage for Sutcliffe to park his car in at his home in Tanton Close.

At around 18.30 the following evening Patricia's boyfriend, Robert Henderson, knocked on her door. There was no reply, which he thought was unusual, so he tried the handle and the door opened. He went inside and checked the rooms as he was walking through. When he reached the bedroom he noticed a pool of blood on the floor. He then looked towards the bed where he saw a bundle and he then noticed Patricia's face and arm sticking out from under the covers. She was pale and it was obvious to him that she was dead. He ran out of the flat and went to the caretakers, where he told him that there had been a murder.

The murder was investigated by Detective Chief Superintendent John Domaille of the Western Crime Area, and an incident room was set up at the headquarters in Bradford.

When police arrived, they found Patricia Atkinson's body still on the bed and it was covered with blankets and a flower-patterned duvet. She was lying face down with her head turned away from the door facing the wall. She was wearing a black bra and the left shoulder strap was visible. A pair of wooden sandals was lying just under the edge of the bed and there were spots of blood on the front of the left sandal.

Her hair was matted with blood, as were the sheets and pillow and her arms were spread out down her side. When Professor Gee, the Home Office Pathologist, examined her further and pulled back the bed covers he could see that her jeans had been pulled down below her knees and her white knickers had been pulled down to expose her buttocks. Her bra had been unfastened and there was clear bruising on her right leg above her knee, possibly indicating that she had been stood or stamped on. Her tights had been pulled down to her ankles and she was wearing just one shoe – a blue denim sling back shoe with a platform sole. The other shoe was found beside the electric fire. Blood spots were found on the front of the chair legs in the room. Professor Gee was also shown a short leather jacket which was heavily bloodstained in the middle of the floor.

There were oblong marks and grazes on her stomach, from the claw end of the hammer. It was also clear that she had been stabbed six times in the stomach with a knife and stabbing attempts had been made on her back. None of the stab wounds would have proved fatal and death occurred from the four hammer strikes to her head.

Later vaginal swabs indicated the presence of semen from several hours before her death and it was believed that this was from Robert Henderson. A blood sample also showed that Patricia had consumed around twenty measures of spirits.

Patricia's keys were also found on the bed. The mortice key was found amid the blood and semen-stained bedsheets in front of her knees and the Yale key was found below her right knee, trapped between her body and her bed clothes.

At the scene, police discovered a bloody footprint on a sheet on the bed that appeared to come from a size 7 Dunlop Warwick wellington boot and it was later matched to the boot print found at the scene of Emily Jackson's murder.

The Scene of Crimes Officers concluded that the following had happened:

> Patricia Atkinson was struck on the head from behind as she entered the room. She fell to the floor bleeding and lay where she fell for some minutes. [*Had Sutcliffe then masturbated?*]. The killer moved the unconscious body to the bedside where probably her leather coat was removed before being dumped in the corner of the room. The jeans could have been undone at this stage and pulled down, together with her underclothes, and this caused the loss of the left shoe. Bloodstaining on the carpet, the handbag, and the smearing on the leg of the bedside chair, showed probably that another blow to the skull had been struck and that the head had moved about on the floor. The killer, with wet bloody hands, manoeuvred the body onto the unmade bed, probably by clambering on to the bed and dragging the body, rather than by lifting it. In doing so a bloody footwear impression was left on the bottom sheet beneath the body and the wall. The bloodstream distribution on the bed indicated further blows to the head and a great deal of blood being lost as a result of the wounds sustained. He also believed the stabbing injuries to the abdomen were probably sustained on the bed. The killer then began a process of 'tidying-up', during which the jeans were partially pushed or drawn on to the legs. The bedding was then piled on top of the body and straightened out sufficiently to cover it almost completely, leaving the injuries and the greater part of the bloodstaining hidden from view.

Patricia Atkinson's body was identified by her ex-husband, Ramen Mitra, at Bradford City Mortuary.

It was quickly established that Patricia often used taxis and an inquiry began into interviewing all taxi drivers in the Bradford area. Approximately 1,200 were seen, but no useful information was found.

Finger and palm prints found at the scene were compared with those of Patricia Atkinson and her known associates but, even though a man who had returned to Africa was traced and eliminated, nothing emerged.

The day after the discovery of Patricia's body, Detective Chief Superintendent Domaille told the local press:

> This was a brutal murder, a very brutal murder. The man we are looking for could be a maniac. The leads that we are following are that there are a number of people in the area that I know knew this lady. I have her diary. This lists a lot of people, names a lot of people, and I would like to see all those people, I shall be making enquiries to trace them. I shall treat as a matter of complete confidentiality any information that comes to me. Anyone can ask to see me personally and I think it might be helpful to some people if they came forward to see me, rather than me making enquiries about some of the facts I know.

The Byford Report stated that at this stage the murder of Emily Jackson was linked to that of Wilma McCann as they were both committed in Leeds, both involved prostitutes and in both cases the victims had suffered severe head injuries followed by exposure of the body and repeated stabbing. They were thus regarded as having a common author, as were the murders of Irene Richardson and Patricia Atkinson which occurred in Leeds and Bradford respectively. A Criminal Intelligence Bulletin also provided details of the Land Rover enquiry, the tyre tracks, the use of two weapons and the lack of evidence stemmed so far.

At this stage the criteria for inclusion of crimes in the series were:

- That the victim should be a prostitute.
- That she should have been hit over the head with a hammer.
- That her clothing should have been disarranged to expose her body.
- That stab and/or slash wounds should have been inflicted to the body.

A woman called Barbara Kathryn Miller soon came forward and told detectives that she had been violently attacked in Bradford two years previously. She was a professional stripper and was also known to be an active sex worker in Wolverhampton, Derby and the Manningham area of Bradford. She said that she knew Patricia Atkinson and wanted to help all she could. She told them that a man with a beard had picked her up in a pub in Lumb Lane and had driven a Land Rover with a hard top. She said that it was blue with a dirty cream top. It was in a dirty condition and had a six-inch tear in the black vinyl of the passenger seat. He drove to a quarry in the Bolton Woods area and told her to get out of his car. When she refused, he dragged her out of the car and punched her in the stomach, chest and face. He drove off when she started to fight back.

She described him as being 35–40 years old, 5ft 8in, of stocky build and untidy ginger hair, a full ginger beard and moustache. He had blue eyes, possibly an Irish accent mixed with a Birmingham dialect, a scar on his left hand and a blue and red tattoo.

Although this was not an attack by Peter Sutcliffe, the description matched the man who had been seen with Emily Jackson on the night she was murdered and a search was undertaken. This man was never traced.

It took until 9 May for the murder of Patricia Atkinson to be linked officially to the murders of Wilma McCann, Emily Jackson and Irene Richardson in the police 'Special Notice'.

In this one case alone, 3,458 people were seen and interviewed.

Just under three weeks later, on 28 May, Sutcliffe went for a night out with his neighbours, David and Ronnie Barker, and Sutcliffe drove them up to York.

David Barker told the court in 1981 that he had kept a diary since 1974 and recalled that evening: 'It was a Saturday night and the three of us went to York. Peter wanted to go to Manchester, but I thought it was too far to go. It was about 20.00 on a Saturday night, and we had just dropped Sonia off at a part-time job.'

They went to a number of pubs in York and in one, Sutcliffe disappeared while the two brothers played pool.

> We were a bit annoyed because we didn't know how to get back, and at closing time we walked back to the car and Peter was standing near it. It was three-quarters of an hour since we saw him last, and he told us he had followed a lass out of the pub. I can't remember him saying anything else.

On the journey home to Bradford, Ronnie Barker fell asleep in the back of the car. 'When I woke up, we were in Chapeltown, Leeds, and I asked what we were doing there.' Chapeltown was not on their route home.

> Peter was driving and I think he said something about this being Ripper country. The car stopped in Chapeltown somewhere and Peter got out. He didn't say where he was going and we didn't ask. He walked off and was away for about a quarter of an hour to twenty minutes.

Ronnie Barker also told of another time when Sutcliffe was out with them and he suddenly stopped the car and left the vehicle after seeing a girl he liked; he told them he was going after her.

It is highly likely that he was using these trips for reconnaissance, as his next attack was to take place in the Chapeltown area just a few weeks later.

Relevant Statistics

Incident Room set up	23 April 1977
House to House Enquiries	2,356
Actions	3,915
Statements	2,161
Vehicle Enquiries	1,924
Officers Engaged	90
Hours Worked (Not inc. Overtime)	96,028
Incident Room Closed	10 July 1977

Chapter 15

Jayne MacDonald

On Sunday 26 June 1977, 16-year-old Jayne Michelle MacDonald was murdered at around 02.00 in Chapeltown, Leeds – two months after the murder of Patricia Atkinson.

Jayne was born on 16 August 1960 to Irene and Wilfred MacDonald. Irene had been married before and had two daughters from that marriage – Carole and Janet. When Irene married Wilfred they then had three children together – Jayne, Debra and Ian. The family then all lived together at 77, Scott Hall Avenue – just six doors away from previous Ripper victim Wilma McCann. Jayne had, on a couple of occasions, babysat Wilma's children.

Jayne had recently left Allerton High School and had a job as a shop assistant in the shoe department at Grandways Supermarket on Roundhay Road. She liked to spend her wages on clothes and would go out dancing at the weekends, having recently split-up with her boyfriend, 18-year-old Steven Martin, because she thought he was getting too serious.

In the prosecution files, it was noted that, 'she was in the habit of regularly visiting public houses, discos and the like. These places included the Fforde Grene Public House, The Cat's Whiskers Disco, Heaven and Hell Disco and the Hofbrausaus Bier Keller [sic].'

No one had a bad word to say about Jayne; her neighbour, Edith Ferguson, recalled her as being 'a smashing girl, with film-star good looks, but absolutely unspoilt.'

On Saturday 25 June, Jayne went to see her neighbours, Jack Bransberg and his wife, before she went into town to meet her friends. She would often do this before a night out as the MacDonalds didn't have a telephone and she would call the Bransbergs if she was going to be late home. Jack Bransberg would then let her parents know.

Jayne was going dancing at the Astoria Ballroom with some of her work colleagues from Grandways and her sister, Debra, recalled: 'We socialised together too and had arranged to go out together that night, her last night. But she blew us out to go to her first works do. Everyone from Grandways was meeting in town and she didn't want to miss that.'

However, instead of going to the Astoria, Jayne and her friends went to the Hofbrauhaus, a German-style 'bierkeller'. Jayne soon met 18-year-old Mark Jones with whom she danced and drank, and there was clearly an instant attraction between them.

At 22.30, Mark Jones left with Jayne and her work colleagues and went in the direction of Briggate, but the two of them soon walked off together to find somewhere to buy some chips. By the time they had found somewhere and eaten the chips, Jayne had missed her last bus home. The two of them sat on a bench until around midnight talking and laughing. They then walked towards Mark Jones' home on an estate near St James' Hospital, because Mark had said that if his sister was home he would ask her to give Jayne a lift.

When they reached his home, they saw that his sister's car wasn't parked in front of the house, so they carried on walking and went into Beckett Street and in the direction of Jayne's home in Chapeltown. They laid down in a nearby field and watched the stars until around 01.00.

They then walked up to the main gates of St James' Hospital and parted company around half an hour later, agreeing to meet again later in the week. Mark Jones only left her because she had told him that she would get a taxi from the taxi rank at the corner of Harehills Road.

Jayne walked to the cab office but when she didn't get a reply from the kiosk, she decided to carry on walking and ended up outside her place of work. She carried on past the Gaiety pub and walked along Chapeltown Road towards home. She was alone in what Sutcliffe sadistically called 'Ripper Country'.

She was seen walking along in her high 'clog' shoes by several people, including two AA patrolmen who were sat in their vehicle near St James' Hospital, and at about 01.40 she was seen in Bayswater Mount, walking in the direction of Roundhay Road.

She was last seen walking through Chapeltown at 01.45, about five minutes' walk from where her body would later be found.

A woman living in Reginald Terrace recalled that at around 02.00 she heard a banging and scuffling from the adventure playground where Jayne's body was discovered, followed by a voice which sounded 'Scottish', shouting and swearing. Sutcliffe was later known to call his victims names as he was hitting them, so could the witness have got the accent wrong and had actually heard Jayne being murdered by the Yorkshire Ripper?

Sutcliffe had spent the day with Sonia, looking at a house they were hoping to buy. Sonia was working that evening so he decided to go out drinking with his neighbours David and Ronnie Barker, and they dropped Sonia off at work at the Sherrington Nursing Home on the way.

The threesome drank in the pubs around Allerton and Heaton, Bradford, and at around 01.30 Sutcliffe dropped them home on Tanton Crescent. But instead of going home, Sutcliffe turned the car around and drove off towards Leeds.

He recalled in his confession statement:

> The next one I did I still feel terrible about, it was a young girl – Jayne MacDonald. I read recently about her father dying of a broken heart and it brought it all back to me. I realised what sort of a monster I had become.
>
> I believed at the time I did it that she was a prostitute. This was on a Saturday night. I drove to Leeds in my Corsair ... At this time the urge to kill prostitutes was very strong and I had gone out of my mind.
>
> I saw this lass walking along quite slowly towards the crossing near the Hayfield pub in Chapeltown Road. She stopped on the corner before crossing over Chapeltown Road. I anticipated that she was going to walk up one of the streets up past the Hayfield. I drove my car into the Hayfield pub car park and got out.

I took my hammer out of the car. I think it was the claw hammer. I also had a knife with me that time, it was a kitchen type knife with a black ebonite handle and a thin blade.

I walked towards the narrow street behind the Hayfield to see where she was, and just as I got there, she was walking up. I walked behind her, I was very near to her, I followed her for a short distance, she never looked round. I took the hammer and I hit her on the back of the head and she fell down. I then pulled her by the arms face down into a yard behind a fence. I recall that her shoes were making a horrible scraping sound on the ground. I pulled her into the corner of this yard. I hit her another at least once, maybe twice, on the head. I pulled her clothes up exposing her breasts, and I stabbed her several times with the knife on the chest. Before this I stabbed her in the back.

I left her lying in the corner. I cannot remember whether she was lying face up or face down. She was wearing a jacket and a skirt. I walked back down the same street to where I parked my car. As I got to the car park, I saw a group of people walking up the narrow street [Reginald Street] from Chapeltown Road. I got into my car and drove away into Reginald Terrace, into Chapeltown Road, and drove straight home. I think my wife may have been working that night. I have remembered that my wife started working some Friday and Saturday nights at Sherrington Private Nursing Home in Bradford. That is why I have done a lot of my attacks on a Saturday night.

I don't think I had any blood on me following this one. I cannot recall what I was wearing then. I cannot remember what I did with the knife, I must have taken it home with me and washed it. I feel I may have left it in the Corsair when I scrapped it. The hammer may have been the one I threw over the wall at Sharps Printers.

When I saw in the papers that MacDonald was so young and not a prostitute, I felt like someone inhuman and I realised that it was a devil driving me against my will and that I was a beast. When the Ripper came up in conversation at work or in a pub I was able to detach my mind from the fact that it was me they were talking about, and I was able to discuss it normally. This amazed me at times that I was able to do this.

When Sutcliffe was asked why he thought Jayne was a prostitute, he replied: 'I were quite certain she were a prostitute, absolutely positive. She were walking along in the red light district for one thing, and then I saw her stop and chat to a couple of girls on a street corner. I felt sure she were one of them.'

Jayne MacDonald's body was found at 09.45 by two children who were playing in the area. It has often been described as a playground, but was in fact little more than an area of concrete. There were certainly no swings and roundabouts. When police arrived they quickly found spots of blood on the pavement on Reginald Street which pointed to where Jayne had first been attacked. There was a clear trail of blood, together with drag marks in the dry soil, leading from Reginald Street and down the slope towards the fence that her body was concealed behind. Her imitation leather handbag was found lying beside the path, a few feet from Reginald Street. Adjacent to it was a piece of rough paper which appeared heavily bloodstained.

Jayne's body was completely hidden from the street. She was lying face down with her head roughly 6ft from the brick wall. Her legs were stretched out straight with her feet crossed, the left over the right. Her left arm was bent up with her hand beneath her head and her right arm was stretched out beside her body. Around her body lay various disused and broken household items, such as an old spring mattress and a rolled-up length of carpet, as well as some old tin cans and broken bottles.

Her grey jacket had been partly pulled up towards her shoulders, leaving the bare skin on her lower back visible (which was smeared with blood from where Sutcliffe had clearly wiped his knife) and her skirt was raised to the upper part of her thighs. One of her yellow high-heeled 'clogs' was still in place and the other lay beside her foot. Her black tights had a visible hole in the left heel. On closer inspection detectives could see blood soiling her head and left hand, as well as her jacket and skirt. Vertical trickles of blood ran downwards from the back of her chest across the sides of her body.

Jayne was wearing a pale blue underskirt which had also been raised slightly upwards. Her tights were still in the normal position and beneath them she wore a pair of black knickers and an external sanitary pad. It was obvious she had not been raped.

As the Pathologist, Professor Gee, removed her jacket at the scene, it revealed her top had been bunched up in the upper part of her back and beneath it was a single stab wound.

Confirmation of Jayne having been dragged from the street to where she was found was shown by some debris which had been caught up in the straps of her top and a piece of paper which was found in the folds of the left side of her skirt in front of her stomach.

When her body was turned over, detectives saw blood soiling her face. She wasn't wearing a bra and where her top had ridden (or been pulled) up it had exposed the nipple on her left breast. In the front of the central upper region of her abdomen was a large wound which had a piece of a broken bottle top with screw lid embedded in it.

When her body was removed to the mortuary, two more pools of blood were found – one where her abdomen had been and one where her head had been.

At the post-mortem, Professor Gee found three semi-circular lacerated wounds to Jayne's scalp which were the same as other Ripper killings. The blows had caused depressed fractures of the skull. In addition to the large wound near her abdomen with the bottle top in it, there were a series of long scratches and cuts to her chest. One large stab wound to Jayne's back was found to have penetrated her heart, lungs and kidneys. A thin-bladed weapon, not less than 6½in long, had been thrust through the two openings on the front and back of Jayne's body. Multiple thrusts, possibly as many as twenty, had been made in and out of the same wound, causing it to become much enlarged.

At the later trial, the Attorney General said:

> Doctors formed the view she had been hit on the head once and fallen, hit once more where she lay, dragged to where she was found and there stabbed on the front of the body and then turned over and stabbed repeatedly in the back. Unfortunately, she did not die until after some of the stab wounds had been inflicted.

Professor Gee was able to state this due to the large volume of blood in each chest cavity.

The killer had then finally removed his knife from the wound in Jayne's back and attempted to wipe it clean on her back, as evidenced by large smear marks left on her skin.

Sutcliffe would later claim that he did not deliberately embed the bottle into her chest and that it must have happened as he dragged her through the rubble on the playground. The post-mortem examination showed that she had not consumed any alcohol.

This latest murder, of a 16-year-old girl who was not connected to sex work, brought national press attention to the case and the general public became outraged. A combination of these factors forced the Chief Constable of West Yorkshire Police, Ronald Gregory, to appoint his most senior detective, Assistant Chief Constable for Crime, George Oldfield, to lead the investigation.

An incident room was immediately set up at Millgarth Police Station where incident rooms dealing with the Emily Jackson and Irene Richardson murders were already operating. Jayne MacDonald's murder was immediately linked by detectives with those of Wilma McCann, Emily Jackson, Irene Richardson and Patricia Atkinson.

A description of a man seen talking to Jayne MacDonald shortly before she was murdered was quickly obtained but led to nothing.

A Leeds taxi driver, Terrence Hawkshaw, was someone the police had suspected of the other crimes for some time and he was interviewed at length, but no connection between him and the murders could be established.

Static observations now began on vehicles moving through the Chapeltown red light area during the evenings. Vehicle registration numbers were recorded and put on lists in the incident room which were to be examined should there be any further murders.

Assistant Chief Constable George Oldfield made a direct appeal to the public for information:

> It looks very much to me as if he is selecting these women of the streets as his targets. I think it was a mistake that he attacked Jayne MacDonald: probably in her case he mistook her for being a lady of the streets because she was out in that area at the time she was.
>
> Innocent women who may have been propositioned by a kerb crawler who could be the Ripper trying to pick up a prostitute must contact the police urgently. Because it may have been the only time they were ever propositioned in this way, the man's face, peering out of his car window, should still be clear in their minds. While there are a number of men who do this, particularly in the Chapeltown area of Leeds, we believe the man we want must have tried it more than once and been turned down. If such a woman is frightened of telling her husband she should contact the police and she will be dealt with in confidence. This killer will strike again and the public hold the key to the success or failure of the police inquiry.
>
> The public have the power to decide what sort of society they want. If they want murder and violence they will keep quiet. If they want a

law-abiding society in which their women folk can move freely without fear of attack from the likes of the individual we are hunting, then they must give us their help. It is the little bits of apparently insignificant information so far as the public is concerned which is the vital information we want. This man has got to be caught. He has got to be stopped for the public good and the good of himself. There is no doubt in my mind that he will strike again. The big questions are 'When', 'Where', and 'Who' is going to be his next victim? We have a clear picture in our minds now of the type of man we are looking for, and obviously no woman is really safe until he is found. We believe he is probably being protected by someone because on several occasions he must have returned home with heavily bloodstained clothing.

In using the phrase 'innocent women', Oldfield epitomised the attitudes of society at the time: sex workers were 'guilty women', and were therefore in some way deserving of their fate. It is little wonder the public were reluctant to come forward with information when, from the very beginning of the investigation, the police indoctrinated them to believe that the lives of sex workers mattered less. It begs the question, had Jayne MacDonald been a prostitute and not an 'innocent woman', would Chief Constable Ronald Gregory have brought in his top policeman?

Two days on from Jayne's murder, police gave another press conference and told how they believed the murderer was 'from West Yorkshire, certainly with good knowledge of Leeds and Bradford, and has possibly developed a psychological hang up about prostitutes, either at the hands of one or because his mother was one ... All the girls were "good time girls" except Jayne MacDonald, who could have been attacked by mistake.'

They concluded that they were looking for 'a psychopathic killer who had a pathological hatred of women he believes are prostitutes ... We now have a clear picture in our minds of the type of man we are looking for.'

Again, there is the insinuation that all the previous victims were prostitutes and as such the police – and most of the public – just considered murder as an 'occupational hazard'. It was only with the murder of Jayne that the police and public became outraged. As stated in the *Sunday Mirror*: 'There wasn't much sympathy for dead prostitutes. It is a high-risk business for girls whose hearts are as cold as their hands.'

House-to-house enquiries were made; 600 taxi drivers interviewed and many women working in the Leeds area were re-interviewed. Files relating to the previous murders were re-examined and fifteen men who fell within the suspect category were re-checked. A man, 6ft 1in tall, with blonde hair and a ginger beard, was seen by a witness in the area on the night of the murder. A man with a ginger beard became of significance again.

A police reconstruction was quickly held with WPC Susan Phillips playing the part of Jayne MacDonald. The feelings of the locals were made clear by the graffiti behind the policewoman in a photograph taken by the press – 'Scott Hall Says Hang The Ripper!'

Jayne MacDonald

It wasn't until 2 July 1977 that Assistant Chief Constable George Oldfield announced that he had reopened the file into the attack on Anna Rogulskyj in July 1975, which he said bore 'certain similarities' to the murder of Jayne MacDonald.

He did not, however, connect the case with those of Gloria Wood, Olive Smelt, Tracy Browne, Rosemary Stead, Marcella Claxton, Maureen Hogan or Debra Schlesinger. Had they done so, they would have quickly discovered an identical description from each incident of a man with a local accent, dark crinkly hair, beard and moustache.

Relevant Statistics
Incident Room set up	26 June 1977
House to House Enquiries	2,994
Actions	5,979
Statements	3,804
Vehicle Enquiries	10,305
Officers Engaged	173
Hours Worked (Not inc. Overtime)	77,199
Incident Room Closed	1 August 1977

Chapter 16

Maureen Long

On Sunday, 10 July 1977, 42-year-old Maureen Elizabeth Long was attacked at around 03.00 in Birkshall Lane, just off Bowling Back Lane, Bradford – two weeks after the murder of Jayne MacDonald and just a five minute drive from the scene of the attack on Gloria Wood.

Born Maureen Waterhouse in 1934, she married a man called Ronald Long when she was 20. They had three children together and after the birth of their third child in 1966 Maureen began to suffer with anxiety. This contributed to the break-up of her marriage the following year.

In 1974 Maureen, aged 40, met 52-year-old Ken Smith and she and her youngest daughter, Jacqueline, moved in with him at 22 Donald Street, Farsley, Leeds. The two elder children, Denise and Ronald, had already left home.

On the evening of Saturday, 9 July 1977, Maureen left home and went for a night out in Bradford. She visited a few different pubs and in one of them bumped into her ex-husband Ronald. They still got on well and she made arrangements to stay at his home at 1 Rendel Street, Laisterdyke, Bradford, later that night.

When it got to closing time at 22.30, Ronald made his way home while Maureen said she was going to the Mecca nightclub for a dance and would get a taxi back to his later. Many people recalled seeing her dancing with various men that night and when she left at 02.00 she appeared to be very drunk. She admitted herself that she had drinks bought for her 'off various men'.

Sutcliffe had spent his evening out drinking around the local pubs in Bradford with David and Ronnie Barker again. When it came to closing time Sutcliffe took the brothers home to Tanton Crescent, via the red light area, but instead of then going home himself, he drove back out to look for another victim.

At Sutcliffe's trial in 1981, Ronnie Barker told the court that at this time in 1977 Sutcliffe sometimes told him about the girls he had been with.

> He said he went with a nurse at one time. He also said something about having two girls follow him back to the car the previous night. He said that he had one of them in the back and one over the bonnet. He told me that in 1977. Sometimes he would shout to girls from the car. He was fascinated by the red-light areas and always wanted to look at whores. Sometimes he got out of the car and followed them. I don't know why he resorted to them, because he had such a lovely wife sitting at home...

I always wanted to go home but Peter seemed to want to go round the red-light districts. These excursions would last between a quarter and half an hour. Peter never said why he wanted to go. It happened three or four times in 1977.

When giving his confession in January 1981, Sutcliffe recalled:

I was driving along Manningham Lane towards the City Centre one Saturday night in July 1977. It was late at night. I saw her walking on the same side as the Mecca, towards Bradford Centre. She was wearing a maxi length dress and a jacket sort of coat.

She was just past the hamburger stand when I saw her. I stopped my car and said, 'Are you going far?' She said, 'Are you giving me a lift?' I said, 'If you want one?' She got in. She told me she had been to the Mecca. She told me where she lived, and that she lived with a man who was an ex-boxer and that he was a spoil sport and would not take her to the Mecca.

She directed me where to drive to her house, which was somewhere off Leeds Road to the left [Rendle Street]. She pointed out a house in a row of terraced houses where she said she was going. She told me not to stop outside but to drive past. I drove about 20 yards past and stopped. She got out of the car.

She told me that if there was no one in the house we could go in. She had asked me if I fancied her and I told her that I did, just to please her. She went and knocked at the door of the house and she was banging away for a minute or two. Then she came back and got into the car and told me she knew a place where we could go.

She told me where to drive, and I drove eventually into Bowling Back Lane and turned right down a cobbled street. I stopped the car some way down the street. There was some spare unlevelled land on the left and a big high wall on the right. She got out of the car and said she was going for a piss first and she went to the spare land and crouched down and had a piss.

I had my hammer ready as she got out of the car and I also had a knife. I think it was the same knife I had at MacDonald.

I got out of the car while she was having a piss and as she was crouching down I hit her on the head with the hammer. She slumped down. I pulled her by the hands further onto the spare ground. She was not making any sound. I pulled up her clothes and I stabbed her three or four times with the knife in her chest and back. I did see a caravan with a light on over the spare land, but it didn't put me off what I was doing. I thought that I had stabbed her enough when I left her. I went back to the car, got in, and drove off.

I was under the impression that the street I was in may be a cul-de-sac, so I reversed my car by turning it round in the street I was in. No, I didn't, I remember that I backed out of the street into Bowling Back Lane facing towards the City. I drove along Bowling Back Lane towards the general direction of the City Centre, and drove home ... I believe my wife may have been working that night, or else she was in bed. I don't think I found any blood on myself on that occasion.

Unknown to him at the time of the attack, a night watchman called Frank Whitaker had been patrolling some premises next to the waste ground and was alerted to something by his barking Alsatian. As he approached the road he saw what he believed to be a white Ford Cortina Mark II with a dark roof (it was actually Sutcliffe in his white Ford Corsair) driving away from the waste ground at high speed and with no lights on. Thinking this highly suspicious, he noted the time as 03.27. It was to be another five hours before Maureen Long was found.

Maureen recalled:

All I remember was trying to pick myself up, grabbing hold of the grass to try and get up and I kept falling and I wondered what was wrong with me and I kept falling back and I was trying to pull myself up. I fell again and then I was screaming and I heard this dog barking and I heard someone say 'You're alright' and that's all I remember about that night.

She had been found by two women who were walking their dog and had heard some feeble cries, like a baby whimpering, so they had gone to investigate.

It was obvious to those that found her that Maureen's bra had been pulled down to her waist and her tights and knickers had been pulled down to her knees. The rest of her clothing was also displaced, with her dress having been pulled down from the shoulders and up from the waist. An ambulance was called and she was taken to Bradford Royal Infirmary, where doctors managed to save her life.

It was established that she had suffered a blow to the back of her head from a ball pein hammer which had left her with a large depressed fracture of the skull. She had also been stabbed five times in the front of her trunk and left shoulder. One of the stab wounds had penetrated her liver and another ran from between her breasts to just below her navel. There was evidence of stabbing through the clothing this time. She also had three fractured ribs, indicating that her attacker had kicked or stamped on her too. She spent nine weeks in hospital recovering.

A police fingertip search of the scene managed to find a partial bloody palm print on a piece of broken sink and they were convinced it had come from her attacker. Missing from the scene was Maureen's left shoe and her large brown imitation-leather handbag, indicating that Sutcliffe had taken them as a trophy.

Sutcliffe recalled:

The next day, or the day after, I heard on the news, or read in the paper, that the woman was still alive. I got a nasty shock and thought it was the end of the line there and then. I thought she would be able to identify me. I think it was about that time that I threw the hammer over Sharps wall. A few days after, I read that Long was suffering from memory loss and this made me less worried about being caught.

> My desire to kill prostitutes was getting stronger than ever and it took
> me over completely. I was in a dilemma, I wanted to tell someone what
> I was doing, but I thought about how it would affect my wife and family.
> I wasn't too much bothered for myself.

On the night she was attacked, Maureen Long could remember going to the cloak-room at the club and then walking towards the city centre. She remembered a white Ford car with a black roof pulling up, but unfortunately then described her attacker as a white male, well-built, aged 36 or 37, 6ft 1in, puffy cheeks, thickish eyebrows, collar-length wiry blond hair and noticeably large hands. It's highly probable that the combination of alcohol, blood loss and head injury meant that she could remember some things but not others of that night.

The attack was immediately linked with those being investigated by Assistant Chief Constable George Oldfield, who told a press conference:

> It is quite apparent now that we have a desperate and dangerous individual
> at large in this area. A person who is going to continue to strike until he
> is caught. I feel now that with the publicity which these cases have had,
> somebody somewhere must know who we are looking for. We need all the
> help we can get from the public and I would like them to bear in mind that
> the next victim could be a wife, sister, daughter or niece.

Two witnesses were found who said that shortly before Maureen Long left the premises a man, purporting to be a taxi driver, attempted to pick them up outside the dance hall. He was described as 35–39 years of age, stocky build with ginger wavy hair and of untidy appearance. They thought the car he was driving was a white Ford Cortina, which linked up with the description given by the night-watchman of the vehicle he had seen.

During the enquiry a woman volunteered information that in 1975 she had been attacked by a man with a ginger beard and who had been driving a Land Rover. This tallied with the description given in the Emily Jackson case.

The collective weight of the various pieces of information led to a major line of enquiry being pursued to trace this man. Enquiries were made at plant hire firms, civil contractors, etc., and 117 suggestions were made of persons with ginger beards. Sixty-one were never traced and there was no real clue as to their identity. Fifty-six were traced, interviewed and eliminated.

Immediately following the attack the observations being kept on vehicles using the Chapeltown red light area of Leeds were extended to include the Manningham Lane area of Bradford. This meant that officers were diverted away from the 'Tracking Inquiry', which had been running since the Irene Richardson murder to trace the car that had left the tyre marks on Soldiers' Field. Of the original 53,000 owners of a vehicle who could have left the tyre marks, 20,000 people remained to be seen. Peter Sutcliffe was one of these.

The index cards made out during the 'Tracking Inquiry' were filed in vehicle registration number order and were marked with the owners' name, but no index cards were made out for names. Despite creating double the amount of paperwork for this part of the inquiry, had this been done it would – and should – have been the first reference to

Peter Sutcliffe by name, and the information of his vehicle would have been available to detectives who later interviewed him.

Due to Frank Whitaker's mistaken insistence that he had seen a white Ford Cortina Mark II leaving the scene of Maureen Long's attack (which couldn't have left the tyre tracks on Soldiers' Field), the 'Tracking Inquiry' was then discontinued and the details of 5,000 owners of Mark II Ford Cortina's living in West Yorkshire were instead obtained. Eventually, 3,000 owners of such vehicles were traced and interviewed but, unsurprisingly, no positive information was gathered. In total, more than 300 police officers collected 12,500 statements and had checked around 36,000 cars.

Relevant Statistics

Incident Room set up	10 July 1977
House to House Enquiries	638
Actions	1,914
Statements	911
Vehicle Enquiries	7,000
Officers Engaged	100+
Hours Worked (Not inc. Overtime)	72,204
Incident Room Closed	1 October 1977

Following the attack, Maureen's youngest daughter Jacqueline was taken into care as Maureen struggled to cope with what had happened to her. She suffered from blackouts, headaches, nightmares and fits and was terrified of going out. She continued to receive out-patient treatment for some time after the attack, and was left heavily scarred. It also altered her behaviour.

A few months following the attack, Maureen agreed to help the detectives by going out on Thursday, Friday and Saturday nights with Detective Sergeant Megan Winterburn and PC Andrew Laptew to see if she could spot her attacker in the local pubs and clubs. Male undercover officers kept watch from across the room and were ready to pounce if she spotted him. PC Laptew was given £15 expenses for the first night, but ended up spending £78 because Maureen 'liked a drink'.

In March 1978, Maureen was involved in a fight in Bradford and was struck on the back of the head with an iron bar. Again, she was lucky to escape with her life. Later that year she appeared at Bradford Magistrates' Court, charged with theft from three city centre shops. The court took into account her background, and the confusion and panic attacks from which she suffered, and fined her £75.

Sutcliffe knew the police were looking for a white car and knew that he needed to change it quickly in order to carry on his murderous rampage. He purchased a second-hand red Ford Corsair (PHE 355G) and insured it on 17 July – exactly one week on from the attack on Maureen Long. He sold his white Corsair to his friend, Ronnie Barker, but it soon broke down and Sutcliffe was forced to give him his money back. Sutcliffe then stripped it for parts and sold it to a car breakers yard on 3 September 1977.

On 26 September Sutcliffe and his wife Sonia made an even larger investment – their first house. Sonia had just finished her teacher training course and began working as a supply teacher at Holmfield First School. She and Sutcliffe had enough money saved up to get a mortgage for a four-bedroom detached house at 6 Garden Lane, Heaton, Bradford. It had a large garage on the side of the house which meant Sutcliffe could work on his various vehicles – and also meant that after his attacks he could clean himself up without his wife finding out. As well as a front door, there was another entrance on the side driveway by the garage which led straight into the kitchen. This meant that once he had taken off his bloody clothes in the garage he could nip straight into the kitchen and put them in the washing machine without his wife suspecting a thing.

Following the attack on Maureen Long, special inquiry teams were assigned to the surveillance of two suspects – neither of whom were Peter Sutcliffe.

Taxi drivers in Leeds and Bradford had already been targeted as potential prime suspects and Terrence Hawkshaw was again looked at closely. His physical appearance was similar to the description given by Maureen Long of her attacker – he was 36 years old, 6ft tall, weighed 15 or 16 stone and had long fair hair brushed back, a fresh complexion and a round face. He lived with his 67-year-old mother in an old terraced house in Drighlington, which was between Leeds and Bradford and, crucially for the investigating officers, drove a white Ford Cortina with a black roof.

He had been interviewed already regarding the murder of Jayne MacDonald but there was no evidence to connect him to the crime, so he was marked out as one to be seen should there be another attack or murder. He then came under even closer scrutiny when he was seen in his taxi near the Mecca Ballroom on the night of Maureen Long's attack. It was quickly established that he was known as someone who would drive prostitutes and their punters around and would allow them to have sex in the back of his taxi. Assistant Chief Constable George Oldfield suspected that Hawkshaw got his sexual thrills out of watching the prostitutes at work. His accounts were searched and they revealed taxi receipts that proved he had the opportunity to have carried out several of the Ripper attacks as he was in close proximity to the sites at the right time. He was known to have visited the pubs and clubs frequented by Emily Jackson and Irene Richardson too, including the Gaiety.

However, there was not enough hard evidence to arrest him, so George Oldfield arranged to virtually kidnap him and make him assist with their inquiries. This was against protocol.

Hawkshaw was taken to the top floor of the Detective Training School at Bishopsgarth in Wakefield, which was a thirteen-storey accommodation block across the road from the force headquarters. There were no courses being run so no one knew he was there apart from those officers who needed to know.

He was questioned by detectives for thirty-six hours and at the same time forensics were going over his car and home with a fine tooth comb. They found two hammers, but they were of a different dimension and weight to those used in the attacks.

When he was released from questioning he was immediately put under twenty-four hour surveillance and this lasted for quite some time. Eventually he realised he was being followed, but also that there was nothing he could do about it.

Chapter 17

Jean Jordan

On Saturday 1 October 1977, 20-year-old Jean Bernadette Jordan was murdered at around 22.00 in Chorlton, Manchester – four days on from Sutcliffe moving in to 6 Garden Lane.

Jean was born on 11 December 1956 at Motherwell Maternity Hospital in The Neuke, Wishaw, Scotland, to hospital maid Catherine Jordan.

In October 1973, aged just 16, she ran away from home and took a train to London and quickly drifted into sex work. There she met a man called Alan Royle, who said he was working as a chef in a Kensington hotel at the time. A year into their relationship and while she was pregnant, Royle claimed that Jean told him she wasn't actually a receptionist as she had led him to believe, but was actually a 'call girl', whose clients booked appointments with her by telephone and either visited her at a place on Mayfair's Curzon Street, or sent a car to collect her. He recalled:

> It didn't matter to me at all. I was hooked and I loved her but, after she told me, she stopped it there and then, and said she wanted to move in with me. She said the only time she would ever do it again would be if her family was absolutely starving. We bought a flat and I started working for Mecca in the Empire, Leicester Square. Life was good and we were doing fine. We had to move around the country a bit then because of my job.

By the time they moved, Jean had given birth to their first son, also named Alan, in London and their second son, James, was born three years later when they were living in Buckinghamshire.

Life was going well for the young couple but things changed when Alan was made redundant. They settled in Manchester and found a small flat in Wythenshawe's Newall Green, before moving to Lingbeck Crescent in August 1977, but he recalled: 'We were living in a rented place and were not getting on very well.' He had become a heavy drinker and would disappear on two- or three-day benders with his friends, leaving Jean at home with the two young children. When he returned, Jean would then disappear back up to Scotland by hitching a ride to see relatives, before returning a few days later.

She soon drifted back into sex work and was known by other prostitutes as 'Scotch Jean'. She was arrested at 23.45 on 15 June 1977 in Heywood Street, Cheetham, for loitering for the purposes of prostitution and gave her name as Jean Scott. She was taken to the local police station and, not finding any record of previous convictions, she was cautioned and released. She was arrested again at 23.50 on 14 September 1977, again on

Heywood Street. This time, she gave her name as Eileen Fisher. Again, no convictions were matched with that name so she was cautioned and released.

She had made a friend, Anna Holt, on the streets and the two of them would use the same flat, rented by a mutual friend, to take their clients to in the winter. In the warmer months, however, they would take their clients to an allotment next to the Southern Cemetery.

Manchester City Corporation had a series of garden allotments on the west side of Princess Road, Chorlton, which were rented off to private individuals. The allotments adjoined land belonging to Manchester Southern Cemetery, on the north side of the cemetery. During 1977, all the old allotments were fenced off on the Manchester City centre side.

Incidentally, Lesley Ann Downey, one of the children killed by the Moors Murderers Ian Brady and Myra Hindley, is buried in the Southern Cemetery

The allotments were entered by a driveway on Princess Road, 200 yards on the north side of its junction with Nell Lane. There was no gate to the old allotments capable of being locked, and so there was public access day and night and people would walk their dogs there.

It was accepted that the area was used by both courting couples on foot and in their cars, and also by sex workers who took their clients there during all hours of the day and night.

On the evening of 1 October, Alan Royle had gone out drinking with his friends and when he returned he found that the children were asleep in bed but there was no sign of Jean. He assumed that she had gone out with friends.

What he didn't know was that Jean had gone out to earn some money by selling her body. She was last seen in the Princess Hotel in Chorlton in the company of two men – one of whom was a fellow Scot from Dundee called Angus – at around 21.40.

Meanwhile, Sutcliffe had spent the day working on his new red Ford Corsair and wanted to go out for a test run. Sonia had recently miscarried and this had caused tensions in their relationship, they argued frequently and Sutcliffe was full of anger and resentment towards women; he knew a prostitute would be his safest target. He also knew that the Leeds and Bradford red light areas were being watched by police, so he decided on somewhere further away – Manchester. He had been there before for work and also when he had gone out drinking with David and Ronnie Barker, so he knew which areas were best to go to for a target. Having thrown his ball pein hammer away following his last attack, he found two heavy walling hammers in the garage of his new home that had been left behind by the previous owners and decided to use these.

During his confession to police in 1981, Sutcliffe recalled:

> I realised things were hotting up a bit in Leeds and Bradford. People had dubbed me the Ripper. I decided to go to Manchester to kill a prostitute. I had read in a paper somewhere, or a magazine, of a priest chastising what went on in his parish at Manchester where there obviously was prostitutes.
>
> One Saturday night in October 1977 I drove over to Manchester. I believe it was in my red Corsair. I had a look at my map in Road Atlas to see where Moss Side was and I drove there.

I went through Manchester town centre, Princess Street I think it was, followed it all the way down past the university, which eventually came out near the Moss Side area. It was a rundown area and almost immediately on arriving there I saw several girls plying for trade. I pulled up at the kerbside and asked a girl if she wanted business. She was very slim with light coloured hair, not bad looking. She told me if I waited further along the road she would meet me there. I drove on two hundred yards and made a right turn, then a 3-point turn to face the main road once again.

After a couple of minutes the girl drew level. She saw my car just as she was going to get into another car which had stopped for her. I think this was an 1100, a light coloured one, either grey or fawn. She didn't get in but came over to me, which I suppose was the biggest mistake she ever made. She came up and got into my car. She told me she was going to go with the man in the other car until she saw me.

She told me she wanted a fiver for business, and she told me she knew a place. I drove at her direction until we came to an allotment. I said to her, 'Fancy coming here, you see that greenhouse?' I pointed to a greenhouse that was about 30 yards away. 'That belongs to my uncle.' I said this to her thinking she would get out of the car to use the greenhouse for business. I told her there was plenty of room and some heating in there.

I was wanting to see her off. She then asked for the money, she said: 'You're not forgetting about the money, are you?' I said, 'Of course not', and I promptly gave her a five pound note. She got out of the car and headed for the greenhouse. I followed her, and seeing there was no entrance into the greenhouse from where we were, I told her we would have to climb over a low fence.

While she was starting to climb over the fence I hit her over the head with the hammer. She fell down and was moaning quite loudly. I hit her again and again on the head until the moaning stopped. At this time I saw some car headlights suddenly come on. They were from a car parked further into the allotments than I was. I had turned sharp right when I drove in and I was parked up close to the hedge. This car was parked about 60 yards further into the allotment.

The car started up and I knew it would be moving within seconds, so I pulled the girl under the bushes, the perimeter bushes, and threw her belongings, handbag, etc., out of the way. On reflection I think there was just her handbag. I stood with my back to the hedge and threw the bag diagonally to my right. I stayed where I was, I saw the car out into the road. [He had actually put an old door on top of her body too.]

No sooner had the car gone, when another car driving along the road, which was a dual carriageway, slowed right down. I saw through the bushes it was indicating left to come into the allotments. Thinking this was a very dangerous position to be in, I hid behind my car.

I saw this car drive into the allotments, the car drove up the road, turned round, and stopped in the same place the other car had just left from. I didn't wait any longer, I jumped into my car and drove off towards the centre of Manchester, and drove home.

The hammer I used that night was the one I had found in my garage after I had taken over my house. I took the hammer back with me. Having driven half way back, I realised suddenly that this didn't put me in the clear, because I had given her from my wage packet a brand new five pound note. I was working at Clarks then. I was in a dilemma once again. I kept on driving towards home, I didn't realise whether she would be found or not. I decided I could not risk going back to retrieve my £5 note, and I carried on home. My wife was either working, or in bed, when I got home.

I was puzzled when no mention of this was made in the newspapers or TV over the next few days. I decided before a week was out that she was lying there undiscovered and that I would go back to retrieve the £5 note.

It was Sunday 9 October when the perfect opportunity presented itself for Sutcliffe to go back to the body of Jean Jordan and retrieve his £5 note. He and Sonia had decided to throw a small house-warming party just for family.

Sutcliffe recalled:

My mother and father, brothers and sisters came from Bingley to my house, and at the end of the party I ran them home. Then I made my return to Manchester. This was about 11 pm … I drove to the allotments in my red Corsair and arrived there within 45 minutes. I turned left off the dual carriageway into the allotments. To get to there I had to drive to a roundabout and double back to that side.

I turned right when I got into the allotments, as I had done before, and parked up about the same place. I found the body still hidden in the place I left it. I pulled it out from the bushes and pulled off her clothes and boots. I went through them desperately trying to find the £5 note. I just threw the clothes about as I took them off.

I realised that she hadn't got the £5 note in her clothes, and that it must have been in her handbag. I roamed about all over the allotments frantically searching for the bag, but I couldn't find it. I was cursing the girl and my luck all the time.

Having not found the £5 note, I gave vent to my frustrations by picking up a piece of broken pane of glass and slashing it across her stomach. When I did this there was a nauseating smell which made me reel back and immediately vomit, it was horrendous.

I forgot to say that before I did this it was my intention to create a mystery about the body, I felt sure this was the end for me anyway. I had taken a hacksaw out of my car intending to remove her head. I started sawing through her neck, the blade might have been blunt because I was getting nowhere at all, so I gave it up. If I had cut the head off I was going to leave it somewhere else to make a big mystery out of it. The glass I used was about ¾ of a pane with the corner missing.

I was very frustrated not having found the £5 note, and thinking that my time was up. I remember I kicked her a few times, and I rolled her over before I left her. I then drove away realising I should stay looking for the fiver, but I thought I had been there long enough.

I got home and went to bed. When I got home I was very surprised to see I had not got much blood on me, just a bit on my shoe and at the bottom of my trousers on one leg, and some on the back of my hand. I washed my hands. I was wearing a pair of casual grey trousers, one of my old pair, the blood wouldn't come off these. I put them in the garage in a cupboard to dispose of later. I was wearing my soft slip shoes, dark brown. I wiped these clean. I don't think I have got them now. I later burned my trousers with some garden rubbish at the other side of our garden wall on the field.

I read about the body of Jean Royle being found and sat back waiting for the inevitable, as I had assumed that the line of enquiry about the £5 note would follow. I read about the note being traced to a Shipley bank, I knew Clarks got the wage money from a Shipley bank, and that a local enquiry would be made, and by some miracle I escaped the dragnet.

I've had at least three hacksaws, I don't know which one it was I took to Manchester. I threw the blade away in the dustbin. One of my hacksaws broke after this and I threw it in the bin.

At around 10.30 am on Monday 10 October, two allotment holders, Jimmy Morrisey and Bruce Jones (who would later play the character Les Battersby in Coronation Street) found Jean Jordan's body while searching for house bricks. It lay near an old wooden shed and was within 20ft of a well-used pathway.

Bruce Jones recalled:

> I found Jean Jordan – the most horrific body – mutilated. I had an allotment with a friend I worked with and we bought a big second hand shed. So I decided to get the wheelbarrow, hammer and chisel and go to the waste-ground over there and get the bricks for the base of the shed and I'd rode the 'barrow over this girl five times. As I went back the sixth time it had all been moved and she was there and I didn't realise at first it was a body. I thought it was a tailor's dummy.
>
> I shouted my mate over, and the guy came over with his little Jack Russell. I ran over the road, phoned the police and within minutes there were that many police cars there you wouldn't believe it.

A police report found:

> Most of the top clothing was badly bloodstained and crawling with fully developed maggots. Under the privet hedge which separated the allotment from the pathway was a depression which was absolutely teeming with maggots, and leaning next to the adjacent wooden shed was a wooden interior house door. It was deduced that the victim had been murdered

some days before; that her body had been put into the depression near the hedge and covered with the wooden door; that the murderer had returned to the scene on the night prior to the body being found and had removed it from its place of concealment, stripped away the clothing and then had mutilated it before attempting to cut off the head.

The pathologist's report found:

The body lay in grass near a wooden hut, next to a cinder track. It was completely naked, the head twisted to the left, the trunk and legs in a semi-prone position with the arms spread apart. A coil of intestine was wrapped around the waist. The head was blackened due both to injuries received and changes brought about by putrefaction. The rest of the body was clean and white. The skin on the trunk and the upper legs showed numerous yellowish areas caused by physical damage and degeneration. There were clear wounds to the abdomen and scalp, and small pieces of paint on the skin matched that on an old door found nearby. There was a large area of bloodstaining under the bushes.

There were eleven injuries to Jeans head, some causing depressed fractures of the skull, some fairly superficial, others in a cluster of wounds each about one inch in diameter and all with fractures of the skull beneath. She had been hit with enough force in the mouth to loosen the middle four teeth in her upper jaw and there were tooth fragments in her mouth. Her head was practically flattened.

Moving to her shoulder, neck and trunk, he found a series of nineteen massive injuries, dark brown in colour, on her arms and upper chest, caused by a hammer. Further down were more savage wounds – cuts to the front of her trunk. Other slashing wounds were found on her right thigh. As the Pathologist examined her body, he felt sure the wounds were made in a series of slashes from the left shoulder to the right knee. His report states: 'Eighteen wounds were seen on the abdomen and chest and six on the right thigh. The largest wound on the abdomen was seven inches long and the intestine protruded through it.' There was a neighbouring large wound through which a part of her gut protruded. It had been made with such ferocity that the intestine had been cut, the wounds extending deep into the abdomen and into the front of the spine. He could see fly eggs present but no maggots in this wound. 'This indicates that the wound had not been exposed to flies as long a time as the head.' More wounds were on the left side of her trunk.

The report concluded: 'There were indications suggesting that the body had been clothed for some days after death and then stripped a day or so before the body was found. The age of the maggots indicated that death had occurred nine or ten days before being found.'

At the request of the police, details of the attempt to sever her head from her body were omitted from his report. Clear marks in two separate places on her neck clearly showed that a saw had been used in an effort to decapitate Jean. Detective Chief Superintendent Jack Ridgeway, who was the lead investigator, wanted this information kept top secret. It was one of the facts only the killer would know, and if anyone came forward claiming false ownership of the murder it meant they could be eliminated from the inquiry if they failed to mention this. No traces of semen were found in her body.

When the details of the murder and a brief description of the victim were published in newspapers, Alan Royle telephoned the police to say that the body could be that of his partner Jean Jordan, and he was able to identify the clothing she was wearing on the day she went missing. Her friend Anna Holt had also read the reports but had gone to the police and they allowed her to identify the body. Up until she did this and gave her statement, police didn't think that Jean was a prostitute. They had already spoken to Alan Royle over the telephone and gathered some background details on Jean and they told the gathered press: 'It could be that while she was walking, some motorist stopped and offered her a lift and that she expected she might have been able to get a lift up to Scotland. She has hitchhiked on occasions before.'

Anna Holt confirmed:

> That's Scotch Jean. She's on the game – she worked the same patch as me. Poor Jean was not really cut out for it. She was guilty about her kids. Just recently she told me she was going to give it all up, pack it all in, settle down to a decent home life again.

Final confirmation that the body was Jean Jordan's came when, after an extensive search of their flat where they had not found her finger prints (with Alan Royle having done most of the housework) her left thumb print was finally found on a lemonade bottle.

Jean Jordan's handbag was finally found at 10.00 on Saturday 15 October by an allotment owner called Mr Cox. He had gone to his new allotment on Princess Road and found the bag concealed in some long grass underneath the fence which separated the old and new allotments.

When he found the handbag, it was 189 ft from where Jean's body had been discovered and it was lying open. In the main compartment was some makeup, cigarettes and matches; £14 was missing from the handbag, but Sutcliffe's brand new £5 note and a £1 note were found in a small side pocket on the outside of the handbag. Sutcliffe had somehow missed it.

Detectives quickly discovered that the £5 note had come from a batch issued in pay packets just days before the murder but, unfortunately, the delay in its discovery meant that too much time had passed to narrow the search further for its owner. Another factor was the delay by the police in announcing its discovery and serial number to the public in the hope they may be able to help.

It was discovered that the £5 note had been part of a consignment of 5,000 £5 notes delivered to the Manningham, Shipley or Bingley branches of the Midland Bank on 29 September 1977.

The investigation into Jean Jordan's murder, which was being run by Detective Chief Superintendent Jack Ridgeway, quickly recognised the possibility of a link with the crimes committed in West Yorkshire. Within hours, he was in contact with Assistant Chief Constable George Oldfield and Detective Chief Superintendent Jim Hobson and, within a few days, they were all certain that they were looking for the same man.

As part of the investigation into who had had possession of the £5 note, detectives from Manchester went up to West Yorkshire to find out which companies could have received it. Sutcliffe's employers, T. & W. H. Clark (Holdings) Limited were one of the possibilities and, as such, all employees were interviewed. At this time, his name was one of 8,000 possibilities in this line of inquiry.

On this point, the Byford Report states:

> The first phase of the police inquiry failed to identify any £5 note remotely connected with the note held by the police. A number of new £5 notes were traced, however, and were so far removed in serial numbers from the Jordan note that the people who held them and their employers could be eliminated from the inquiry.
>
> Before starting the second phase of the inquiry officers involved attended a briefing at which they were given as much evidence as was available which might help them to identify the murderer. Little evidence was, in fact, available at this time particularly in light of the fact that only the murders of McCann, Jackson, Richardson, Atkinson and MacDonald and the assault on Maureen Long were regarded as being in the series. The earlier assaults on Rogulskyj, Smelt and Claxton were not linked at this stage and the evidence from them was not given to members of the Inquiry Teams.

(At the time the Byford Report was written, the attacks on Gloria Wood, Tracy Browne, Rosemary Stead, Maureen Hogan, Debra Schlesinger and the later murder of Carol Wilkinson were being treated as separate assaults).

The Byford Report continued:

> The principal evidential items available at that time were:
>
> 1. That the murder weapon was thought to be a hammer
> 2. That an unknown cutting/stabbing instrument was also used
> 3. The murderer had previously worn wellington or industrial boots about size 7
> 4. The vehicle used by the murderer might be fitted with two India Autoway tyres (this evidence came from the Richardson murder eight months previously and was not rated very highly because it was thought that the tyres in all probability had been replaced).
>
> These points were brought to the attention of members of the Inquiry Team during a briefing at which visual aids were used to reinforce the comments of the senior investigating officers, Assistant Chief Constable Oldfield and Detective Chief Superintendent Ridgeway.
>
> Mr Oldfield also asked the Inquiry Team members to ask people being interviewed whether they had used taxis during the relevant period and paid their fare with one of the new £5 notes. A Leeds taxi driver (Terrence Hawkshaw) was at this time a strong suspect and Mr Oldfield hoped that the £5 note inquiry might lead to him.

To assist inquiry officers an aide-memoire was prepared listing the points to be covered at interview including, in particular, the whereabouts of interview subjects on the night of Jordan's murder (1 October 1977) and on the night of the 9/10 October 1977 when it was believed the murderer had returned to the scene and inflicted further injuries to the body.

Detective Chief Superintendent Ridgeway, who was in charge of the Manchester end of the investigation, decided not to disclose to the West Yorkshire officers or to his own Inquiry Team members that the post-mortem examination of Jordan had revealed an attempt to saw off her head with a hacksaw. He wanted to keep this vital fact from the press so that it could be used in the future as an important corroborative clue...

Detective Chief Superintendent Ridgeway's decision to withhold the knowledge that an attempt had been made to sever Jordan's head was in some ways understandable but on balance was wrong. Since it had been clearly established that a hacksaw had been used on Jordan's body officers should have been briefed to take possession of hacksaws so that they could be subjected to forensic examination.

Sutcliffe's time to be interviewed came at 19.45 on 2 November when he was visited at home by DC Edwin Howard and DC Leslie Smith. They found him at home with his wife, Sonia, where he appeared relaxed and casual. He told them that on the night of the murder of Jean Jordan he had been at home and had gone to bed at around 23.30.

When he was questioned about the second date, when the killer had returned to the body, Sutcliffe told them all about his house-warming party – giving him a cast-iron alibi. His wife, Sonia, gave him an alibi for both dates. He also told the detectives that he was unable to produce any of the £5 notes that he had received in his pay packet on 29 September and, when Sonia was out of the room making a drink, denied using prostitutes. He said that he never went out to Manchester but had delivered to there once about twelve months previously for work, but couldn't remember the address.

The detectives found nothing to arouse their suspicions and filed a five-paragraph report stating that Sutcliffe denied using prostitutes and that his wife had given him an alibi for the night of the murder. However, they also reported that Sutcliffe didn't own a car, which was clearly wrong, and when Sir Lawrence Byford wrote his report, the detectives couldn't remember whether Sutcliffe had told them this, or they had assumed it because they had not seen a car at the house. It was deemed that he was 'not connected' to the murder of Jean Jordan.

Six days on from the first interview with Sutcliffe, detectives went back to his home on Garden Lane for a follow-up interview to see if further detail could be obtained to corroborate his account for the two material dates. This time he was interviewed by DC Rayne from Greater Manchester Police and DC Smith from West Yorkshire Police.

The detectives reported details of Sutcliffe's occupation, employer, his personal description, the vehicle he owned and his previous car disposed of two months prior to their visit.

Sutcliffe and his wife both gave the same version of events as they had in the first interview, and this time they allowed their house to be searched, but nothing incriminating was found. As one of 6,000 people interviewed it is not clear how thorough this search was. On this occasion, Sutcliffe was questioned about his car as it was believed his make of car (the Ford Corsair) could have left the tyre marks at the scene of Irene Richardson's murder, but the detectives were not alerted to anything suspicious.

Detectives then went to visit Sutcliffe's mother, Kathleen, as he had told them that he had given his parents a lift home after the house-warming party, and she confirmed that she had been at the party and that her son had given them a lift home.

It is believed that at the time of these two interviews, the tyres on Sutcliffe's red Corsair were the same as the ones he had had on his white Corsair. These would have linked him conclusively to the murder scene of Irene Richardson and it is clear that the interviewing detectives did not examine the vehicle. Had they done so, it is highly likely that the inquiry would have taken a very different turn. This was the first time Sutcliffe would slip through the net. It would not be the last.

The Byford Report found:

> It is now obvious that the interview with Sutcliffe ... was not the in-depth probe which had been intended and amounted, in fact, to a fairly superficial questioning and to answers which were accepted at their face values. Further questioning about the house-warming party in particular might have allowed what was regarded as a concrete alibi to be broken and so pave the way to further investigation of Sutcliffe and his identification as a suspect.
>
> It is highly probable that at the time this interview was conducted Sutcliffe's car had on it similar tyres to those which left the tread marks at the Richardson scene. The failure to examine the car and its tyres was therefore significant, more particularly in the light of the fact that Sutcliffe was to use the same car at the time of his assault on Marilyn Moore a little more than a month later.
>
> The interviewing officers clearly failed to comply with their instructions that the house, garage and motor car of interview subjects were to be searched and so lost an opportunity to confirm or deny the factors spelled out to them during their briefing.
>
> While the officers had no reason to suspect Sutcliffe any more than any other person being interviewed there was a distinct possibility that the person to whom the Jordan £5 note had been paid would be seen during the inquiry, and therefore, their attitude was not as positive as it should have been.

As can be seen from the evidence, at this stage Sutcliffe's house and vehicle were not examined properly. The tyres from his car would have put him at the scene of Irene Richardson's murder, his wellington boots which left the footprints at the scenes of Emily Jackson's and Patricia Atkinson's murders were in his wardrobe, and he was alibied only by his family members. The hacksaw he had used to try to decapitate Jean Jordan with was also probably hanging up in his garage. Without doubt, Peter Sutcliffe *should* have been arrested at this point in the investigation.

Sutcliffe bragged to his best friend Trevor Birdsall about these interviews and at this point Birdsall began to think that his friend may well have been the Yorkshire Ripper. He discussed the conversation with his wife, but he later recalled: 'My suspicions were not strong enough to tell the police. I found it hard to believe that Peter, a friend of mine, could be the Ripper.'

Following Jean Jordan's murder, an intelligence operation was mounted in West Yorkshire, South Yorkshire, Greater Manchester and Humberside to gather information about prostitutes and their associates, the areas where they solicited and the places to which they took their punters.

But before all this, as Bruce Jones was stumbling across Jean Jordan's body, Peter Sutcliffe believed that his time was up and, frustrated not to have found his £5 note, he struck again.

Chapter 18

Carol Wilkinson

At around 10.45 on the morning of Monday 10 October 1977, 20-year-old Carol Wilkinson was murdered on Woodhall Road, Bradford.

Born in 1957, Carol's parents split when she was 4 years old. Her mother went on to marry a George Wilkinson. Carol and George did not get on and there were frequent rows between the two. These got worse in 1967 when Carol's sister Wendy, who was seven years older than Carol, moved out.

Carol got in with a bad crowd from Bradford's Ravenscliffe Estate, where she was living, and George didn't like them, which led to further rows. Just before Carol left school at the age of 16 in 1973, she went missing for a couple of days, having gone out on a Saturday night. She said that three men had started talking to her at a bus stop as she was heading home and had then taken her to a nearby garage where they gang-raped her. This rape doesn't appear to have been reported at the time.

Carol got a job in Empire Stores in Bradford, which was, at the time, one of the biggest mail-order firms. The job didn't last long and in 1974 she got a job as a clerk in the wholesale department of Almond's Bakery.

In 1975 Carol got engaged to her boyfriend of just over a year, Kevin Best; in 1977, she left home following yet another huge argument with her stepfather.

At first she moved in with her sister, Wendy (now going by the name of Worsley), who lived on the other side of the estate. Kevin Best lived just across the road from Wendy, and Carol and Kevin were soon living together in a house a little further down the estate at 131 Ranelagh Avenue. Kevin also got a job as a butcher on Ravenscliffe Avenue.

On Saturday 8 October, Carol went to Bradford to buy some new shoes. She returned home in time to have lunch with Kevin before they both went to the local supermarket. That evening, Carol went out with some of her friends from work and ended up on a pub crawl around Shipley.

She was seen talking to a rugby player in one of these pubs before the two of them disappeared. Carol was next seen in the early hours of the following morning at home, getting out of a taxi in a very drunken state. Carol and Kevin argued but had made up by the Monday morning.

Kay Lintern, who lived opposite Carol's mother and stepfather, recalled that morning vividly:

> I was 14 and my stepfather was a friend of Peter Sutcliffe. One day our new fridge broke down and Sutcliffe turned up to fix the motor. From then

I kept spotting Sutcliffe near where we lived. He would follow me when I walked to school. It was creepy.

On the day Carol died I had an ear infection and stayed off school. At 08.25 I looked out of our landing window and saw Sutcliffe. I thought he was waiting there to follow me to school again.

Carol had left home a short time later and gone to visit her mother. Kay Lintern continued: 'I saw Carol coming out of her parents' home. She would have been walking to work ... Sutcliffe had already been run off the estate for being a Peeping Tom.'

He had been run off the estate in February 1977 because a man called Paul Hodgson had repeatedly found Sutcliffe outside his 19-year-old sisters' home and called the police. 'I think he was looking out for a victim. Lynne lived in the same street as Carol's family.'

After visiting her mother, Carol then visited Kevin at work on her way to her shift at the bakery. She was wearing her new shoes and was walking to work because there was a local bus strike. She took a shortcut down a lane and into Woodhall Road which ran along the back of Almond's Bakery.

Shortly before 10.00, hospital cook Stephen Smith took the same shortcut on his way to work and found Carol lying face down in a pool of blood on Woodhall Road. She had been hit over the back of the head with either a walling hammer (which we know Sutcliffe was using at this time) or a rock, and partially stripped: her trousers and knickers had been pulled down and her bra lifted up (in typical Ripper fashion). But she was still alive.

She was rushed straight to hospital where surgeons discovered that her skull had been fractured in multiple places and that she had severe brain damage. After two days on a life-support machine, her doctors concluded that the machine was the only thing keeping her alive. The machine was switched off on the morning of 12 October and she passed away.

Detective Chief Superintendent Jim Hobson was put in charge of the investigation but, despite the similarities between this murder and those previously, a decision was made to exclude this attack from the list of Ripper victims. Once again, it seemed that because she wasn't a prostitute and was attacked in broad daylight, the police presumed she couldn't have been attacked by the Ripper. Had detectives kept a more open mind they may have discovered that Peter Sutcliffe was known to have argued violently with Carol's stepfather. The Ravenscliffe Estate residents would have told them that during the previous summer (1976) Sutcliffe had carried out jobs for families on the estate and it was due to one of these jobs that he got to know George Wilkinson. However, George Wilkinson and Peter Sutcliffe quickly fell out and George threatened to beat Sutcliffe up because he was constantly trying to pick up Carol.

Professor David Gee, the Home Office Pathologist who carried out all the post-mortem examinations on the Ripper victims, said that there were similarities between the murder of Carol Wilkinson and the later murder of Yvonne Pearson by Sutcliffe, committed just three months later. At both post-mortems, Professor Gee thought that a large rock had been used to hit the victim on the head, but Sutcliffe later confessed that he had used a walling hammer, rather than the usual ball pein hammer, to attack Pearson with. Surely it is now obvious that Sutcliffe, who had also used the walling hammer on Jean Jordan, had also used it here just days later.

A man named Anthony Steel was later convicted of Carol Wilkinson's murder, in one of the gravest miscarriages of justice in British criminal history. He spent twenty years in prison for the murder before finally having his sentence quashed at the Court of Appeal in February 2003, due to the new evidence from both defence and Crown consultant psychologists indicating that Steel 'is and was mentally handicapped and at the borderline of abnormal suggestibility. He was therefore a significantly more vulnerable interviewee than could be appreciated at the time of the trial.'

Anthony Steel received an official police apology and about £100,000 in compensation from the government, but he was in poor health following his release from prison. He died from a heart attack aged 52 in September 2007. None of the police officers involved in the wrongful conviction, including Jim Hobson, were reprimanded or prosecuted.

Chapter 19

Marilyn Moore

On Wednesday, 14 December 1977, 25-year-old sex worker Marilyn Moore was attacked at around 20.30 in Chapeltown, Leeds – two months after the murder of Carol Wilkinson.

Born in Leeds in 1952, Marilyn left home aged 15 and was married a year later. The couple went on to have two children together, a boy and a girl, but the relationship quickly soured and Marilyn moved out, leaving the children with their father. They soon divorced and Marilyn was forced to turn to sex work as the only way of supporting herself. The children were soon taken into care.

She would travel to London, Slough, Bradford and Leeds to ply her trade, receiving her one conviction for soliciting earlier in 1977, and didn't have a home to call her own. When she was in Leeds she would live with a man called Peter Sucvic, described as a 'good friend'. The 51-year-old had a flat in Harehills, just a short walk from the Gaiety pub.

On the evening of 14 December, Marilyn told Peter that she was off to see her friend Beverley who lived on Gathorne Terrace, just behind the Gaiety pub. Later that evening she was out looking for punters on Gipton Avenue and spotted a car driving slowly. As she walked along Spencer Place the car drove past her, so she crossed the road onto Leopold Street in anticipation of the car coming back. At the junction with Frankland Place she saw the same car parked up and a man standing beside the driver's door, who appeared to be waving to someone in one of the houses.

Sutcliffe recalled:

> I had been taken over completely by this urge to kill and I couldn't fight it ... I drove into the red light district in Chapeltown. I was driving along a street, I now know as Leopold Street, where I saw her walking along Spencer Place, from the phone boxes at the end. I saw her reject a man in a car who had stopped and she carried on. I turned left into Spencer Place, turned first left, and left again into a narrow street, and stopped near the corner of the road I had just been on. [Frankland Place with junction of Leopold Street].
>
> It was my intention to get her into my car with the minimum of fuss. I knew she had refused to get in one car, so I got out of my car and walked to the corner. She was only a few yards away walking towards where I stood. I walked back to my car and as she came into view I shouted, 'Bye now, see you later', and 'Take care', and I waved towards the houses on my left. I did this to give her reassurances that I was all right. I got in and

started the engine and opened the passenger window. I asked her if she was doing business. She glanced at the house, said 'Yes', and got in.

She told me where to drive. She asked my name, I told her it was Dave. We had some conversation in the car but I cannot remember what I might have said. She directed me to this place which was up a narrow lane and I can only describe it as an oasis of mud. It was an open area with a building to one side. I parked up.

They talked about what Sutcliffe had been doing that day and he told Marilyn that he had been saying goodbye to his sick girlfriend when she first saw him. He also mentioned in conversation two other prostitutes he knew, called Gloria and Hilary, and that Hilary had a Jamaican boyfriend. She listened carefully as she gazed into his 'come to bed eyes'.

They had driven to Scott Hall Street, and then turned on to Buslinghtorpe Lane, and driven to some waste ground behind Brown's factory (Stonegate). They were now just 200 yards from the Prince Phillip Playing Fields, where Sutcliffe had murdered Wilma McCann two years previously.

Marilyn recalled:

I started unbuckling my right shoe, thinking we were going to stay in the front seat, but Dave said he wanted to go in the back of the car. It was a bit unusual, but I didn't mind because he seemed such a nice bloke. So I fastened my shoe and got out.

Sutcliffe later stated:

When she got out, I got out with my hammer, which I had on the floor at my side. I went round the front of my car and up behind her. I took a swing at her with the hammer but I slipped on the mud and lost my balance. I only caught her a glancing blow on the head.

She cried out and I hit her again on the head. She was still screaming. After the second blow, she fell down.

Marilyn recalled:

I didn't know what was happening. I didn't really feel the blow but I put my hands up over the back of my head for protection and he hit my thumb with the second blow. The third one really hurt and I began to go down. I could hear him screaming at me 'filthy prostitute' and the next thing I knew, I was lying on the ground and everything seemed to be a haze.

Marilyn's screaming alerted some local dogs who started barking, and Sutcliffe recalled:

I saw some people walking along about 40 yards away on the narrow road at the top. I jumped in my car and started it up. I put my foot down but the back wheels started spinning and I couldn't drive off at first. When the car got a grip I slewed round to the right and I drove away with a lot of wheel spin. I drove straight home.

That night I was wearing the old brown car coat, which you've got, and a pair of blue jeans and a pair of Doc Martins boots.

When Marilyn Moore regained consciousness, she staggered towards the road to get help. Luckily, a couple found her and the man ran to get help while the woman tried to comfort Marilyn. The ambulance took her straight to Leeds General Infirmary (LGI) for emergency surgery, where it was discovered that she had been hit eight times with a ball pein hammer which had left lacerations of between 1–4 inches on her head along with a 4 inch depressed fracture of the skull. She required fifty-six stitches to close the wounds. She also had cuts and bruises on her thumb and hand where she had tried to protect herself from the blows.

The attack was investigated by Detective Chief Superintendent Jim Hobson. When she was well enough, Marilyn was interviewed and was able to give her first photofit of her attacker.

Both Marilyn and the police made mistakes at this early stage of the investigation. The police believed that she had been hit only three times with the hammer, and that she had only got out of the car after her attacker had refused to pay her before intercourse. Marilyn had made the mistake of recalling her attacker as having a Liverpudlian accent, but more importantly that the car she believed he was driving was a dark coloured or maroon vehicle, about the size of a Morris Oxford, which had two rear-view mirrors. As such, it was difficult to link this to the previous murders and attacks.

When she came out of hospital, the police sat her in various makes of cars but, unfortunately, she ruled out the Ford Corsair and two other similar models. She considered the Austin A55 Farina to be the car she was in; 404 such vehicles were traced and all but thirty-six were eliminated.

The tyre tracks found at the scene were eventually found to be similar to those left at the scene of Irene Richardson's murder on Soldiers' Field.

The two sex workers that the attacker and Marilyn seemed to know, Gloria and Hilary, were also interviewed and that resulted in a further 198 women being interviewed. Indices in the Incident Room showed that 1,037 men called Dave had so far been seen and eliminated; they were seen again.

The 1983 'Report into the Investigation of the Series of Murders and Assaults on Women in the North of England between 1975 and 1980' found that:

> The officers involved tended to regard the information given by Miss Moore as unreliable because of her head injuries and conflicting recollections after surgery. This proved to be unfortunate as the first photofit was a good likeness. It is difficult to understand why so little weight was given to the physical description, yet so much reliance placed on her description of the vehicle which proved to be misleading.

In January 1978, the search for the person who received the £5 note and had given it to Jean Jordan was discontinued by the police. Detective Chief Superintendent Jack

Ridgeway, who was in charge of the investigation, told the press: 'We have just about exhausted the enquiry. It has drawn a blank.' His assistant stated: 'I personally don't believe that we have yet met the killer in our multitude of interviews. When we do I am positive we will realise and nail him.' He was clearly wrong.

While Sutcliffe was lucky in that respect, it was in early 1978 that he contracted a Sexually Transmitted Infection (STI) – almost certainly from a prostitute. He claimed to his wife Sonia that it must have come from 'a still warm toilet seat', but almost certainly shows that he was using the services of prostitutes still. This, together with the fact that he knew some prostitutes who Marilyn Moore knew, is further evidence that he was using the services of prostitutes, as well as attacking and killing them. Sutcliffe himself always denied using prostitutes, but did tell the police: 'If I was late home it was easy to explain. I'd say I'd been on a long trip or been loading the wagon for the next morning.'

Due to the severity of Marilyn Moore's injuries, the police thought that her description of her attacker might not be reliable, and it was later revealed by Chief Constable Ronald Gregory that she had been taken to Leeds University Hospital to be questioned under hypnosis. She was able to give a clearer description of her attacker, stating that he had a small gap between his upper front teeth and had 'come-to-bed' eyes. The police soon released an updated photofit and it was a remarkable likeness to Peter Sutcliffe.

Relevant Statistics

Incident Room set up	14 December 1977
House to House Enquiries	103
Actions	839
Statements	149
Vehicle Enquiries	404
Officers Engaged	71
Hours Worked (Not inc. Overtime)	6,741
Incident Room Closed	31 January 1978

When Tracy Browne, Sutcliffe's youngest victim at 14, saw the updated photofit published in the newspapers she immediately recognised him as the same man who had attacked her. She went with her mother, Nora, straight to the police station at Keighley to tell them, but the policeman on the front desk thought that she was making the story up. Tracy's mother showed him the photofit in the newspaper and told him how he had attacked her daughter, but the policeman just said: 'We are all having fun and games today, aren't we?!' When Nora Browne wouldn't let the matter drop, the policeman simply gave them a form to fill in. With this, Mrs Browne began shouting and a detective, who just happened to be walking past, tried to calm her and Tracy down. He took their details but they were never followed up.

Incensed, Nora Browne called her brother, Mr Monty Featherman, who was a local magistrate and personal friend of Chief Superintendent Jim Hobson, to see if he could make the police listen, but he was unable to make any progress.

The later review in 1981, by Deputy Chief Constable Colin Sampson, recognised the importance of Marilyn Moore's photofit, stating that it was a remarkable likeness which should have provided the police with the turning point in their enquiries:

If her photofit had been compared with those provided by other survivors, the similarity is so striking that it is beyond belief that they would not all have been linked and considerable emphasis given to tracing the bearded man described ... While publicity was given to the description of Miss Moore's attacker, little weight was given to this aspect during the investigation. Had this been done, and linked with others, the investigation might have been resolved much earlier.

A possible explanation for the police failing to follow these obvious links could have been the direction from the very top of the force. After what would prove to be the biggest police investigation in British history, West Yorkshire Chief Constable Ronald Gregory didn't even know the facts of the case! In his memoirs, he stated:

> Marilyn Moore's description was suspect. When she had been found, badly injured but still alive in December 1977, I prayed we at last had our breakthrough – a witness who had seen the Ripper face to face. Her recovery had been a medical miracle – her skull had been fractured and she had been stabbed eight times – but she proved an unreliable witness, or so we thought at the time. Three times she phoned us to say she had just seen the Ripper in a public house. Three times it proved a false alarm ... Moore had been drunk when attacked.

As can be seen from the facts above, Marilyn Moore was not stabbed eight times – in fact she hadn't been stabbed at all. She also was not drunk on the night of her attack. On top of this, Anna Rogulskyj, Olive Smelt, Marcella Claxton, Maureen Long – and especially Tracy Browne – had all given a description of their attacker having been face to face with him and spoken to him, but the police were not interested.

The attack on Marilyn Moore was not conclusively linked to the Ripper until the 12 May 1978.

The 1983 'Report into the Investigation of the Series of Murders and Assaults on Women in the North of England between 1975 and 1980', states:

> The turning point in the enquiry should have occurred following the attack on Marilyn Moore because:-
>
> a) She was struck on the head
> b) She provided photofits of her attacker, again with a beard
> c) She provided a description of her attacker's vehicle
> d) If her photofit had been compared with those provided by other survivors, the similarity is so striking that it is beyond belief that they would not all have been linked and considerable emphasis given to tracing the bearded man described

While there were doubts about the weight that should be placed on the description given by Moore of her attacker, this would have been dispelled had the other two descriptions been properly linked. In any event, the subsequent identification of men closely resembling Moore's photofit should have strengthened, not weakened, her credibility. The police certainly accepted her credibility in the identification of the car and, as a result, embarked on a mammoth line of enquiry.

The fact remains that, following Moore's attack, if the beard index had been enlarged to include black beards, or all beards, one name that would certainly have emerged was that of Sutcliffe as he had already been seen, and his description provided, on the £5 note enquiry in November 1977.

If Sutcliffe had been re-interviewed at any point soon after Moore had compiled her photofit picture in December 1977, the officers would have seen his striking resemblance to the photofits provided by the survivors.

All the previous matters are factual and were available to investigating officers at the time. One further point needs to be added, and it involves a degree of speculation. If the events had transpired as described, what other evidence might have been found that an enquiring detective could act on? The answer is that Sutcliffe had in his possession, at that time, a red Ford Corsair, which had been used in the attack on Moore and which could be matched to the tyre tracks found at the scene of her attack, a vehicle he did not dispose of until August 1978.

This was not the first, nor last, time that Chief Constable Ronald Gregory would make major mistakes in the Ripper investigation.

Chapter 20

Yvonne Pearson

On Saturday 21 January 1978, 21-year-old Yvonne Anne Pearson was murdered on waste ground on Arthington Street, at the back of Drummond's Mill, in Bradford at around 21.30 – just over a month after the attack on Marilyn Moore.

Yvonne was born in Leeds on 2 February 1956 to John and Rose Pearson. She had three siblings and left home aged 17. The reason is probably because she had fallen out with her Roman Catholic parents. Certainly, she had been in trouble with the police by this point; she appeared at Leeds City Juvenile Court in January 1968, where she was fined £5 for stealing, and then again in August 1970, charged with theft of money and theft from a shop. She was fined a further £10 and put on probation for two years. Then one day, quite out of the blue, Yvonne appeared on her parents' doorstep.

Yvonne had been in a relationship with a Jamaican man and they had two children together – 3-year-old Colette and 6-month-old Lorraine. Yvonne's partner, Roy Saunders, later told the press: 'We had an understanding that if either of us wanted someone else, that was OK. After all, I never put a ring on her finger.'

Because he didn't work, it was up to Yvonne to earn the money and the only way she could was to turn to sex work. Her first conviction for prostitution was in January 1974, and she would appear in front of Leeds and Bradford Magistrates a total of fourteen times before her murder. She had previously been questioned by the police regarding the Ripper murders and was afraid of becoming his next victim, but she was forced out onto the streets by her pimp.

She knew Patricia Atkinson quite well and had often drunk in the same pubs as her. It was as a direct result of Patricia's murder that Yvonne no longer took punters back to her home on Woodbury Road and would always use their car instead.

Yvonne's last appearance in court was at Bradford Magistrates' Court on 5 January 1978 when she was charged with loitering for the purpose of prostitution. She was bailed on that date to reappear at Court on 26 January on the condition being that she remained at her home address between the hours of 17.00 and 09.00.

Roy Saunders had returned to Jamaica to visit relatives and so Yvonne, who knew the chances were that she would go back to prison, had made arrangements for the children to be taken care of by friends.

At around 16.00 on the evening she was murdered, Yvonne left the two children in the care of 16-year-old babysitter Selma Turley, saying she was going to visit her mother to ask for some money and would be home by 19.00. However, Yvonne didn't go to see her mother and instead went to the Flying Dutchman pub and left around 21.30 to go 'earn some money' as she told a friend before she left.

That day, Sutcliffe had been helping his parents move to a new home nearer to the centre of Bingley. They were moving from Cornwall Road to Rutland House, near Mornington Road, due to Kathleen's failing health. Instead of caring for his wife, however, John Sutcliffe used her health as an excuse to carry on his womanising. He soon had an affair with a woman called Marion Dean and he assured her that his wife was practically an invalid.

As day turned to night, Sutcliffe decided against having a drink with his brother Mick and his father John to celebrate the completion of the move. His brother and father assumed that he wanted to get home to Sonia, but Sutcliffe had other ideas.

He recalled that when he left his parents' new home, he was driving home to Garden Lane when a car backed out of a side street in front of him which forced him to stop suddenly. This was on Lumb Lane – a known area for prostitution and not on his route back home. It was also only 100 yards from where he had picked up Maureen Long. Clearly, he had gone looking for someone to attack and would use the excuse that the move had taken longer than expected if his wife Sonia questioned him.

He recalled:

> She stepped straight up to the car as I stopped and tapped on the window. She asked me if I wanted business ... I still had a hammer in the car on the floor, under my seat. I told her to get in. She suggested that I turn the car round and she told me where to drive.

In fact, he had put the walling hammer back under his car seat, as he had killed with the attacks in which he had used it (Jean Jordan and Carol Wilkinson) and had failed in his last attempt (Marilyn Moore) with the ball pein hammer.

He continued:

> I drove back along Lumb Lane, past Drummond Mill, turned right down a road onto White Abbey Road, and I was directed to turn by Yvonne left into a street behind Silvio's bakery. I drove to the very end of this street where there was a large open space like a parking space and parked the car.
>
> I asked her how much she wanted. She said, 'It depends how much you can afford. A good time £5, more than a good time £10.' She had very few words to say after that, the last words she said was, 'Shall we get into the back?' We both got out and she went round to the back door of the car on the nearside, she tried to open it but it was locked. I opened the front passenger door, reached in, and opened the rear door catch.
>
> As she opened the door, I hit her from behind twice on the head with the hammer. She fell down and started to moan loudly. I dragged her by her feet on her back about 20 yards or so to where there was an old settee lying on its back on some spare land. When I got her to the settee she was still moaning loudly. At that moment a car drove up and parked next to my car.
>
> I saw there was a blonde woman in the car and a man driving. To stop her moaning, I took some filling [horsehair] from the settee, I held her nose and shoved the straw into her mouth, then I shoved it down her throat.

I was kneeling behind the settee, hiding from the motor car, keeping hold of her nose.

I let go after a while to see if she was still making a noise through her nose, but when I did, she started again, so I took hold of her nose again. The car seemed to be there for ages before it drove away. I stayed still, petrified with fear while the car was there.

When the car had gone I was seething with rage. Her jeans were nearly off, because she had undone them at the car, and when I was pulling her by her feet I nearly pulled them off. I pulled her jeans right off. I think I kicked her hard to the head and body. I was senseless with rage and I was kicking away furiously at her.

He had actually bared both of her breasts by raising her bra but, finding he hadn't picked up a knife, he kicked her to death. At one point he jumped on her chest with the weight of both feet. He then hid her body by throwing soil, rubble and turf over her.

He continued:

After this, I remember acting very strangely, I talked to her and apologised for what I had done, but she was dead. I put the settee on top of her. I was very distraught and I was in tears when I left her. This was the first time I had apologised to someone I had killed. I drove home, I cannot recall the time, but it was after 9 pm. I can't remember if Sonia was in the house or not.

I remember stopping on the way home and I just sat in the car trying to work out why I had done this killing. My mind was in a turmoil. Oh, I've just remembered it might have been a walling hammer that I used on Yvonne, there was two walling hammers in the garage of the house when I moved in. I remember I put one in the car when I threw the other one away at Sharps. It might still be in the garage somewhere.

I kept reading the papers and I found it incredible to believe that she hadn't been found. I read a story that she had gone to Wolverhampton.

Then, to cover the fact that he went back to the body later, he stated: 'I didn't dare go back to where she lay, there was no reason to go back.'

When Yvonne Pearson didn't return home, the babysitter put the latch on the door and stayed the night with the children. When there was still no sign of her the following morning, the babysitter telephoned the friends who had agreed to look after the children should Yvonne be sent to prison. When she failed to arrive for her appointment with her solicitor the following Monday, the police were called.

She was reported as missing and the police noted that, as there were concerns for her life because she was a prostitute and they knew the Ripper targeted them, it was also possible that she had 'gone to ground' to avoid her court date and probable imprisonment.

Unfortunately for the investigation, an associate of Yvonne Pearson's told the police that Yvonne had absconded to London to avoid her court appearance. Another associate then later told detectives that she had seen Yvonne in London after the date of her disappearance.

However, a week later there was still no sign of her, so the police held a press conference on 30 January to discuss her disappearance. They disclosed that the last sighting of her had been where Patricia Atkinson was seen shortly before her death and there was a possibility that the same man might be responsible for Yvonne going missing.

Yvonne Pearson's body would not be found until 26 March and, by then, the Ripper had struck again.

Relevant Statistics

Incident Room set up	21 January 1978
House to House Enquiries	511
Actions	966
Statements	331
Vehicle Enquiries	1,155
Officers Engaged	55
Hours Worked (Not inc. Overtime)	11,582
Incident Room Closed	2 June 1978

Chapter 21

Helen Rytka

On Tuesday 31 January 1978, 18-year-old Helen Rytka was murdered at around 21.15 in Huddersfield, West Yorkshire – just ten days after the murder of Yvonne Pearson.

Helen, whose twin sister was called Rita, was born Elena de Mattia on 3 March 1959 in Armley, Leeds. Her mother was an Italian named Bernardina, and her father was a Jamaican named Eric. Helen had younger siblings, Anthony and Angela, born in 1960, who were also twins.

The siblings were put into the care system when their parents broke up in 1969 and their mother later claimed that this was because she didn't have a home big enough for two sets of twins, but people close to them insisted that it was because their mother had remarried in 1970; she beat them and her new husband didn't want to raise four children that weren't his.

When they were 14, Helen and Rita wrote a poem to the *Yorkshire Post* newspaper looking for foster parents, and told the editor that it would be like winning £1,000 on the pools if they were fostered together, but it took another two years before this happened.

Aged 16 and as soon as she was able, Helen Rytka got herself a job working at a bakery; unfortunately, she was made redundant after one month. She then got a job as a packer in a sweet factory in Heckmondwike earning £20 a week. In a bizarre twist, one of Helen's friends was a girl who happened to be related to Sutcliffe's former neighbours and friends, the Barker brothers, and Helen was a frequent visitor to Tanton Crescent in the years when Sutcliffe was living with his in-laws.

When the sisters reached 18 years of age, local authority responsibility for them ended. They didn't want to move far because they wanted to be close to their brother and sister, so social workers found them a flat and they moved to Manningham. Once Anthony and Angela reached 18, the four of them shared a flat in a high-rise block in Laisterdyke, Bradford. Helen would then travel the seven miles to work each day on the bus.

Rita had fallen out with her mother, but the other three children maintained contact with her. Barnardina recalled that Helen was 'always my favourite daughter. She would always come to talk to me and tell me her problems. She cared for me and I cared for her.'

In the lead up to Christmas, Rita had become withdrawn and she dropped out of college. A short time later she then disappeared altogether.

It was over the Christmas break that Helen managed to track her sister down and found her living over forty miles away in a shabby bedsit at 13 Elmwood Avenue in Huddersfield. Rita had resorted to sex work as a way of supporting herself and showed Helen how much money she was making. Just two weeks later, Helen quit her job at the sweet factory and moved to Huddersfield to live with her sister. She too turned to sex work.

The two sisters had only been working the streets for a matter of weeks but had devised a plan to make sure that the risk of any possible harm to them was minimal. They would each take punters at roughly the same time and give them no longer than twenty minutes, before meeting back up at the same place, which happened to be a block of public lavatories at the market end of Great Northern Street, which was also a meeting place for homosexuals.

On the evening of 31 January, the sisters left their flat at around 20.30 to go and look for punters at their usual spot. Approximately forty minutes later, Rita saw her sister get into a dark blue car on the other side of the street. Rita was then quickly picked up by a man driving a Datsun and she took him back to the flat. Helen arrived back at the meeting point first and it was then that Sutcliffe drove by and persuaded her to go for a 'quickie'.

Sutcliffe recalled:

> Before Yvonne was found I had committed another murder in Huddersfield, Helen Rytka. I did not know the Huddersfield red-light area, but one day I had to make a delivery in Huddersfield in the afternoon. I noticed a few girls plying their trade near the Market Area. Two or three nights later I decided to pay them a visit.
>
> The urge inside me to kill girls was now practically uncontrollable. I drove to Huddersfield in my red Corsair one evening. When I got to the red-light area I came across one or two girls walking round the street. I stopped and asked one girl if she was doing business. She said yes, but I'd have to wait, as her regular client was picking her up at any minute. She was a half-caste girl. I drove off, and after going about 50 yards round the corner I saw another half-caste girl. I stopped and asked her and she got in.
>
> She told me she shared a flat with her sister, but she was quite willing to have sex in the car. She said it would cost £5. She told me where to drive, which was only about 80–90 yards away in a timber yard. I drove straight into this yard and parked in an area at the end of the lane that ran between the stack of wood.
>
> On the way to the yard we passed the half-caste girl I had tried to pick up. She told me that it was her sister. Afterwards, when I read about it in the papers, I realised that I had seen these two Rytka sisters in Clayton where they used to live.
>
> I must have given her some money, but I can't recall handing it over to her, because she started to undo her jeans and started to pull them down. Then she hesitated and said it would be better in the back of the car. I agreed thinking that it was what I wanted her to do anyway.
>
> We both got out, she went to the rear nearside door. I picked up a hammer from under my seat and walked round the front. By the time I got to her she had opened the rear door and was getting in. I hit her on the head with the hammer as she was practically into the car. The hammer struck the top door sill and diminished the impact with her skull to a mere tap.
>
> She jumped back in alarm out of the car, at the same time letting go of her jeans, which fell down around her knees, and she exclaimed, 'What was

that?' To which I replied, 'Just a sample of one of these,' and I hit a furious blow to her head which knocked her down. She just crumpled like a sack. She was making a loud moaning sound, so I hit her a few more times on the head.

On looking up, I realised that I had done this in full view of two taxi drivers, who were no more than 35 yards up the right-hand side of the woodyard. Their cars were parked one behind the other facing me. The drivers were stood talking to each other. I dragged Helen by the hands to the end of the woodyard. I then pulled off her jeans and her knickers and her shoes or boots. She had stopped moaning, but she wasn't dead. I could see her eyes moving. She held up her hand as though to ward off any further attack from me.

I told her not to make any more noise, and she would be all right. By this time, I was aroused sexually, so I had intercourse with her. I just undid my fly, I spread her legs out, and did it. It only took a few minutes before I ejaculated inside her. Her eyes appeared to be focusing on me when I was doing it, but she just laid there limp, she didn't put anything in to it.

When I'd finished, I got up, and she began moaning once again and started to move as well. We were out of sight of the taxi drivers, but I knew they could quite possibly have heard the sounds. I couldn't drive away for obvious reasons, one being that she was still showing signs of life. I was worried sick that I was about to be discovered, and was furious that she could not keep quiet. I took my knife from my pocket, I think it was the one with the rosewood handle, which is probably still at home in my knife drawer. I plunged the knife into her ribs and again into her heart, I did this five or six times. Before I did this I had taken all her clothes off, apart from her jumper. I threw these over the wall.

I dragged her by the arms to where I thought she would not be discovered, which was behind some bushes in a gap between a woodpile and a wall. There wasn't much room, I had to part lift, part pull her in. Then I covered her up with a piece of asbestos sheet. I stayed in the woodyard for some minutes and when I looked the taxi drivers had gone. I reversed out of the yard and drove off. The operation had taken about half an hour.

I drove straight home. I found that I had some blood on one of my fawn court shoes. I rinsed it off. I had my Levi jeans and I think I had a dark blue pullover on, but I couldn't see any blood on these. I kept the hammer, I'm not sure which one it was, but I don't think it was the walling hammer.

Sutcliffe then gave a second statement to the police on the 26 January 1981 in order to correct certain aspects of the above confession and said that he had confused some of the account with the murder of Irene Richardson. He stated:

From the outset, the one purpose I had in mind was to kill her at the first opportunity, but things were made difficult from the moment I parked the car because Helen unfastened her trousers and seemed prepared to start straight away.

It was very awkward for me to find a way of getting her out of the car. We were there five minutes or more, while I was trying to decide which method to use to kill her. Meanwhile, against my wishes, she was in the process of arousing me sexually. I found I did not want to go through with this, so I got out of the car on the pretext of wanting to urinate.

I didn't urinate, but I managed to persuade her to get out as well, as we'd be better off in the back of the car. As she was attempting to get in, I realised this was my chance, so I hit her from behind on the head with the hammer. Unfortunately, during the downward swing the hammer caught the top edge of the door frame and gave her a very light tap on her head. She apparently thought I had struck her with my left hand, and she said, 'There's no need for that, you don't even have to pay.' I expected her to immediately shout for help as there were a couple of taxis in view about a distance of 40 yards or so.

She was obviously very scared. I then pushed her forward onto the ground and she stumbled and fell somewhere in front of the car just out of sight of the taxi drivers. I jumped on top of her and covered her mouth with my hand, it seemed like an eternity and she was struggling. I told her if she kept quiet she would be all right. As she had got me aroused less than a minute previously, I had no alternative than to go ahead with the act of sex as the only means thereby of persuading her to keep quiet, as I had already dropped the hammer several yards away. After what seemed like several more minutes, I got up and saw that the cars had gone so I started to grope around looking for the hammer. I found it, and as I was turning towards her she tried to run past between me and the car, this is when I hit her a heavy blow to the head.

I then dragged her back in front of the car, and may have hit her again before I dragged her back. I began gathering her belongings and throwing them over a wall. She was obviously still alive then. I took the knife from the front of the car and stabbed her several times in the heart and lungs. After this, I pulled her to a place a few yards away where I thought she wouldn't be found so quickly, when I got there I covered her with a sheet of asbestos or corrugated metal.

When Rita returned to the usual meeting place she found no sign of her sister. She stood and waited for a while, but when it became obvious that she wasn't going to turn up, she headed back to their flat. It would be another three days before she would overcome her fear of being prosecuted by the police for soliciting and report Helen as missing.

One curiosity of the case is that at that time, a man driving a brown van was getting his sexual kicks out of watching prostitutes and their punters. He would follow them and watch them from a distance, before creeping up closer to watch through the windows of the punter's car once their attention was elsewhere. It is unfortunate that on the night in question, he had followed Rita and not Helen. He was questioned by the police but they took no further action against him.

On the morning after the murder, men working at Garrard's timber yard noticed a blood-stained patch in the mud and they also found a pair of black, blood-stained lace knickers in the yard which a lorry driver had pinned to the door of a nearby shed. Apparently, this was nothing out of the ordinary as the owners knew the yard was frequented at night by prostitutes and homosexuals and so didn't raise an alarm.

It wasn't until 3 February that Rita finally went to the police and reported her sister as missing. Not wanting to get herself or her sister into trouble for soliciting, it took her a while to admit in the interviews that they had both been acting as prostitutes on the night Helen disappeared.

Armed with this knowledge, Assistant Chief Constable George Oldfield was called for and he immediately set up an incident room in Huddersfield Police Station and he sent a policeman with a sniffer dog to the area where Rita had last seen her sister. At 15.00 a search of Garrard's timber yard began and within ten minutes the sniffer dog had found Helen Rytka's body in a narrow space behind a pile of timber and a disused garage. She had been deliberately covered with a sheet of asbestos and wedged into an 18in space between a brick wall and the timber. Her legs and the front of her trunk were visible but neither her head or arms were. A chest wound was clearly visible and there was some bloodstaining on the surrounding skin. Blood had run from the wound towards her naval and then dropped to the ground.

Home Office Pathologist Professor Gee was called for and he soon removed the asbestos sheet. He immediately saw Helen's body tilted on its right side, with her head covered by what seemed to be cloth or tarred paper. She was virtually naked, wearing only dark-coloured socks and a black bra which was entangled with a black woollen jumper that had been pulled up over her chin, exposing her breasts in typical Ripper fashion. There were oblong marks on her thigh which left a depression, as if something like a plank of wood had been placed over her. Helen's arms were stretched above her head and around her upper arm was a piece of blue material. Professor Gee noticed a silver cross at the front of her neck, apparently from a necklace, though the chain appeared to be missing. There was a large laceration on Helen's forehead and when he felt behind with gloved hands, he discovered another wound at the back of her head. There were also three clear but separate stab wounds to the chest.

Only a tiny amount of blood soiled the pieces of wood, tarred paper and strips of metal that had been beneath Helen's body, but nearer to the back of the main building, behind another stack of timber, was an area of blood which was soiling the ground. The immediate assumption was that Helen had been killed there before being moved to where she was found and covered with the asbestos sheet.

At the post-mortem, they found the tiny silver chain which had held the small silver cross found earlier. They also found pubic hair in her mouth, which raised the possibility that she had been preforming oral sex on Sutcliffe shortly before she was killed, or that he had put his penis in her mouth after she was murdered. There were six lacerated wounds on her head – one in the centre of her forehead, three on the right side and two to the back and there were semi-circular fractures with some of these wounds which indicated that the hammer blows had been struck with considerable force.

The stab wounds to Helen's chest had caused injuries to both lungs, her heart, her aorta, her liver and her stomach. The knife, which was estimated to have a blade 6–7 inches long, had been thrust through the same openings at least thirteen times, which caused the injuries to her internal organs. There were also scratches on her chest.

Helen Rytka

Assistant Chief Constable George Oldfield sent out an immediate telex to neighbouring forces:

> AT 3.10 PM ON FRIDAY 3RD FEBRUARY 1978, THE NAKED BODY OF HELEN RYTKA BORN 3/3/59, A HALF-CASTE JAMAICAN WOMAN WAS FOUND PARTIALLY CONCEALED IN A TIMBER YARD OFF GREAT NORTHERN STREET, HUDDERSFIELD. THE BODY HAD SEVERE INJURIES TO THE HEAD WITH A BLUNT INSTRUMENT AND STAB WOUNDS TO THE BODY. NEITHER INSTRUMENT HAS BEEN FOUND. IT HAS NOT YET BEEN ESTABLISHED WHETHER THE DECEASED HAD BEEN SUBJECT TO SEXUAL INTERFERENCE.
>
> THE DECEASED, WHO WAS AN ACTIVE PROSTITUTE, HAD ONLY LIVED IN HUDDERSFIELD FOR THE PAST TWO MONTHS BUT IT IS KNOWN THAT SHE TOOK CLIENTS TO THE WOODYARD WHERE HER BODY WAS FOUND. SHE FORMERLY LIVED IN BRADFORD.
>
> SHE WAS REPORTED MISSING FROM HOME ON THE 2ND FEBRUARY 1978 HAVING BEEN SEEN BY HER SISTER, ALSO AN ACTIVE PROSTITUTE, AT 21.10 HOURS ON TUESDAY 31ST JANUARY 1978 IN GREAT NORTHERN STREET HUDDERSFIELD, AT WHICH TIME SHE WAS SEEN TO GET INTO A DARK BLUE-COLOURED SALOON CAR, POSSIBLY AN AUDI 100LS DRIVEN BY A WHITE MALE ABOUT 35 YEARS OF AGE AND OF SMART APPEARANCE. ATTENTION IS DRAWN TO PREVIOUS OFFENCES OF MURDER OF PROSTITTUES WHICH HAVE OCCURRED IN THE WEST YORKSHIRE METROPOLITAN POLICE AREA SINCE 22/7/75 DETAILS OF WHICH HAVE BEEN CIRCULATED IN POLICE REPORTS 634, CASE 1 (23/7/75 – MCGOWAN)
> 703-1 (31/10/75 – MCCANN)
> 758-1 (21/1/76 – JACKSON)
> 1021-1 (6/5/77 – RICHARDSON)
> 1071-1 (24/4/77 – ATKINSON)
> 1113-1 (26/4/77 – MCDONALD)
> 1123-1 (10/7/77 – LONG)
> 1234-1 (14/12/77 – MOORE)

The inclusion of Ms Renee McGowan in the list above is a curious one. Assistant Chief Constable George Oldfield had obviously been looking back on previous attacks similar to those he had already classed as being carried out by the Ripper and decided at this point that this too was one. Yet, it was a completely different MO to those he was certain were Ripper murders.

Renee McGowan was 55 years old and had been found strangled, partly clothed and with her wrists tied behind her back in her high-rise flat in Bradford. She was a member of a Lonely Hearts Club but had met someone and had been planning to get married when she was murdered. She was not a prostitute (as seemed to be the main requirement to be included as a Ripper victim), there were no head injuries, no stab wounds, she had been strangled and she had been restrained by having her hands tied behind her back – none of this had been seen in any of the other Ripper attacks.

It demonstrates just what a state the investigation was already in; it seems obvious that the murder of Renee McGowan had not been committed by the Ripper, yet attacks and murders which bore his signature such as those on Gloria Wood, Anna Rogulskyj, Olive Smelt, Tracy Browne, Rosemary Stead, Marcella Claxton, Maureen Hogan, Debra Schlesinger and Carol Wilkinson were being ignored.

A number of people who were in the area around the time of Helen Rytka last being seen were traced, interviewed and eliminated from inquiries. The details of three cars wanted for elimination were then circulated – a Morris Oxford saloon, a Ford Cortina Mark I and a white coloured Datsun 160/180B. The owner of the dark blue Audi 100 LS in the telex was quickly traced and eliminated.

The Ford Cortina and Datsun were then quickly eliminated too, and the police focused their attention on the Morris Oxford saloon and the BMC 'Farina' range of similar cars.

Because some of the vehicles in the range did not fit the tyre track of the Irene Richardson murder, a new vehicle inquiry – referred to as the 'Farina Index' – was started. This was a considerable commitment of manpower and was still running when Peter Sutcliffe was arrested almost three years later.

The 1983 'Report into the Investigation of the Series of Murders and Assaults on Women in the North of England between 1975 and 1980' states that '7,000 vehicles of three types of manufacture were traced and drivers seen, which illustrates how police resources can be dissipated in pursuing information given by witnesses in good faith but, with the benefit of hindsight, proves to be useless information.'

The following day, forensic scientists returned to the scene of Helen Rytka's murder at Garrard's timber yard and this time, in daylight, they found a thin metal bangle, a gold hinged-stud earring, a button and some coins, several feet from where Helen Rytka's body had been found. They searched further afield too and discovered Helen's sling-backed platform-soled shoes over the fence and half-way up the railway embankment. Her dark denim jeans and fake fur jacket were also found by the fence on the woodyard side.

On the 13 February, Rita Rytka appeared at a press conference to ask for help in finding her sister's killer. She said:

> Helen was a very happy girl and her main ambition in life was to sing. The circumstances did not allow her to fulfil that ambition. She was very close to me. No loss could be greater than of her. I hope the public will not forget her. I am helping the police all I can and I hope anyone who has information will show sympathy and come forward.

Following Helen Rytka's murder, the nominal indexes and vehicle indexes from the Wilma McCann, Emily Jackson, Irene Richardson, Patricia Atkinson, Jayne MacDonald and Maureen Long cases were centralised at Millgarth Police Station in Leeds and subsequently amalgamated into an integrated index. This incident room continued to monitor the Ripper series inquiry until Sutcliffe's arrest in 1981.

However, just five days after the police had again interrogated Terrence Hawkshaw, a new prime suspect entered the fray – and this one would lead the investigation completely off the rails.

Relevant Statistics
Incident Room set up	31 January 1978
House to House Enquiries	1,800
Actions	21,250
Statements	7,921
Vehicle Enquiries	15,500
Officers Engaged	110
Hours Worked (Not inc. Overtime)	197,407
Incident Room Closed	18 March 1979

Chapter 22

The Letters

On the 9 March, Assistant Chief Constable George Oldfield received a letter that had been post marked 'Sunderland 1.45 pm 8 March 1978.'
It read:

> Dear Sir,
> I am sorry I cannot give my name for obvious reasons. I am the Ripper. I've been dubbed a maniac by the Press but not by you, you call me clever and I am. You and your mates haven't a clue that photo in the paper gave me fits and that bit about killing myself, no chance. I've got things to do. My purpose to rid the streets of them sluts. My one regret is that young lassie McDonald, did not know cause changed routine that nite. Up to number 8 now you say 7 but remember Preston '75, get about you know. You were right I travel a bit. You probably look for me in Sunderland, don't bother, I am not daft, just posted letter there on one of my trips. Not a bad place compared with Chapeltown and Manningham and other places. Warn whores to keep off streets cause I feel it coming on again.
> Yours respectfully
Jack the Ripper
>
> Might write again later I not sure last one really deserved it. Whores getting younger each time. Old slut next time I hope. Huddersfield never again, too small close call last one.

A second letter was sent four days later, this time to the Chief Editor of the Daily Mirror newspaper and was postmarked 'Sunderland 10.00 am 13 March 1978.'
It reads:

> Dear Sir,
> I have already written to Chief Constable George Oldfield 'a man I respect' concerning the recent ripper murders. I told him and I am telling you to warn them whores I'll strike again and soon when the heat cools off. About the MacDonald lassie, I didn't know that she was decent and I am sorry I changed my routine that night. Up to murder 8 now you say seven but remember Preston '75. Easy picking them up don't even have to try you think they're [sic] learn but they don't. Most are young lassies, next time try older one I hope. Police

haven't a clue yet and I don't leave any I am very clever and don't look for me up there in Sunderland cause I not stupid just passed through the place not a bad place compared with Chapeltown and Manningham. Can't walk the streets for them whores. Don't forget warn them I feel it coming on again if I get chance. Sorry about lassie I didn't know.

Yours respectfully
Jack the Ripper

Might write again after another week gone Liverpool or even Manchester again. To hot here in Yorkshire. Bye. I have given advance warning so its yours and their fault.

No immediate action was taken in regard to the letters – after all the police had received many letters claiming to be from the killer – but there was a suspicion among some detectives that the writer knew more than simply what had been printed in the newspapers.

At midday on 26 March, Yvonne Pearson's body was finally discovered. A passer-by was walking along the waste ground on Arthington Street when he looked across at the upturned settee and happened to see an arm sticking out from underneath. He thought it was probably a tailor's dummy but went to have a closer look and as he got closer the smell of a decaying body hit him. He immediately telephoned the police.

The old settee had most of its covering missing and the springs and wooden frame were clearly visible. When the police arrived they found Yvonne Pearson's head was badly decomposed and showed obvious injuries. Her right forearm, which was the one sticking out from under the settee, was completely dark and discoloured. A shoe and a piece of wood were lying on the ground on the left side of the body. Another platform shoe was found about 20 yards away at the top of the ridge that overlooked the murder scene and that matched the one found under the settee. Nearby, police found a purse, a pair of tights and a condom. There was a large stone on the ground near the sofa, as well as several others nearby.

Once the settee had been overturned, the lower part of Yvonne Pearson's body became visible. Underneath her right hand was a copy – sports page up – of the *Daily Mirror* newspaper, dated 21 February 1978, a full month after Yvonne had been murdered and reported missing – meaning Sutcliffe had returned to the scene and made her arm visible to ensure she was found.

The rest of her body was hard to see and was well covered with sods of earth, springs from the settee, grass, other debris and horsehair stuffing from inside the sofa. Her left arm was raised above her head, stretching out in rigor mortis, because it had been stuck in the springs of the sofa.

The rest of Yvonne Pearson's body was also badly decomposed. There were several holes in her skull, and a small metal comb had been placed upright between her thighs, which were themselves covered in dried grass and horsehair from the settee.

She had been wearing a greenish-yellow jacket with a zig-zag design, a black polo-neck jumper and a white bra, all of which were pushed up to expose her breasts in typical Ripper fashion. Her knickers had been rolled down slightly around her upper thighs, but her legs and feet were bare and there was a pair of dark blue slacks sticking to the under-surface of Yvonne's body. A small bottle of perfume and a leather handbag were close by. There were also a small number of maggots on the surface of Yvonne's body, especially around the neck.

At the post-mortem (again carried out by Home Office Pathologist Professor Gee), as Yvonne's throat was being dissected, the large oval-shaped ball of horsehair was discovered. It completely filled the back of her mouth and the upper part of her throat, blocking her larynx.

Professor Gee later commented: 'So badly damaged was the head, that in order to reconstruct the actual pattern of the fractures, we had to rebuild the skull around a large ball of modelling clay, so that it could be photographed in roughly the form it must have been at death.' It had fractured into seventeen pieces.

Professor Gee could not see any clear signs of a ball pein hammer being used and there were no stabbing or slashing wounds to the body. It also became clear during the post-mortem that Yvonne had fractured ribs and various ruptured organs, including her liver – it seemed to him that she had been stamped and kicked to death.

There was no significant blood soiling in her lower air passages, in spite of the fractures of the skull around her nose and upper jaw and this proved that the ball of horsehair had been introduced to the back of her throat very soon after the injuries were inflicted.

Professor Gee's report stated: 'Considerable force would have been necessary to cause the damage to the skull. It is possible for this damage to have been caused by one impact on the head by a heavy object.'

He concluded:

> The most probable circumstances are that the deceased's injuries were caused by a deliberate attack on her ... apparently causing the head injuries by a blow with some heavy object, causing the injuries to the trunk either by a blow with a similar object or, for instance, by a kick, and pushing into the throat a mass of the material found at the scene. The clothing could have been disturbed either before or after the attack.

Remarkably, in the notes later found at the Bradford Coroner's Office, there was a crucial piece of information – Professor Gee had come to the conclusion that whoever had murdered Yvonne Pearson had also murdered Carol Wilkinson! It was an official document – yet West Yorkshire Police either overlooked or – worse – ignored it.

The murder wasn't immediately linked to the others in the Ripper series, mainly because the police believed that her head injuries had been caused by a rock and there had been no stab wounds to the body. It is possible that the police had read Professor Gee's report and wrongly concluded that because Carol Wilkinson wasn't a prostitute, and the same person had killed both her and Yvonne Pearson, then neither could be attributable to the Ripper. What changed their mind in May 1978 to include Yvonne Pearson as a Ripper victim isn't quite clear – and it is even less clear why Carol Wilkinson wasn't also included at that point. The only conclusion that can be drawn is that the investigation was too unwieldy by that point to include every attack.

One unexplained factor was the copy of the *Daily Mirror* dated 21 February 1978 (exactly one month after she was last seen alive) which was found under the right side of

Yvonne's body. The newspaper had been placed there intentionally and could not have been in that position accidentally. Surely this was proof that Sutcliffe had returned to the body. When he put the newspaper under the body, he must also have left the arm exposed in the hope that someone would see it, as it is almost unfathomable that had her arm been there the whole time it would have taken so long for it to be spotted.

The murder was investigated by Detective Chief Superintendent Trevor Lapish of the Western Crime Area and another incident room was established at Bradford. Because of the time that had elapsed between the death and the discovery of the body, there was little evidence forthcoming.

A police reconstruction of Yvonne Pearson's last movements was then held in late March, with WPC Lena Markovic taking the place of Yvonne.

On 25 April, the Special Homicide Investigation Team was set up at Millgarth Police Station in Leeds. It was more commonly referred to as the 'Ripper Squad', as opposed to the 'SHIT' squad. It was led by Detective Chief Superintendent John Domaille, with Detective Superintendent Jack Slater as his deputy. The team was completed by two Detective Inspectors, four Detective Sergeants and four Detective Constables.

They were appointed following increasing concern within the West Yorkshire police force that the administration side of the investigation was becoming overwhelmed by the amount of information being gathered.

Included in the very wide terms of reference given to the team was the task, 'To examine all reported attacks on women in general and prostitutes in particular and endeavour to find any common link or pattern to formulate any new and profitable line of inquiry.'

The following day, 26 April, Detective Chief Superintendent Domaille contacted the Police Scientific Branch to ask for help in reducing the paperwork. Members of the Branch and the Police Research Services Unit visited the force on 4, 22 and 25 May and agreed to arrange for the results of the vehicle observations in red light areas to be processed on the Police National Computer.

The team went through each case in turn and decided whether any further action was required. In some cases they re-interviewed victims, witnesses and some investigating officers. Their conclusions were put onto a large wallchart and the selected offences discussed with Assistant Chief Constable George Oldfield and other senior detectives. Finally, a criminal intelligence 'Special Notice' and wallchart were produced and circulated to all police forces in the country.

Finally, on 12 May, the attack on Marilyn Moore was linked to the other Ripper attacks when it was shared with other forces in a West Yorkshire Police circulation, along with the murder of Yvonne Pearson.

Their report was submitted to Chief Constable Ronald Gregory in December 1979.

It was around this time that Sutcliffe bought a black Sunbeam Rapier, registration number NKU 888H, meaning that for the next three months he had access to two vehicles.

Chapter 23

Vera Millward

On Tuesday 16 May 1978, Sutcliffe struck in Manchester for the second time and 40-year-old Infirmary – four-and-a-half months after the murder of Helen Rytka.

Vera was born in Liverpool on 26 August 1937. Not much is known about her early years, but when she was in her late teens she met Yusef Mohammed Sultan, a man eleven years older than her. They went on to have five children together, all of whom were taken into care.

In 1967, aged 30, she first appeared before Manchester City Magistrates' Court, charged with loitering for prostitution, and was placed on probation for two years.

Vera then moved to London and appeared before Camberwell Green Magistrates' Court on 9 June 1971, again charged with soliciting for prostitution and was placed on probation for another two years. She moved back to Manchester and continued her relationship with Yusef Mohammed Sultan, but he passed away later that year.

Her health began to suffer, and in 1972 she had an operation to remove one of her lungs at St Mary's Hospital.

Knowing that the money was better in London, she moved back there but was again arrested on the same charges of soliciting for prostitution and went before Camberwell Green Magistrates' Court on 3 July 1973, where she was found guilty and given the choice of a fine of £20 or one day's police detention, which she served.

Vera then moved back to the Moss Side area of Manchester where, before long, she was living with a Jamaican man called Cy Birkett.

On 26 November 1973 Vera appeared for the last time at Manchester City Magistrates' Court on two charges of loitering for the purposes of prostitution and was put on probation for two years. She was known to use the aliases Anne Brown, Mary Barton and Eva Birkett. Cy Birkett knew that Vera was a prostitute, and on the nights she went out, usually a Tuesday and Thursday to meet a regular punter, he would stay at home in Greenham Avenue, Hulme, and look after their children.

Vera's regular punter, who would pick her up from outside her home, drove a Mercedes and would often pay her for her company with food for the children or cigarettes, helping Vera to keep up with her forty-a-day habit.

She had a hysterectomy in 1976, and two further operations in 1977, leaving her with complaints of constant pains in her stomach.

At 22.00 on the evening of Tuesday, 16 May 1978, Vera, who had been suffering from chronic stomach pains, went out, telling Cy Birkett that she was going out to get some cigarettes. He knew she was actually going to meet her regular client and that she wouldn't be back for a couple of hours. However, the regular punter didn't turn up and so Vera went out to earn some money on the streets. It was just bad luck that Peter Sutcliffe was the first person to drive past her that night.

Sutcliffe recalled:

> The urge inside me still diminished my actions when it came to the fore. The next time I felt this way I paid another visit to Manchester one evening a few months after Rytka. I went there in my red Corsair to the red light area.
>
> When I got there, there was no sign of any girls, so after reaching a night club on a corner in a small labyrinth of terraced houses about ¾ mile square, I took the 3rd left after the nightclub, which was a long street running from one end to the other of this area. I drove down to the bottom end and there I saw a woman obviously waiting to be picked up. It was Vera Millward. I stopped and asked her if she was doing business. She said, 'Yes', but it would have to be in the car. The price was £5, she got in and I drove off.
>
> She told me where to drive and I followed her directions, which led us into a hospital grounds. I stopped the car in an area near a narrow road, from where I could see an archway obviously used by pedestrians. I parked up the car and suggested to her that it would be better in the back. I don't think I'd paid her.
>
> She got out of my car and went to the back door. I picked up my hammer from under the seat and walked round the back of the car. As she was opening the rear door I hit her on the head with the hammer, and she dived backwards past where I was stood. She was on her hands and knees when I hit her again at least once. She fell flat on her face. I pulled her by her wrists over to the edge of the area where there was either a fence or bushes.
>
> I took out my knife I was carrying. I think it may have been the same one I used on Rytka, but I'm not sure. I pulled her clothes up and slashed her stomach either vertical or diagonal. It opened up her stomach. Then I rolled her over onto her stomach and left her lying there. I drove away. I think I had to reverse out to get back again.
>
> I didn't get any blood on me on that occasion. I think I was wearing my brown car coat, which you've got.

At 08.00 the following morning, Vera's body was discovered when workers arrived to do some gardening at the Manchester Royal Infirmary. While unloading tools from the back of one of the vans, one of the men, Jim McGuigan, saw what they thought was a tailor's dummy lying near a temporary fence. He moved closer to get a better look and then became alarmed when he realised it was the body of a woman.

The police were called and Professor Gee was again sent for. Before he arrived, the detectives could clearly see that just four yards from the body there were clear marks in the mud where a struggle could have taken place and, crucially, some tyre tracks.

When Professor Gee arrived, close to the body he found a pool of blood which had hair and brain tissue in it. There were also scrape marks and blood splashes leading to Vera's body. She lay face down on her right side in a semi-prone position, arms folded beneath her, legs straight and her feet extended towards the pool of blood. Her blue/brown reversible checked coat with a blue collar and cuffs was open and covered her from her knees to her neck. Her blue canvas wedge-heeled sling-back shoes had been neatly placed on her body, and a piece of paper covered her head. When the coat was removed it became clear that her tights and slacks were in place but her blue cardigan, floral-patterned yellow sleeveless dress and under slip had been pulled up to expose her abdomen. Her blue and white bra still covered her breasts, which was unusual for one of Sutcliffe's victims. There was a large wound on her stomach through which a coil of intestines protruded and she had severe head wounds covered in blood. Brain tissue was found on her clothing.

At the post-mortem, it was found that she had several skull fractures and a disc of bone had been displaced and had lacerated her brain. She had probably been attacked about the head from the right side. One chest wound passed between her ribs and penetrated her left lung, her liver and her stomach. It was thought this had been caused by three separate thrusts through the same wound, without the weapon being fully withdrawn. Another wound in the stomach area, eight inches long, had jagged edges caused by a large number of separate cutting movements. It was this that led the intestines to protrude. Her right eyelid had also been punctured and the eye bruised. There was no sign of a handbag.

The attack had been so violent, and the wounds so horrific, that court officials were ordered to remove photographs of her body from the files handed to the jury at Sutcliffe's trial.

An examination of the scene concluded that from the position of the tyre tracks, footprints, blood, and the spot where the body was found, it was likely that the murderer had driven through the opening in the wire mesh at the southern end of the compound and had veered sharply to the right; he had then reversed the vehicle until it was pointing towards the exit, ready for a quick getaway. Cast impressions were made of all four tyres of the vehicle and from these casts and the measurements obtained, the scientists at North-West Forensic Science Laboratory were able to prepare a list of only eleven vehicles within the suspect range, one of which was a Ford Corsair.

The tyre tracks were similar in size, but with a different combination of tyres to those left at the scene of the Irene Richardson murder and the attack on Marilyn Moore. This led to many more enquiries being pursued in connection with vehicles.

As with the murder of Jean Jordan, this murder was investigated by Detective Chief Superintendent Jack Ridgeway and an incident room was established at Longsight Police Station, Manchester. As a result of their investigations into the tyre tracks at the scene, the Greater Manchester Police were satisfied that they were not made by a car from the 'Farina' range, but the West Yorkshire Police were not as convinced as their Manchester colleagues on this point and continued their inquiry.

Research conducted by an officer at Greater Manchester Police was at variance with the findings of the West Yorkshire Metropolitan Force.

The Manchester report excluded the Farina from their range of suspect vehicles because their research established that for vehicles in this range manufactured in 1957,

58 and 59, although the 13in tyre size was applicable, the track axle widths did not fit. The report conceded that a Farina manufactured from 1960 onwards could have fallen within the suspect range *only* if two of the tyres at the scene of the Richardson murder, and one tyre at the scene of the Millward murder, were 'rogue', that is to say a 13in diameter tyre fitted to a 14in axle stub. It is known that this permutation can occur without seriously affecting the operation of the brakes and steering.

Greater Manchester Police prepared a list of eleven vehicles within the suspect range and this included the Ford Corsair, which was the actual vehicle that mattered. Unfortunately, the West Yorkshire Force excluded the vehicles contained in the Greater Manchester list.

Examination of the measurements and physical details of the vehicles listed by Greater Manchester later showed that by applying the technical data known to the West Yorkshire Metropolitan Force, their schedule of eleven vehicles could have been reduced to only two, one of which was the Ford Corsair.

The officer conducting the research drew attention to the divergence of views between himself and his counterpart, but he failed to place sufficient emphasis on the two vehicles which could not be eliminated on the technical information available.

In June 1978, Detective Chief Superintendent Domaille issued a 'Special Notice' to all forces regarding the assaults and murders they considered were now part of the Ripper series. After reviewing twenty-one previous similar attacks, they had decided that the ten crimes definitely committed by the Ripper were: Anna Rogulskyj (linked for the first time), Olive Smelt (linked for the first time), Wilma McCann, Emily Jackson, Irene Richardson, Patricia Atkinson, Jayne MacDonald, Jean Jordan, Helen Rytka and Vera Millward.

They were also fairly confident he had committed the attacks on: Joan Harrison (linked because of the letters from Sunderland), Maureen Long, Marilyn Moore and Yvonne Pearson.

The members of Domaille's team applied very narrow criteria so that a number of similar assaults where good descriptions or photofit pictures of the suspect were available were not included. The extremely narrow criteria were:

a) Wounds to the head caused by hammer blows
b) Wounds to the body and abdomen (scratch or stab wounds) caused by a knife and/or star-shaped instrument

There was also an inference that the attack should have been committed against a prostitute or in a red light area. The seven attacks wrongly dismissed at this point were: Gloria Wood, Tracy Browne, Rosemary Stead, Marcella Claxton, Maureen Hogan, Debra Schlesinger and Carol Wilkinson.

By 19 June the staff at the Police National Computer and Police Scientific Development Branch had completed their arrangements for the computerisation of information gathered from twenty-six observation points in the red light districts of Leeds, Bradford and Huddersfield. Initially, the vehicle registration numbers were recorded and fed into the computer at Hendon and were printed out for inquiries where the same vehicle was identified as having been seen in two of the separate areas.

The first print-out of 'Cross Area Sightings' came a week later on 26 June, and lists were then issued on a weekly basis.

Greater Manchester Police joined the system the following month with observations from thirteen points in the Moss Side area.

Sutcliffe sold his red Ford Corsair on 7 August, leaving him just the one car – his black Sunbeam Rapier. Six days later, he was interviewed by the police for the third time and this was due to the 'Cross Area Sighting' inquiry. DC Peter Smith visited him at home at 6 Garden Lane, Heaton, Bradford, because his red Ford Corsair had been spotted six times in the Manningham Lane red light area of Bradford and once in the Chapeltown red light area of Leeds – the last sighting had been on 7 July 1978. As there was a delay between the cars being reported and the data being printed (and then actioned), unknown to DC Smith at the time, Sutcliffe's Sunbeam Rapier had also been spotted on a further nine occasions in the Manningham area of Bradford. The interval of five weeks before he was interviewed gives an indication of the workload being created by the volume of 'double-area sightings', bearing in mind that the operation only started in June.

DC Smith had been briefed to ask drivers of the vehicles to account for their movements on one or more of the murder dates by providing proof of diary entries, passport stamps, holiday booking forms, hospital records or family anniversaries. He (and the other officers doing similar inquiries) was told that on no account were they to tell the interviewee that police observations were going on in the red light areas and that their cars had been spotted, and on no account were ball pein hammers to be mentioned.

DC Smith was aware of Sutcliffe's two previous interviews during the £5 note inquiry following Jean Jordan's murder and had the relevant paperwork with him. He was also aware of the loose alibi Sutcliffe had provided before, and it was his intention to obtain a strong alibi for the murder of Vera Millward.

When he arrived at Sutcliffe's home he found him and Sonia dressed in overalls and decorating the kitchen. Sonia remained present during the interview and they explained to DC Smith that they had recently bought the house and spent most of their spare time decorating and making home improvements. They said they hardly ever went out and that when they did, they were always together.

Initially, they were unable to remember their movements on the evening when Vera Millward was murdered, but it was Sonia who then told the detective that on the night in question her husband 'would have come home from work and stayed with her all evening'. They then both made written statements to that effect.

However, Sonia also told the detective that she and her husband had been at a disco in Leeds called Rockafella's on the night of one of the other murders.

While Sonia was out of the room, DC Smith asked Sutcliffe whether he used prostitutes. Sutcliffe denied the need to use them and when he asked why the detective was asking, DC Smith told him that he was just asking general questions about what his car was used for in the evenings. Sutcliffe was then able to satisfy the detective that the sightings of his car around the red light area of Manningham in Bradford could be accounted for by his having to drive through it to get to and from work. Sutcliffe would later say: 'I told him I couldn't say exactly what I'd been doing, but that I had to drive

Above: Peter Sutcliffe (pale sweater) at work in Bingley Cemetery.

Below: Back Lindum Terrace, where the 'stone in the sock' attack took place.

Above: Anna Rogulskyj crime scene.

Left: Sonia Szurma and Peter Sutcliffe on their wedding day.

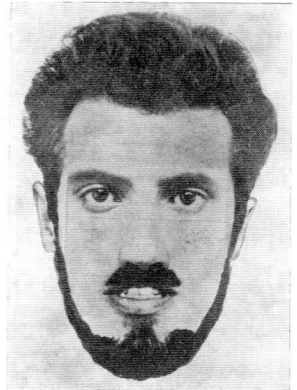

Right: Tracy Browne's poster.

Below: The Gaiety was renowned as a rough pub where pimps, prostitutes and their clients gathered.

Above: Wilma McCann was brutally murdered on this slope on the Prince Philip Playing Fields.

Below: Irene Richardson's body lay on Soldiers' Field where Marcella Claxton had been attacked previously.

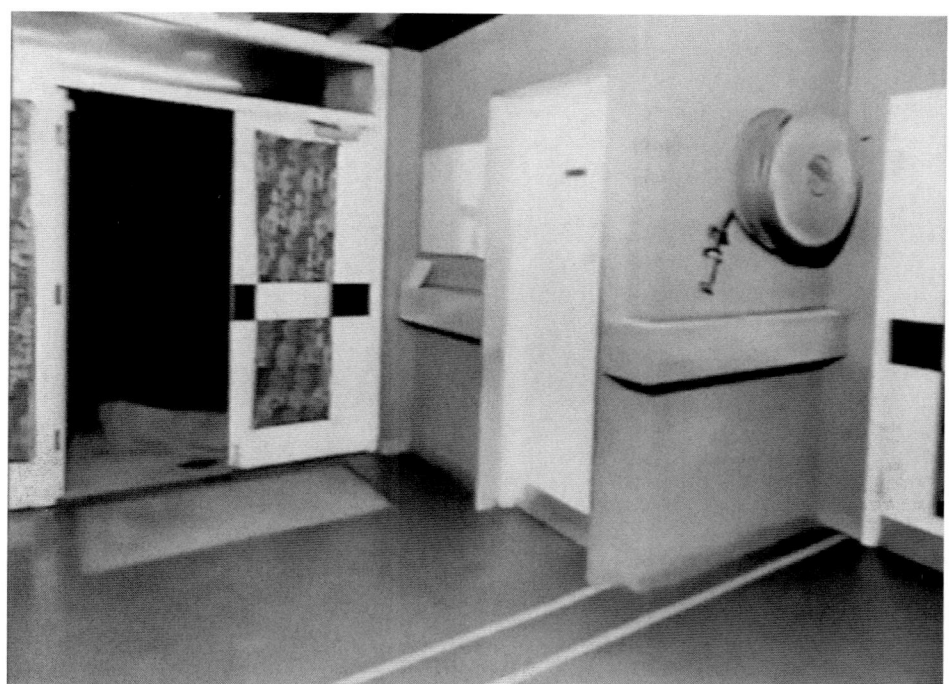

Above: Debra Schlesinger murder scene. Her body lay just outside the door where she collapsed.

Below: Blood marks the spot on the floor where Patricia Atkinson's body lay briefly.

Above: Sutcliffe's home at 6, Garden Lane, Heaton, Bradford.

Below: (L-R) Standing – Mick, his wife and Peter. Seated – John, Kathleen, unidentified woman, Carl and Sonia.

Marilyn Moore was attacked here at Stonegate, just off Buslingthorpe Lane, Leeds.

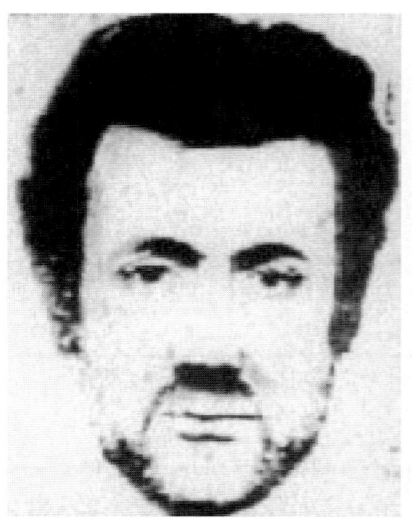 

Above left: Marilyn Moore's second photofit of her attacker. It bares a striking resemblance to Peter Sutcliffe.

Above right: Peter Sutcliffe.

Above: Josephine Whitaker's body on Savile Park, Halifax. You can see where she was dragged from where her shoe came off to where she lay.

Below: Helen Rytka's body was found hidden in the piles of timber between the two sheds.

Above: (L-R) DS Dick Holland, ACC George Oldfield and Det Ch Supt Jack Ridgway play the tape for the gathered Press.

Right: Peter and Sonia Sutcliffe.

ACTION FORM—SUPPLEMENTARY REPORT

ACTION No.: 7/13291

(Action reference must be shown. All minutes should be numbered consecutively, dated and signed by the person making them with the rank and name clearly shown)

FOR USE IN THE INCIDENT ROOM ONLY.

Redacted under FOI exemption section 40(2).
Detective Superintendent Holland

With regards to the marginally numbered Action I report as follows:-

On Saturday 29th July 1979 Peter William Sutcliffe b. 2.6.46 at Shipley of 6 Garden Lane, Bradford 9, WRC No 5235/65 was interviewed at his home address.

At the times of the Cross Area Sightings he was the owner of a black Sunbeam Rapier fast back, 2 door saloon motor car, reg no NKU 888H which he sold on June 15th 1979.

He currently owns a grey coloured Rover 3.5 litre, 4 door saloon reg no FHY 400K which he acquired some 2 months prior to disposing of the Sunbeam Rapier. (The Rover may become the subject of further Cross Area Sightings as it has already been registered on the VDU)½

Mr Sutcliffe was interviewed at length about the use of the Rapier motor car which was sighted at the Leeds (2), Bradford (36) and Manchester (1) observation points.

His explanation as to its use is as follows:- with regards to the Bradford sightings it was ascertained that he passed observation points en route from his place of work (Shipley Engineering, Singleton Street, Canal Road, Bradford) to his home at Heaton, Bradford 9 - which is reasonable.

His explanation for the Leeds sightings was that he ▉▉▉▉▉▉▉ ▉▉▉▉▉▉▉▉▉▉▉▉▉▉▉ visited Cinderella/Rockerfella's Night Club, Leeds.

However with regards to the Manchester sighting he denied ever being there (enquiries made by the reporting officers confirmed the Manchester sighting as an accurate and positive one.)

▉▉▉▉▉▉▉▉▉▉▉▉▉▉▉▉▉▉▉▉▉▉▉▉▉▉▉▉▉▉▉▉▉▉▉

Sutcliffe is employed by T & W H Clarke, Shipley Engineering Head Office, Perseverence Iron Works, Low Forge, Leeds Road, Shipley, Tle No 584031, but he operates from the Transport Yard situated at Singleton Street, Bradford as an HGV Class 1 haulage driver.

He drives a red and white Ford Transcontinental articulated vehicle reg no FHD 214S. His work consists of picking up and delivering heavy engineering component parts (e.g. axles and shafts for heavy plant machinery). He delivers throughout the U.K. and is on a regular run to Coles Cranes at Sunderland. His other runs involve travel through or nearby the sites of the Yorkshire and Lancashire prostitute murders and assaults.

7/S3377

VEH IND.

7/S3328

7/B 47018.

VEH IND.

FILE 7/S128

The Laptew Report part 1.

ACTION FORM—SUPPLEMENTARY REPORT

ACTION No.: 7/13291 cont....

(Action reference must be shown. All minutes should be numbered consecutively, dated and signed by the person making them with the rank and name clearly shown)

FOR USE IN THE INCIDENT ROOM ONLY.

Redacted under FOI exemption section 40(2).

The only connection with the letter dates he could have is that on the 23rd of March 1979 he travelled up to East Kilbride and Livingstone in the West of Scotland. However the recognised route advocated by the firm is via the M6 motorway which would preclude Sunderland. On the other letter dates and the tape dates he made only local runs.

The impressions gained by the interviewing officers was that there was something 'not quite right' about Sutcliffe.

▓▓▓▓▓▓. He has a pronounced gap in his two middle upper teeth of about an 8th of an inch. His shoe size is 8½ but he wore boots of the soft crepe sole type. His hair and beard is of the frizzy neo-affro type, jet black in colour. He was very quiet and very withdrawn during the interview. His denial of going to Manchester reinforced doubts about him.

An old handwriting sample was obtained ▓▓▓▓▓ and this appears to have certain similarities when compared with the 'Ripper' letters. Also obtained from Sutcliffe's place of work was an invoice delivery book and drivers hours book for further possible analysis.

It is of interest to note that although Sutcliffe does not have a bank account (apart from being in two Building Societies) his firm featured in the Manchester £5 note enquiry.

A CRO check showed Sutcliffe having convictions for theft of tyres 1976 at Dewesbury, going equipped 1969 at Shipley and attempt larceny 1965 at Bingley. He has no convictions for violence.

The Sunbeam Rapier car subject of the sightings is currently owned by ▓▓▓▓▓▓▓. The vehicle since purchase has not been altered. The engine on this vehicle siezed up immediately after purchase and has not been run since the 5th of June 1979. The car is presently situated in the driveway of ▓▓▓▓▓▓▓

The car has been examined by the reporting officers but with negative results. It is available for forensic examination should this be required. The tyres on the vehicle were all brand new (fitted prior to ▓▓▓▓▓ purchase of the car). The tyres are all Vredestein 155 x 13 SR. Mr Sutcliffe does not know his blood group but said he would provide one should this prove necessary.

He has a quiet spoken Bradford accent. He completely denies ever punting. His prints have been checked at WRC with those outstanding but with a negative result.

As can be seen Sutcliffe cannot completely be verified and the reporting officers are not fully satisfied with this man.

It is asked that the handwriting sample and books be returned as soon as possible to the donors after your perusual.

Graham Stuart Greenwood DC 3006. DC 3489 Andrew John Laptew

FILE 7/S128

The Laptew Report part 2.

 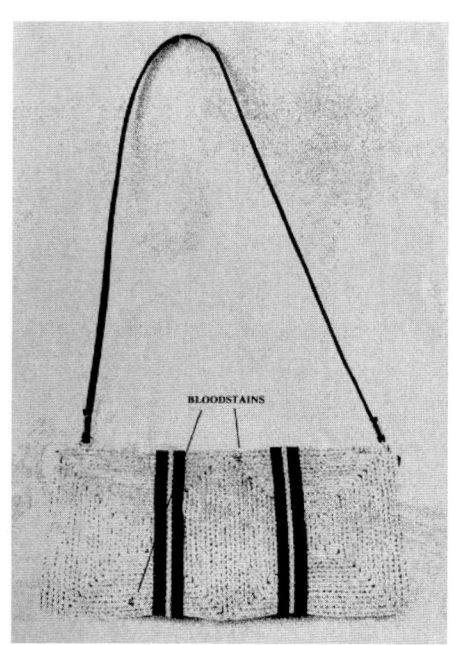

Above left: One of the many posters put out during the 'Flush Out The Ripper' campaign.

Above right: Jacqueline Hill's handbag.

Detectives survey the scene off Alma Road following Jacqueline Hill's murder.

Right: Bus Stop where Jacqueline Hill got off and headed to Alma Road, behind the Arndale Centre.

Below: Home Secretary William Whitelaw visits the Murder Incident Room in Leeds following Jacqueline Hill's murder.

Above: Peter Sutcliffe was arrested here at the Light Trades House in Sheffield.

Below: Olivia Reivers and Denise Hall.

Police Sergeant Robert Ring and Police Constable Robert Hydes arrested Peter Sutcliffe.

Above left: The crowd outside Dewsbury Magistrates' Court make their feelings clear.

Above right: Peter Sutcliffe's mugshot from Armley Prison in 1981.

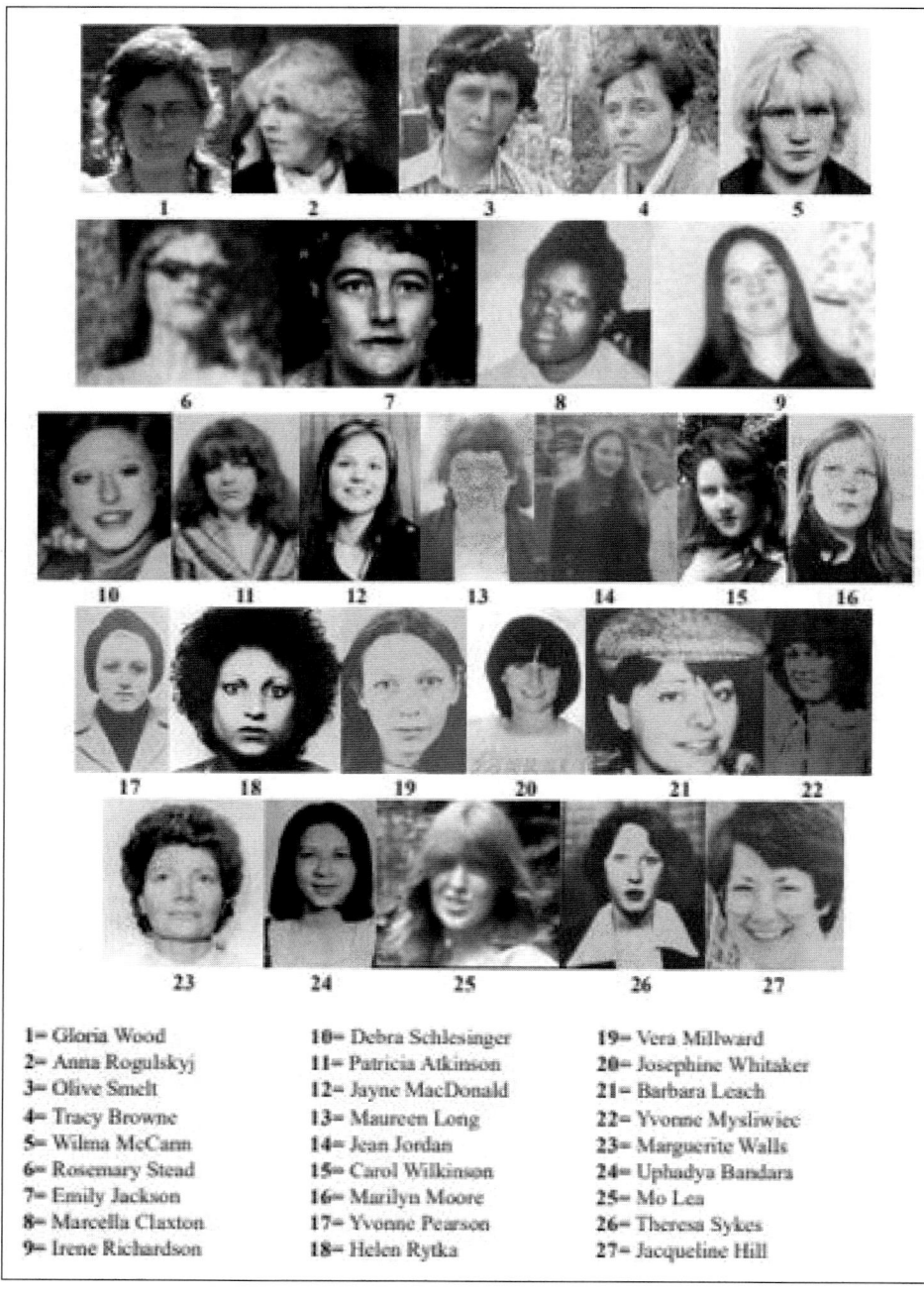

Most of the victims.

that way to work and back.' He completely denied visiting Leeds and DC Smith did not question Sutcliffe any further since he was aware of a fairly high error rate in the 'Cross Area Sighting' inquiry.

DC Smith thought that the Sutcliffe's were just a normal young couple trying to improve their new home, and as they appeared calm and normal his suspicions were not aroused.

He did not check the tyres on Sutcliffe's car and neither did he carry out any search of the house or garage. He later explained that he did not do so because he did not believe that the tyre tracks found at the murder scenes could have been left by a Ford Corsair and because he had seen from previous papers that Sutcliffe's house had been searched during the earlier interviews. This was not accurate.

In regard to Sutcliffe's account of being spotted going through the Manningham red light area, it was unfortunate that DC Smith did not have the actual times of the Bradford sightings when he interviewed Sutcliffe, as these were not available due to the limitations of the PNC print-out. Had they been checked from the input documents it would have revealed that the earliest sighting was at 20.00 and the latest at 00.25, which was hardly compatible with Sutcliffe's assertion that he 'rarely went out in the evenings'.

The officer's report was submitted via his team leader with the observation which culminated with the comment that Sutcliffe could not be connected.

The Byford Report found:

> When DC Smith submitted his report in connection with the previous interview, together with the statements from Sutcliffe and his wife, the results were acceptable to his immediate supervising officer. When the papers were seen by Detective Superintendent Holland, however, he instructed that Sutcliffe had owned two Ford Corsair motor cars (which were within the list of vehicles for the 'Tracking Inquiry') and that the tyres of both vehicles should be checked. He also called for details of Sutcliffe's employers and for his personal banking arrangements to be obtained.
>
> The action was dated 29 August, but because most of the members of the team had been directed to the 'Farina' inquiry it was not actioned until 23 November.

The police investigation ran into further trouble in September when it was discovered that a number of detectives sent to get statements from people spotted in red light areas had actually made some of them up, and an internal audit team of seven officers was appointed to determine the extent of the problem. They checked a sample covering about 10 per cent of completed inquiries but found no other evidence of such misconduct. Two detectives resigned from the force and a further thirteen were subjected to internal disciplinary action.

Things would only get worse for the investigation from here on in; the South Yorkshire Police joined the 'Cross Area Sighting' inquiry in October with four observation points in Sheffield. Humberside Police then joined in November with three observation points in Kingston-Upon-Hull.

It was agreed that inquiries about the 'Cross Area Sightings' from all four police forces would be initiated by the Ripper Incident Room in Leeds, but police were quickly overwhelmed by the sheer number of vehicles visiting more than one red light area.

On 8 November 1978, Sutcliffe's mother Kathleen passed away aged just 58. She had been admitted to Airedale General Hospital earlier in the day having suffered a mild angina attack. This was followed by a second and more severe heart attack which proved fatal.

Fifteen days later, on 23 November, Sutcliffe was interviewed for a fourth time. DC Peter Smith returned to make inquiries about Sutcliffe's banking arrangements and his vehicles, as directed by Detective Superintendent Holland; DC Smith ascertained that in late 1977 Sutcliffe had changed from Barclays Bank to the Halifax Building Society.

DC Smith obtained a statement from Sutcliffe about the last murder (Vera Millward) in which Sutcliffe said he had been at work during the day and at home in the evening with his wife. Sonia made a statement verifying the account.

The Byford Report found:

> It is now obvious that this fourth interview with Sutcliffe was treated as a matter of simple routine to the extent that DC Bradshaw who accompanied DC Smith on his visit to Sutcliffe's home did not even get out of the police vehicle.
>
> The two officers visited the home of the new owners of the red Ford Corsair where they examined the tyres. The tyres were not of the makes recorded at the Richardson, Moore and Millward crime scenes and DC Smith added a note to his action report that the tyres had been fitted after the vehicle had changed hands and that details of the previous tyres were unknown.
>
> This action and its associated papers were returned to the Major Incident Room but then disappeared for eleven months. The inquiry was unable to discover where they had gone.

That report was received at the Incident Room and endorsed by a Detective Inspector to the effect that Sutcliffe was not fully eliminated and that further enquiries were to be made and reported on. That endorsement was dated 30 November 1978.

Five days later, the West Yorkshire Police Authority let it be known that their reward being offered for information leading to the killer being caught was £20,000. This stimulated public response and was reflected in the sudden increase of work generated. For example: 21,250 general enquiries were undertaken; 15,500 vehicle enquiries made; and 8,000 statements taken in connection with the Rytka murder alone.

Peter Sutcliffe's only remaining link with Bingley during 1978 was his best friend Trevor Birdsall. Trevor had split up with his wife Melissa a little over a year after they both appeared at Wakefield Crown Court on a number of charges, including breaking and entering, theft and attempt to defraud.

Trevor would stay over some nights at Sutcliffe's house, always when Sonia was at work at the nursing home on Tuesday, Wednesday and Saturday nights, or when she was away visiting family. On one such occasion, when Sonia was staying with her sister in London, Sutcliffe's brother Carl visited him and recalled:

> I came round one morning on [my] bike and there were Peter an' Birdsall in [the] house and that little boy of Birdsall's who then must have been about three. I asked Pete where Sonia were, an' he said she were at Marianne's for the week. Then he says, looking round right nervously, whispering, 'We just got rid of two birds. Just in time.' An' they had, because he were telling me what had gone off.

Following his fourth interview, Sutcliffe now knew the police must be watching the red light areas he frequented so he decided to change targets. He knew that students walking alone would be a good target and it wasn't long before he struck again.

Chapter 24

The Students

On 17 February 1979, it is highly probable that Sutcliffe struck again. During the early hours of the morning in Harrogate, North Yorkshire, a 16-year-old student was attacked from behind and suffered three severe head injuries from a blunt instrument. She was unable to provide any description of her attacker.

Surprisingly (and probably because the police were overwhelmed with work), the police concluded that she had injured herself by falling on an icy pavement and that no actual crime had taken place. Professor Gee was asked to examine her at Leeds General Infirmary (LGI). On his first visit he was unable to examine her due to a large surgical bandage on her head, but he was shown a sketch done by one of the doctors of the lacerations on her head and he viewed the post-operation X-rays.

There was one linear laceration on the left side of the top of the head 2½in long, and one on the right side of the top of the head 2in long. A third curved laceration at the back of the head was about one inch long.

On his second visit, Professor Gee was able to examine the girl's shaved head. He felt that the wounds on her scalp did not have the curved shape that would have suggested that she had been hit with a ball pein hammer, but he could not conclude what had caused the injuries.

However, years later, an official report noted that the X-rays had clearly shown three semi-circular injuries to the head and that it was certainly not consistent with an accidental fall.

Peter Sutcliffe must at least be the prime suspect for this attack. It certainly has his MO of hammer blows to the back and top of the victims head, on a female alone at night, and he was probably disturbed before he had a chance to stab her. He was certainly still looking for a victim and visiting red light areas at the time of the attack because just a week later, on 23 February, he was printed out as a 'Triple Area Sighting', having been spotted visiting the Moss Side area of Manchester in his black Sunbeam Rapier.

Even Sutcliffe himself recalled:

> Following Millward, the compulsion inside me seemed to lay dormant, but eventually the feeling came welling up, and each time they were more random and indiscriminate. I now realised I had the urge to kill any woman and I thought this would eventually get me caught, but I think that in my sub-conscious this was what I really wanted.

He also commented:

> I had the urge to kill any woman. It sounds a bit evil now. There I was walking along with a big hammer and a big Phillips screwdriver in my pocket ready for the inevitable. I have been taken over by this urge to kill and I cannot fight it.

Chapter 25

Ann Rooney

On Friday 2 March 1979, 22-year-old Irish student Ann Marie Rooney was attacked in Horsforth, Leeds – 289 days since the murder of Vera Millward, but only three weeks after the attack on the 16-year-old student in Harrogate.

Ann got a look at her attacker this time and described him as being in his twenties, 5ft 10in tall, of broad build, with dark curly hair and a drooping moustache. She also believed that she had seen him before the attack watching her on Brownberrie Lane at 19.55, and that he had been sitting in a dark-coloured Sunbeam Rapier. She had thought he was simply there to pick up a fellow student.

Once Ann had walked past his car, Sutcliffe quietly got out and followed her until the two of them were alone in the grounds of Trinity and All Saints College by 20.00. He then struck her three times over the head with a hammer. As she fell to the ground she was able to scream and this made Sutcliffe flee for fear of being discovered.

Ann was soon found by a fellow student and rushed to LGI for emergency treatment. She was examined by Professor David Gee at LGI and this time he thought that the wounds were probably caused by the circular head of a hammer. Luckily, she had sustained no other injuries because Sutcliffe was disturbed.

There were 850 Sunbeam Rapier and Alpine vehicles listed in the 'punters index', twenty-one Sunbeam Rapiers were cross-area sightings, and only three, including Sutcliffe's, had been flagged as 'Triple Area Sightings'. Unfortunately, the officers involved in the investigation into the attack on Ann Rooney were completely unaware of this information and the importance of the data that was available in the system.

At the time, the attack on Ann Rooney was not included in the Ripper series based on the extremely narrow criteria that it was believed the hammer which caused her head injuries was a different size to the one believed to be used by the Ripper – and because she was not a prostitute.

The Byford Report stated:

> Detective Inspector Sidebottom ... obtained a computer printout of all Sunbeam Rapier and Alpine saloons which had been input on the 'Punters Index'. Sutcliffe's Rapier had been sighted on 46 occasions and while there were a few other vehicles which had been sighted more frequently, only three, including Sutcliffe's, had also been printed out as 'Triple Area Sightings'.

Only 21 other vehicles had been printed out as 'Cross Area Sightings'. There is, unfortunately, no evidence that any police inquiries were made on the basis of this computer print-out which established Sutcliffe as one of three prime suspects for the attack, although she was not at the time regarded as a Ripper victim. This was entirely due to a lack of appreciation of the information which the print-out contained.

When the Chief Constable of Cleveland Police, Keith Hellawell, visited Sutcliffe in 1992 and he confessed to the attack on Tracy Browne, he also confessed to this attack on Ann Rooney.

Keith Hellawell later recalled that Sutcliffe's recollection was remarkably vivid; he remembered how, after attacking Ann Rooney, he had tried to escape by car but found himself in a dead-end and had to retrace his route. Sutcliffe then refused to talk about any more attacks. Hellawell recalled: 'Try as I might, and certain as I was that Sutcliffe had committed other crimes, he clammed up. He told me that after his two further confessions Sonia remonstrated with him for not telling her. She said he had betrayed her trust.'

On 23 March 1979, Assistant Chief Constable George Oldfield received another letter that was postmarked from Sunderland, and it again threw the investigation off course:

> *Dear Officer,*
> *Sorry I havn't written, about a year to be exact, but I havn't been up north for quite a while. I was'nt kidding last time I wrote saying the whore would be older this time and maybe I'd strike in Manchester for a change, you should have took heed. That bit about her being in hospital, funny the lady mentioned something about being in hospital before I stopped her whoring ways. The lady won't worry about hospitals now will she. I bet you be wondering how come I hav'nt been to work for ages, well I would have been if it hadnt been for your cursered coppers I had the lady just where I wanted her and was about to strike when one of you cursing police cars stopped right outside the lane, he must have been a dumb copper cause he didnt say anything, he didnt know how close he was to catching me. Tell you the truth I thought I was collared, the lady said don't worry about the coppers, little did she know that bloody copper saved her neck. That was last month, so I don't know when I will get back on the job but I know it won't be Chapeltown too bloody hot there maybe Bradfords Manningham. Might write again if up north.*
>
> *Jack the Ripper*
>
> *PS Did you get the letter I sent to Daily Mirror in Manchester.*

With this third letter, those higher up within the West Yorkshire Police Force (such as Assistant Chief Constable George Oldfield and Chief Constable Ronald Gregory) began to suspect that the author of these letters might actually be the Ripper. The author had gone to a high degree of trouble to ensure that there was little to no forensic evidence on either the letters or the envelopes and analysis of the envelope that belonged to this third letter showed that whoever had licked it was a secretor of the blood group 'B'.

This was considered highly significant to the Ripper Squad because analysis of semen removed from the body of Joan Harrison in Preston in 1975, referred to in the previous letter as 'Remember '75?' showed that the person responsible for that crime was also blood group 'B'. Blood group 'B' secretors made up just 6 per cent of the total male population at the time.

Police inquiries were quickly put in place in the North-East of England to try to find the author of these letters.

Force-wide enquiries were also made to test the authenticity of the Chapeltown encounter with a police officer, but without success.

Chapter 26

Joan Harrison

Let's have a look at the murder of Joan Harrison and try to understand why the police believed she may have been a victim of the Yorkshire Ripper.

Joan Harrison was 26 years old when she was murdered in Preston, Lancashire, on Thursday 20 November 1975 – three weeks after the murder of Wilma McCann.

She was born in Chorley and had been married with two children; at the time of her death she had been living apart from them since 1973. She had become a chronic alcoholic and she was hooked on the morphine contained in cough mixtures. Sometimes she would drink as much as eight bottles a day. She hung around with other alcoholics, drug addicts and sex workers, and it was known in the area that she would accept money for sex so that she could fund her drinking habit, although she didn't have any convictions for soliciting.

In 1974 Joan pleaded guilty to theft and forging a drug prescription when she appeared at Preston Magistrates' Court, and was described in court as 'a complete wreck of a human being'.

By July 1975 she was unemployed and living on social security. She began renting a room in the Avenham Street area of Preston from landlord David Keighley. The two soon began an intimate relationship – with Joan probably paying her rent with her body – and he tried to get her sober, but she was hooked and would disappear on binges and, on occasions, wake up on the streets.

On the day she was murdered Joan had spent most of the day at St Mary's Hostel for homeless men, having worked there on a voluntary basis as a part-time cleaner. According to Ian Pinchen, the hostel's warden, Joan left at lunchtime with some of the other staff for a drink at the nearby St Mary's pub. When she came back later that afternoon she was very drunk and was allowed to sleep it off on one of the rest beds. Shortly after 16.00 she had sexual intercourse with a man at the hostel – possibly Ian Pinchen, in return for the bed.

At around 22.00 that night Joan returned home, sober, and looking for money from David Keighley so she could have a drink. She stormed out twenty minutes later when this request was denied, walking along Church Street towards Preston town centre. She was wearing a light-green three-quarter length coat with imitation fur collar, turquoise-blue jumper with a bright yellow tank-top over it, dark brown trousers, and brown suede calf-length boots. This was the last time anyone saw her alive.

At around 08.00 on Sunday 23 November, Mrs Mildred Atkinson saw her husband, Ronald, off to work and then she left her home on Guilford Road to go to the newsagents to collect her Sunday newspapers. As she walked along Berwick Road, at the rear of

No. 3 Frenchwood Street, which was vacant, she noticed that the door on a derelict lock-up garage on the property was banging in the wind. When the door blew open and she looked closely she saw a body lying face down on the concrete floor, a coat over its head, and blood on the ground beside it.

The murder was investigated by Detective Chief Superintendent Brooks of the Lancashire Constabulary and it was quickly established that Joan's body had been moved a few feet from where the initial attack had taken place. Her dark brown trousers had been pulled down and one leg was out of her knickers and tights, and one of her boots had been removed. Before her coat had been placed over her body, the boot that had been removed had been placed over her leg so that it appeared to be worn. She had been wearing two padded bras, both had been lifted up to expose her breasts, but one of the bras, which had been unfastened, had slipped down again.

The post-mortem was carried out at Preston Royal Infirmary by pathologist Dr John Benstead, who was unable to determine either the exact cause of death, or pinpoint the time of death. The cause of death given on the death certificate was: 'haemorrhage and shock caused by multiple injuries, murder by person or persons unknown'. Joan had one U-shaped laceration on the back of her head and the Lancashire Police concluded that she had been hit with the heel of a lady's shoe, though none was found, and Joan had been wearing boots.

Although the detectives from West Yorkshire had looked at the case when it happened and dismissed it, following the letters from Sunderland they became convinced that the Ripper was actually responsible. They now believed (despite the pathology report) that the head injuries could have been consistent with a blow from a hammer.

Joan also had extensive injuries to her head, face, body and legs, which it was concluded had been caused by violent kicking and stamping. There were no stab wounds.

Joan also had bite marks on her left breast, which were examined by Liverpool dentist James Furness, a specialist in forensic odontology. He concluded that the marks on the breast had been made a short time before death, and that the bruising indicated a clear gap in the front upper teeth.

Pathological examination of the body also found semen deposits, apparently due to vaginal and anal intercourse at around the time of death.

Lancashire Police discovered that Joan Harrison's handbag and purse were missing. Her purse was believed to have contained cigarette lighters, rings, bracelets, an inhaler and possibly a diary. Lancashire Police believed that the murderer was local and familiar with the area because an object from Joan's body, which Detective Chief Superintendent Brooks refused to identify, was found within days in the cistern of a men's lavatory up the road from the garage. The police believed they had further confirmation of this when her purse was found two months later hidden in a bush in Avenham Park, and in June 1976 when her handbag was found carefully hidden in a refuse-tip about 400 yards from where she was murdered.

The murder was not felt by Lancashire Police to be connected to the murder of Wilma McCann the previous month. It was with the murder of Irene Richardson – with the similar arrangement of the boots placed over the legs to make them appear to still be worn, and the covering of the body with a coat, that the Lancashire and Yorkshire Police thought there might be a possible connection, but because of the obvious sexual assault and robbery, elements missing from the Yorkshire Ripper attacks, the murder of Joan Harrison was not conclusively linked. Sadly, it was the letters that finally convinced officers hunting the Ripper that her murder was part of the Ripper series.

Between her murder and the arrest of Peter Sutcliffe, Lancashire Police had interviewed over 50,000 people, including 300 lorry drivers and the crews of twelve ships who were in Preston on the night.

Meanwhile, back in Leeds, the Major Incident Room at Millgarth Police Station was by now completely overrun trying to action over 20,000 'Cross Area Sightings' which had been recorded; at that point, only around 25 per cent of the vehicle owners had been traced and interviewed. The selection for vehicle owners for interview depended primarily on their home address. If they lived in West Yorkshire or Greater Manchester then they would almost certainly be interviewed, but if the owners of the vehicles lived further away then they were given a lower priority.

Chapter 27

Josephine Whitaker

On Thursday 5 April 1979, 19-year-old Josephine Anne Whitaker was murdered at around 00.15 on Savile Park Moor, Halifax – one month after the attack on Ann Rooney. Sutcliffe, who had by now given up trying to kill prostitutes because the red light areas were being watched by police, had been out looking for women who were on their own, hence the attacks on the 16-year-old student and Ann Rooney. His usual hunting grounds had become too hot so he decided this time to try Halifax.

Josephine was born shortly before Christmas in 1959 to Thelma (known as Avril) and Trevor Whitaker, but by 1961 her parents had separated and she moved with her mother into her grandparents' house. Josephine remained extremely close to her grandparents, Tom and Mary Priestley, throughout her young life and would have tea with them every Sunday. Later that year Thelma and Trevor divorced and Thelma started to see another man whom she would go on to live with, and have two further children – Michael and David; that relationship also ended. In 1972 Thelma met a local builder, Haydn Hiley, and they moved to 10 Ivy Street, Halifax.

Josephine went to Highland School and was regarded as a great all-rounder, being both good academically and at sports. She spent her weekends horse riding at Norland Moor Stables and when she left school in 1977 she began working at the local branch of the Halifax Building Society. She worked hard there, gaining a promotion and a pay-rise, which she was keen to get as she wanted to start saving for when she got married and had children; she also had a part-time job working behind a bar at a local hotel. With her first increased wage packet from the Halifax Building Society she treated herself to a new silver watch, for which she paid £60.

This arrived in the morning post on the 4 April and when she got home from work that evening Josephine had an argument with her mother, who thought that she shouldn't be wasting her money on expensive items. Josephine stormed off and went to see her grandparents at 294 Huddersfield Road to cool off, taking the watch with her. Her grandmother was at a church party across the road, so she showed her grandfather the watch. Josephine's grandmother got home around 23.00 and was pleased to see her granddaughter and the three of them carried on talking until around 23.40.

As it was late, her grandparents begged her to stay the night, but Josephine said that she had to go home because the case for her contact lenses was there and she also had to get ready in the morning for work. Her grandfather then offered to walk her home, but as he had health problems Josephine assured them that she would be OK getting home alone. She left at 23.55 for the twenty-five-minute walk to Savile Park, and on to the suburb of Bell Hall and Ivy Street where she lived.

That evening, Sutcliffe had been out drinking with Trevor Birdsall, and shortly after closing time Sutcliffe dropped his friend off at home, before turning the car around and heading for Halifax, arriving at around 23.30.

He recalled:

> I drove to Halifax, I'd been driving round aimlessly, the mood was in me, and no woman was safe while I was in this state of mind. Without realising, or without having a particular destination, I arrived in Halifax late at night.
>
> I drove along through the centre, past the Bulls Head, round the roundabout, past the Halifax Building Society. I came to a wide road with a sweeping curve to it, I took a right turn and eventually came to a big open grass area. I just kept driving round this grassy area until I came to a row of terrace houses about ¼ mile from the grass area [Manor Heath Road].
>
> I saw Josephine Whitaker walking up this street. She was wearing a ¾ length skirt and jacket. I parked up in this street with terrace houses and started to follow her on foot, and I caught up with her after a couple of minutes. I realised she was not a prostitute, but at that time I wasn't bothered. I just wanted to kill a woman.
>
> When I caught up with her I started talking to her. I asked her if she had far to go. She said, 'It's quite a walk.' She didn't seem alarmed by my approach. I continued walking alongside her and she started speaking to me about having just left her grandmother's and that she had considered staying there but had decided to walk home. I asked her if she had considered learning to drive, I think she said she rode a horse and that it was a satisfactory form of transport. We were approaching the open grassland area. She told me that she normally took a short cut across the field.
>
> I said you don't know who you can trust these days. It sounds a bit evil now, there was I walking along with my hammer and a big Philips screwdriver in my pocket ready to do the inevitable.
>
> We both started to walk diagonally across the grass field. We were still talking when we were about 30–40 yards from the main road. I asked her what time it was on the clock tower, which was to our right. She looked at the clock and told me what time it was. I forget the time she said. I said to her she must have good eyesight and I lagged behind her pretending to look at the clock.
>
> I took my hammer out of my pocket and hit her on the back of the head twice. She fell down and she made a loud groaning sound. To my horror I saw a figure walking along the main road from my right.
>
> I took hold of her by the ankles and dragged her face down away from the road further into the field. She was still moaning as I did this. When I thought I was a safe distance from the road, I stopped. Then I heard voices from somewhere behind me to my left. I saw at least two figures walking along the path across the field toward the Huddersfield Road.

> I forgot to mention that on the way up to the grass we passed a man walking a dog. We were within 5ft of him.
>
> As these people were walking on the path, she was still moaning loudly. I took my screwdriver, I remember I first pulled some of her clothing off. I was working like lightning and it was all a blur. I turned her over and stabbed her numerous times in the chest and stomach with the screwdriver. I was in a frenzy.
>
> After I'd stabbed her, she stopped moaning. I left her lying face down. I walked over to the main road, but I thought I saw someone coming up from the bottom, so I went back across the field the way I had come and went over to my car. I drove home, I don't think I had any blood on me, but my feet were covered in mud. I had my black boots on, which had been worn out and thrown in the bin. I had my old brown coat on that night.

At 05.30 later that morning, while driving his bus along Savile Park Road, driver Ronald Marwood saw what he thought was a bundle of rags in the park. When he reached the bus depot, he reported it at the office, but the police were not informed as it was not thought necessary to do so.

At 06.30, Jean Markham was at the bus stop on Free School Lane when she noticed the bundle in the park. She recalled: 'I thought it was a bundle of rags until I saw a shoe nearby.' She went across the road and was about to pick up the shoe when she realised that the bundle of rags was actually the body of a young woman. She then ran home to call the police.

Josephine's brother, 13-year-old David, was on his paper round when he saw the police activity on the field and then he noticed the same shoe that Jean Markham had first seen. He immediately recognised it as one that belonged to his sister and ran home to tell their mother what he had seen. Avril and Haydn had gone to bed the previous night and assumed that Josephine had let herself in and was sleeping in her room. It was only after they checked her room to see that she hadn't been home that they panicked and called the police.

The first policeman on the scene wondered whether she might have been the victim of a hit-and-run and had crawled from the road to where she was found, but it soon became obvious that she had in fact been murdered.

Home Office Pathologist Professor Gee was sent for and when he arrived he noticed the blood streaks on her face, both backwards behind the right ear and downwards and forwards across the right upper eyelid and bridge of the nose. Two large wounds to the head were clearly visible and blood had soiled the surrounding hair.

At the autopsy, it became clear that Josephine had been hit by a single blow to the back of the head and then hit again when she was on the ground. Her skull had been fractured from ear to ear and the fractures were consistent with being struck by a hammer. She had then been stabbed nine times in the front of the trunk and twelve times to her back. Professor Gee also noticed that the stab wounds had been inflicted by a different weapon to previous Ripper victims. They had been caused by an object very sharply pointed which created triangular wounds with rounded corners and with a definite hilt mark reproduced in mud around the wound. Josephine had also been stabbed six times in the right leg.

Professor Gee noticed that around one of the entry wounds was a faint ring of bruising and in some cases the weapon had penetrated the same wound twice. At the front of the left breast, in the areola immediately above the nipple, he noticed a tiny puncture, barely penetrating through the skin, an eighth of an inch in diameter, which looked like a bite mark and showed that the perpetrator had a gap between his top two front teeth. However, after the trial, the *New Statesman* reported:

> the marks which detectives thought might be bite marks were on her right breast. But the detectives conjecture could not be supported by expert opinion. The marks could equally have been caused by the scratching of Sutcliffe's finger nails as he carried out his customary act of dragging his victim's bra upwards, or by the V-shaped wedge of a claw hammer.

More disturbingly, however, was the discovery that Josephine had been stabbed several times through the vagina, with the same wounds having been penetrated several times.

In the wounds police discovered traces of a milling oil used in engineering shops. Unfortunately for the case, similar traces of milling oil had also been found on the envelopes sent to the police from Sunderland, which gave the letters added credence. The police then began to form a theory that the killer could have been a machine tool-fitter, or an electrical or maintenance engineer.

Enquiries were made at tool and handle manufacturers in an attempt to identify the weapon. Various samples were obtained and sent to the Forensic Science Laboratory and the Home Office Pathologist in an effort to identify the weapon, but without success. What they didn't know was that Sutcliffe had sharpened an old cross-head screwdriver down into a bradawl.

At the scene of the crime police had discovered that boot prints found in the mud beside Josephine's body were consistent with those found at the Emily Jackson and Patricia Atkinson murder scenes. Again, they looked to have come from a moulded rubber shoe or boot and the sole impression said they were a size 7. Further enquiries revealed that the type of sole pattern in question had been manufactured in the past twenty-five years and was produced by a number of firms. The right sole showed some wearing and twisting in the centre, possibly from the wearer regularly pressing some sort of pedal with his right foot. Enquiries of the Shoe and Allied Trade Retail Association produced a consensus of opinion that the wear could have been caused by some person operating large plant, mechanical diggers or presses etc. This also suggested that the killer could be a lorry driver with engineering or mechanical connections.

Enquiries were made at firms in Yorkshire with an engineering connection, in the broadest sense, to identify and then check any employees who were absent from work on one or more of the dates when the 'Ripper' letters were posted. The identity of persons who normally resided in West Yorkshire but were engaged in work in the North-East were sought. Handwriting samples were obtained and examined. This line of enquiry led to 3,500 major companies being contacted.

It was obvious from the start that this was another attack by the Yorkshire Ripper and Assistant Chief Constable George Oldfield set up an incident room in Halifax to deal with this murder, but the demand for manpower to help with the new murder was such that inquiry teams attached to the other murders being investigated at Millgarth Police Station in Leeds were dragged away and tasked with investigating this latest murder. Subsequently, the processing of all outstanding actions at Millgarth ground to a halt.

George Oldfield did speak to awaiting journalists briefly, but again showed that they were on the wrong track. He stated: 'If this is connected with the previous Ripper killings, then he has made a terrible mistake. As with Jayne MacDonald, the dead girl is perfectly respectable.'

The following day, Oldfield finally confirmed to the press that the death was being attributed to the Yorkshire Ripper.

> This girl was perfectly respectable, in an open space and legitimately going about her business. We always felt he would strike again, but we are now faced with a new situation. We cannot stress how careful every woman must be. Unless we catch him, and the public must help us, he will go on and on. This was another particularly brutal and savage attack on an innocent young woman who was most respectable. There are many similarities with other murders of women which we have been actively investigating for the past three-and-a-half years. I have good reason to believe that one man is responsible for all those horrific crimes. Clearly, we have a homicidal maniac at large and I believe he lives in West Yorkshire. I have repeatedly said in the past that this man will continue to kill until he is caught. I am still of that opinion and I am more determined than ever to catch him.

Because Josephine was termed 'respectable' and 'innocent' by the police, and clearly not a prostitute, the public came forward in their droves with masses of indirect evidence that almost overwhelmed the investigation. The most significant piece of information, however, appeared to be that a Sunbeam Rapier had been seen cruising the streets at the significant times, but the car and driver were never traced. The driver was described as having dirty blonde collar-length hair, an unshaven appearance and a 'Jason King' moustache. This was clearly Peter Sutcliffe and the appearance of blonde hair can be attributable to the orange street lighting.

The following day, 7 April, Assistant Chief Constable Oldfield appealed for the driver of a white Ford Escort with flared wings and a pre-1969 model to come forward. He added:

> We are receiving information from people all over the country. We are looking for a clever person who, if he is not living with us, is not far out of West Yorkshire. The man is obviously mentally deranged, but now he has changed his pattern. We cannot stress how careful every woman must be. Unless we catch him, and the public must help us, he will go on and on. I warn all women to use lighted streets and to walk home with someone they know. In no circumstances accept lifts from strangers.

The dog walker came forward and told officers that he had seen a woman, whose description and clothing were similar to Josephine Whitaker's, walking with a man he described as being aged 19–22, 5ft 8in, medium build, wearing jeans and a three-quarter-length coloured coat, who appeared not to have shaven for three or four days, and had mousy-coloured, slightly wavy, greasy hair that was brushed right to left.

The last witness said that he was walking by the park at the time of the murder and said that he heard an unusual noise, 'the type of noise that makes your hair stand on end'.

As part of Incident Room records an index ('D/62') was kept of persons coming to light during the investigation who, in the opinion of the Senior Investigating Officer, should have been regarded as a suspect. In the series, however, different investigating officers interpreted the category in different ways, resulting in a lack of uniformity.

The bulk of these suspects appeared in the system after the murder of Helen Rytka, when it was decided to extend the use of the index to include men who could not be positively eliminated from the enquiry. The idea was that if another incident occurred these individuals could be seen quickly after the event and either connected or eliminated.

Between the attack on Maureen Long and Sutcliffe's eventual arrest 458 suspects featured in the index, the bulk of whom were included between the Helen Rytka murder and just after the Josephine Whitaker murder.

After the Whitaker murder the index returned to its more narrow criteria – those who had been entered progressively being eliminated from the enquiry.

The criteria used for entering persons in the index is somewhat unclear. Although Sutcliffe featured in the investigation at this time, his name was never included in this list.

The Byford Report found that the comparatively harmonious relationship between the police and media reporters which had previously existed underwent a significant change with the discovery of the body of Josephine Whitaker. Although the crime was immediately linked with the Ripper series, it marked a change in pattern in that, apparently for the first time, the victim was a 'young woman of good character', murdered in a respectable residential area of the town, and who could not possibly have been mistaken for a prostitute by the murderer. The first rift between the police and the press stemmed from the publication of a photograph showing the dead girl's body and the crime scene.

On 1 May 1979, West Yorkshire Police made a fatal error. An entry in the murder log approved the practice of eliminating suspects on the basis of the handwriting from the three letters from Sunderland. Assistant Chief Constable George Oldfield and his team believed that the letters were most likely from the killer, that he lived local to West Yorkshire, and that it was his work that took him to Sunderland from where he posted the letters.

When drivers were interviewed regarding the 'Triple Area Sighting' inquiry, a small sample of their handwriting was taken and the driver eliminated from inquiries if the handwriting didn't match those from the letters.

On 4 June 1979, Sutcliffe sold his Sunbeam Rapier and bought himself another second-hand car – a brown Rover 3.5L saloon registered number FHY 400K, which he got from Robin Holland, Sonia's sister's husband. Robin had twice been questioned by detectives regarding the murders, and later recalled:

> I had been out with him to pubs in the red light districts and his main topic of conversation was sex and prostitutes he had been with. The man was such a hypocrite. When we were with friends he would go on about men who were rotten beasts for two-timing their wives.

He said that Sutcliffe even sought out prostitutes on his lunch breaks:

> It happened a few times when I was with him. He would just go out for five or ten minutes with a girl and come back again. In the end I stopped having these lunchtime sessions in public houses with him. I found them too sordid.

Relevant Statistics

Incident Room set up	5 April 1979
House to House Enquiries	2,269
Actions	17,178
Statements	4,474
Vehicle Enquiries	4,500
Officers Engaged	133
Hours Worked (Not inc. Overtime)	97,161
Incident Room Closed	3 September 1979

Chapter 28

The Tape

Exactly two weeks later, on 18 June 1979, the police investigation was sent completely off course. It would never recover. Assistant Chief Constable George Oldfield received a tape from Sunderland claiming to be from the same man who had written the letters.

The tape, in a North-East accent, said:

> I'm Jack. I see you are still having no luck catching me. I have the greatest respect for you, George, but Lord, you are no nearer catching me now than four years ago when I started. I reckon your boys are lettin' you down, George. They can't be much good, can they? The only time they came near catching me was a few months back in Chapeltown, when I was disturbed. Even then it was a uniformed copper, not a detective.
>
> I warned you in March that I'd strike again. Sorry it wasn't Bradford. I did promise you that, but I couldn't get there. I'm not quite sure when I'll strike again, but it will definitely be sometime this year, maybe September, October or even sooner if I get the chance. I'm not sure where, maybe Manchester; I like it there, there's plenty of them knocking about. They never learn, do they, George? I bet you've warned them. But they never listen.
>
> At the rate I'm goin', I should be in the book of records. I think it's eleven up to now, isn't it? Well, I'll keep on going for quite a while yet. I can't see myself being nicked just yet. Even if you do get near, I'll probably top myself first.
>
> Well, it's been nice chatting to you, George.
>
> Yours, Jack the Ripper.

No good looking for fingerprints, you should know by now it's as clean as a whistle. See you soon. Bye. Hope you like the catchy tune at the end. Ha-ha.

(This was followed by twenty-two seconds of the song *Thank You For Being a Friend* by Andrew Gold.)

Detectives soon discovered that the saliva used to seal the envelope came from a 'B' secretor blood group and this linked it with the third letter and, as far as they were concerned, the Joan Harrison murder.

The senior detectives now became convinced that the writer of the letters and the sender of the tape were the same person and that person was responsible for the Ripper murders.

Two days after Assistant Chief Constable Oldfield received the tape, a secret conference of the top detectives from West Yorkshire, Manchester, Lancashire and Sunderland police forces took place at the Wakefield Headquarters of the West Yorkshire Police. For the first time outside of George Oldfield and his immediate squad, he played the tape and then gave his views on the authenticity of the tape and letters – including the rare 'B' blood group connection to the Joan Harrison murder, the milling oil link to the Josephine Whitaker murder, and the hospital reference to Vera Millward.

However, the Lancashire detectives remained unconvinced, regarding the link between the Joan Harrison murder and the Ripper murders, and George Oldfield himself was not 100 per cent certain about the tape and its authenticity – mainly because he believed that the letters were more likely to be genuine than the tape, and that he believed the killer was from West Yorkshire, or somewhere very close by.

Other discussions were also had, such as whether the tape (and how much of it) should be released to the public. On the one hand they didn't want to release it in case it caused a panic – or worse that it proved not to be genuine, but on the other hand, if they didn't release it and more murders took place, 'all hell would break loose'. They decided to release the tape soon while they made the necessary preparations, such as making a transcript of the tape and copies of the letters (with some parts redacted) for the journalists who would be in attendance; within a very short time of its preparation, however, a copy of the transcript of the tape was in the hands of a local newspaper, which used some of the information in a report prior to the press conference. This leak, and the lack of cooperation on the part of the press, hardened attitudes among senior police officers, who had no choice other than to bring the press conference forward. They deliberately timed it to enable the TV news to 'scoop the press'. An internal police inquiry failed to find the source of the leak.

It was decided then that the tape would be released to the press and public unedited, except for the shortening of some of the blank spaces on the tape.

At 14.00 on 26 June 1979, Assistant Chief Constable George Oldfield walked into a crowded press conference at the Police Academy, Wakefield, and played the tape. Photographs of the envelopes were also released and this caused the case to become international news. It was extremely rare for a murderer to taunt the police in such a way. That night and the following morning, the tape and the crimes were the lead stories on all radio and television news bulletins across Britain. The story also dominated the newspaper headlines for the next week. In the days following the release of the tape, George Oldfield also released extracts from the letters in an attempt to track down the author.

Prior to the release of the tape, the police forces expected a large public response and had expanded the incident room in Sunderland, including the addition of eleven West Yorkshire detectives, which brought the number of officers waiting to handle the public response up to 100. Once the tape was released, six officers in Sunderland were engaged in handling the telephone calls during most of the day, while four were needed for the 22.00–06.00 night shift. By the end of the third day, 2,500 calls with information had been received by police forces nationally, with the Sunderland incident room handling

560 calls. A 'Dial-The-Ripper' freephone telephone number was also set up to allow people to hear the tape and it was promptly overloaded with calls.

The public response completely overwhelmed the already over-burdened Ripper investigation. A large number of the approximately 250 officers working on the investigation were required in the incident rooms just to handle the volume of calls and letters from the public; all information had to be checked and investigated, reports written and then filed. Even prior to the release of the tape, the filing system was completely overwhelmed and this added work meant files waited even longer to be processed. The floor of the Major Incident Room at Millgarth Police Station had to be reinforced due to the sheer weight of the paperwork.

Detectives in the North-East of the country took copies of the tape and played them at local firms, pubs and clubs. The West Yorkshire police only did the same some weeks later – and it was only then they discovered that the number of people who had listened to the tape was far fewer than they had expected.

Over the coming summer months the focus of the investigation was on the North-East as being the Ripper's location, but Assistant Chief Constable Oldfield consistently said that he believed that the Yorkshire Ripper was actually living in the Bradford/Leeds area.

Because of the very high number of vehicles being printed out by the Police National Computer as having been sighted in two separate red-light areas, this line of inquiry also began to suffer from neglect and a lack of manpower needed to conduct the follow-up action. Of the 21,131 vehicles printed out so far, 15,195 were not pursued by further checks.

As a result of this overloading, compounded by the effects of the Josephine Whitaker inquiry and the Sunderland tape inquiry, a decision was taken to only print out those vehicles which had been observed in at least three separate observation areas, subsequently referred to as 'Triple Area Sightings'.

Dr Richard Totty, a handwriting expert from the Home Office Forensic Science Laboratory in Birmingham, was asked to help and he worked in an office in Wakefield on 10 July where he began to compare the handwriting samples obtained by the detectives who were interviewing the 'Triple Area Sightings' with the three Sunderland letters.

Then, for reasons known only to the police, Assistant Chief Constable Oldfield went to see Tracy Browne. Despite not believing that she was a victim of the Ripper, he took the tape with him and asked her to listen to it. Tracy recalled:

> George Oldfield came round and asked me to listen to the Geordie tape. I said: 'Look – he's not a Geordie, he's a Yorkshireman. I can tell the difference between a Yorkshire accent and a Geordie accent.' But it was like banging my head against a brick wall. I felt 'I don't know whether I'm coming or going': do the police know whether they're coming or going?'

She felt as though George Oldfield was trying to force her to say that the voice on the tape was that of the man who attacked her. He left a frustrated man.

Detectives also spoke to Olive Smelt and asked her to consider undergoing hypnosis because they wouldn't believe that her attacker spoke with a Yorkshire accent as she had claimed, and wanted to know if she remembered anything else. Olive Smelt said to them: 'What's the point? You don't believe what I actually remember consciously!'

Because all members of the Inquiry Teams attached to the Millgarth Major Incident Room had been transferred to Halifax following the Josephine Whitaker murder, no actions were generated by the Millgarth Major Incident Room for a significant period. Five months after Sutcliffe's Sunbeam Rapier had been sighted in Manchester, making it a Triple Area Sighting, Peter Sutcliffe was finally interviewed for the fifth time on 29 July 1979. DC Andrew Laptew and DC Graham Greenwood visited Sutcliffe at his home in Garden Lane, Bradford, because his Sunbeam Rapier had been spotted thirty-six times in the Bradford red light area of Manningham Lane, twice in the Leeds red light area of Chapeltown, and once in the Manchester red light area of Moss Side. This was the only interview where, for the first time, his answers and demeanour did not allow him to avoid the suspicion of the interviewing officers. They were sure that there was 'something not quite right about this man'.

Unfortunately, the two detectives did not know that Sutcliffe had already been questioned during the £5 note inquiry, nor did they know that he had previously been questioned about the frequency of his red Ford Corsair being seen in red light areas, as the papers were then in the backlog of work awaiting attention. It later emerged that at this point, Sutcliffe's file in the Ripper Incident Room was almost two years out of date.

In a later interview with the *Times* newspaper, DC Laptew recalled:

> I remember having a joke with his wife to break the ice. I said to her that now was a good time to get rid of her husband if she wanted to. I expected some reaction or a laugh. But neither her nor her husband seemed to have any sense of humour whatsoever.

Sonia supported Sutcliffe with dates of attacks as he said he couldn't remember his movements on the dates in question, but that if he did go out it was always with his wife; at the same time he was quiet and very short with his answers. Both he and Sonia were calm and answered the questions put to them without difficulty or embarrassment, but they also did not volunteer any additional information.

A sample of Sutcliffe's handwriting was also taken at this point as per the detectives' instructions, in the form of a letter which he had written to his wife.

Sutcliffe again explained that the reason his car had been seen so many times in the red light area of Bradford was because he had to travel through there to get to and from work, and he gave the detectives details of his work and location of the premises. He stated that the reason his car had been seen in the Leeds red light area was because he had visited a nightclub there with his wife and the route he took had taken him through Chapeltown Road. Both Peter and Sonia made written statements to this affect. Sutcliffe then said that the Manchester sighting must have been a mistake as he hadn't visited Manchester.

He was also asked if his job ever took him to Sunderland, and Sutcliffe admitted that he had been there for work on numerous occasions.

At one point during the questioning Sonia left the room and the detectives asked Sutcliffe if he ever used prostitutes; if he did, they would arrange to talk to him somewhere where his wife was not present, but he denied it and said that he didn't need to because he hadn't been married very long.

As he sat in the living room opposite Sutcliffe, DC Laptew realised that everything the police knew about the Ripper seemed to fit him. Sutcliffe was the same height and build as the man described by two of the survivors, he had a beard, a 'Jason King' style moustache, collar-length black hair, dark complexion, and smallish feet – sized 8½. He also had a smallish gap between his top two front teeth, as noted in Marilyn Moore's photofit and as a possible injury to Josephine Whitaker's right breast. The detectives noted that Sutcliffe spoke with a soft, quiet, Bradford accent.

DC Laptew recalled:

> He stuck in my mind. I was not 99 per cent certain, otherwise I would have pulled him in. But he was the best I had seen so far and I had seen hundreds. The gap in his teeth struck me as significant. He fitted the frame and could not really be taken out of it.

The interview lasted for almost two hours. Both DC Laptew and DC Greenwood did a cursory search of Sutcliffe's car and garage before they left, but found nothing to connect him with any crime.

DC Laptew and DC Greenwood were not satisfied with the outcome of the interview and they discussed a couple of points arising from it:

a) The loose alibi.
b) Sutcliffe's denial of having been to Manchester after a positive sighting of his vehicle.

A few days later, DC Laptew discovered that Sutcliffe could also have owned the £5 note found at the Jean Jordan murder scene. Continuing to follow up on Sutcliffe, he also found out through the Regional Criminal Records Office that Sutcliffe had been convicted for 'Going equipped to steal' in 1969. Unfortunately, he did not check with the Criminal Records Office at Scotland Yard, where there were two more important and vital details – the burglary tool had been a hammer and Sutcliffe had earlier been arrested in a stationary car in a red light area.

DC Laptew was able to verify that the Manchester sighting was definitely Sutcliffe's car, but was unable to pursue it himself because detectives had been told not to alert anyone they interviewed to the police surveillance in the red light areas.

He checked Sutcliffe's work records and was able to establish that Sutcliffe had indeed been to Sunderland on various deliveries/collections, but that he had not been there for work when the letters and tape were posted.

The detectives also managed to trace the Sunbeam Rapier that Sutcliffe had sold, and recorded the details of the tyres that were currently fitted. They also searched it, but found nothing incriminating. They then made arrangements with the current owner for the car to be made available for forensic examinations should his senior officers feel that this was warranted.

The officers checked Sutcliffe's fingerprints against those found at the Atkinson murder scene, with negative results. Sutcliffe said he did not know his blood group, but would provide a sample if required.

DC Laptew's two page report, detailing his and DC Greenwood's suspicions about Sutcliffe and their recommendation that a follow up should be done by more senior detectives, was passed on into the volumes of paperwork already unsanctioned in the Major Incident Room on 2 August 1979. It took nine months for it to be looked at by two Detective Superintendents – one of whom was Detective Superintendent Dick Holland, second-in-command of the overall investigation to George Oldfield.

The report states:

Detective Superintendent Holland

With regard to the marginally numbered Action I report as follows:-

On Saturday 29 July 1979 Peter William Sutcliffe b. 2.6.46 at Shipley of 6 Garden Lane, Bradford 9, WRC No 5235/65 was interviewed at his home address.

At the time of the Cross Area Sightings he was the owner of a black Sunbeam Rapier fast back, 2 door saloon motor car, reg no NKU **888H** which he sold on June 15 1979.

He currently owns a grey coloured Rover 3.5 litre, 4 door saloon reg no FHY 400K which he acquired some 2 months prior to disposing of the Sunbeam Rapier. (The Rover may become the subject of further Cross Area Sightings as it has already been registered on the VDU).

Mr Sutcliffe was interviewed at length about the use of the Rapier motor car which was sighted at the Leeds (2), Bradford (36) and Manchester (1) observation points.

His explanation as to its use is as follows:- with regard to the Bradford sightings it was ascertained that he passed observation points en route from his place of work (Shipley Engineering, Singleton Street, Canal Road, Bradford) to his home at Heaton, Bradford 9 – which is reasonable.

His explanation for the Leeds sightings was that he and his wife, Sonia, visited Cinderella/Rockerfella's Night Club, Leeds.

However, with regard to the Manchester sighting he denied ever being there (enquiries made by the reporting officers confirmed the Manchester sighting as an accurate and positive one).

Sutcliffe is employed by T & W H Clarke, Shipley Engineering Head Office, Perseverance Iron Works, Low Forge, Leeds Road, Shipley, Tel No 584031, but he operates from the Transport Yard situated at Singleton Street, Bradford as an HGV Class 1 haulage driver.

He drives a red and white Ford Transcontinental articulated vehicle reg no FHD 214S. His work consists of picking up and delivering heavy engineering component parts (e.g. axles and shafts for heavy plant machinery). He delivers throughout the U.K. and is on a regular run to Coles Cranes at Sunderland. His other runs involve travel through or nearby the sites of the Yorkshire and Lancashire prostitute murders and assaults.

The only connection with the letter dates he could have is that on the 23 of March 1979 he travelled up to East Kilbride and Livingston in the West of Scotland. However, the recognised route advocated by the firm is via the M6 motorway which would preclude Sunderland. On the other letter dates and the tape dates he made only local runs.

The impressions gained by the interviewing officers was that there was something 'not quite right' about Sutcliffe ... He has a pronounced gap in his two middle upper teeth of about ⅛ of an inch. His shoe size is 8½ but he wore boots of the soft crepe sole type. His hair and beard is of the frizzy neo-afro type, jet black in colour. He was very quiet and very withdrawn during the interview. His denial of going to Manchester reinforced doubts about him.

An old handwriting sample was obtained ... and this appears to have certain similarities when compared with the 'Ripper' letters. Also obtained from Sutcliffe's place of work was an invoice delivery book and driver's hours book for further possible analysis.

It is of interest to note that although Sutcliffe does not have a bank account (apart from being in two Building Societies), his firm featured in the Manchester £5 note enquiry.

A CRO check showed Sutcliffe having convictions for theft of tyres 1976 at Dewsbury, going equipped 1969 at Shipley and attempt larceny 1965 at Bingley. He has no convictions for violence.

The Sunbeam Rapier car subject of the sightings is currently owned by XXXXX. The vehicle since purchase has not been altered. The engine on this vehicle seized up immediately after purchase and has not been run since the 5 June 1979. The car is essentially situated in the driveway...

The car has been examined by the reporting officers but with negative results. It is available for forensic examination should this be required. The tyres on the vehicle were all brand new (fitted prior to XXXXX purchase of the car). The tyres are all Vredestein 155 x 13 SR. Mr Sutcliffe does not know his blood group but said he would provide one should this prove necessary.

He has a quiet spoken Bradford accent. He completely denies ever punting. His prints have been checked at WRC with those outstanding but with a negative result.

As can be seen Sutcliffe cannot completely be verified and the reporting officers are not fully satisfied with this man.

It is asked that the handwriting sample and books be returned as soon as possible to the donors after your perusal.

Unfortunately, it is now obvious that the letters and tape from Sunderland took preference over the real crime scene clues and descriptions from survivors and they played their part in allowing Sutcliffe to both avoid further intense questioning and from becoming a prime suspect.

Sutcliffe's handwriting did not match that of the letters, and so DC Laptew's and DC Greenwood's report was simply marked 'Type up and index statements into S system. This file out on handwriting', which meant that it languished with thousands of others in the enormous backlog of reports still to be filed in the system.

The 1983 'Report into the Investigation of the Series of Murders and Assaults on Women in the North of England between 1975 and 1980' found that:

> It is considered that any experienced detective reading the report following the fifth interview irrespective of the handwriting criteria, would have immediately directed that an in-depth enquiry be made. Why this report was overlooked cannot be determined.
>
> What happened to the report thereafter can only be conjecture but it seems likely that it was left pending because it contained a request that the handwriting samples be returned. It was not entered in the main index system until March 1980 and this delay resulted in details of this interview, which clearly left the interviewing officers with the feeling that there was something 'not quite right' about Sutcliffe, being unavailable to officers who subsequently saw him. It was also the second report to be absorbed in the massive backlog of reports and actions which the investigation was generating.

At this point in the inquiry Assistant Chief Constable George Oldfield and other senior detectives on the case consulted senior FBI Special Agents John Douglas and Robert Ressler in an effort to construct a psychological profile of the killer. After playing the hoax tape to Ressler and Douglas, Ressler said to Oldfield: 'You do realise, of course, that the man on the tape is not the killer, don't you?' Unfortunately, Oldfield chose to ignore this observation and on 6 August 1979 he developed what was officially described as a 'chest infection' – but was in reality a series of heart attacks, having been showing increasing signs of stress and strain. He would remain off-duty on sick leave until 6 January 1980.

The Byford Report showed just how much pressure George Oldfield was under at the time and a lot of the blame must be put at Chief Constable Ronald Gregory's door:

> The decision that Assistant Chief Constable Oldfield should, in addition to his routine responsibilities, take charge of the overall inquiry and at the same time act as senior inquiry officer in the MacDonald murder was also a mistake. It would have been perfectly proper for Mr Oldfield to have assumed responsibility for the whole series but to attempt to take personal command of routine investigations of the MacDonald, Long, Rytka and Whitaker cases was clearly inconsistent with his wider responsibilities.
>
> Once committed to these tasks Mr Oldfield's working days started in the morning in his office in Wakefield where he dealt with his ordinary responsibilities as Assistant Chief Constable (Crime) which involved the

supervision of all CID operations within the force area. He would then often travel to the Incident Room covering the current murder, frequently returning to his Wakefield office late at night to clear his paperwork.

Once the amalgamated Incident Room at Millgarth had been opened after the Rytka murder he also visited it during the day so that his return to his Wakefield office was still further delayed. That this situation led to the breakdown of Mr Oldfield's health is not at all surprising and the fact that he was allowed to work to this extent is clearly a reflection, not only on his own judgement, but on that of his Chief Constable who should have seen that his senior detective was overloaded and have made arrangements for him to be relieved of his routine responsibilities. The appointment of an Acting Assistant Chief Constable would not have caused any difficulty in a force of West Yorkshire's size and indeed, took place in connection with the appointment of the external Advisory Team in November, 1980.

In George Oldfield's absence, Detective Chief Superintendent Jim Hobson assumed responsibility for all crime matters in the West Yorkshire area, but at the same time continued to act as the senior detective in the Eastern Crime area of the force. No arrangements were made for him to assume the rank of Acting Assistant Chief Constable.

Although this meant that Chief Superintendent Hobson had command of the overall Ripper inquiry, day-to-day decisions in connection with the investigation of crimes in the series were taken by Detective Superintendent Dick Holland.

The Byford Report also found:

> Equally important in connection with leadership was the Chief Constable's failure to take positive action when Mr Oldfield had to stop work as a result of illness. An Acting Assistant Chief Constable should have been appointed at that stage and clear directions should have been given about ultimate responsibility for the Ripper inquiry.
>
> In practice, Detective Chief Superintendent Hobson, who was Mr Oldfield's deputy, took over the responsibility for CID matters within the force and, by implication, for the Ripper inquiry. However, Mr Oldfield had undoubtedly suggested to the Chief Constable that Detective Superintendent Holland should take charge of the Ripper inquiry and this, in effect, is what happened, at least until the appointment of Chief Superintendent Gilrain as the investigating officer for the Leach murder.

When DC Laptew heard nothing from his senior officers regarding his report on Sutcliffe, he went to see Detective Superintendent Holland. DC Laptew told DS Holland (whom he admitted he revered 'like a God') of his unease about Sutcliffe, and finished off by explaining the similarity of Sutcliffe to Marilyn Moore's photofit. Rather than heeding DC Laptew's thoughts and beliefs, DS Holland instead lambasted him. DC Laptew recalled that DS Holland shouted: 'Anybody who mentions photofits to me will draw uniform and do traffic for the rest of their career!!!'

Six weeks after the release of the Sunderland tape, voice and linguistic experts Stanley Ellis and Jack Windsor Lewis of Leeds University, had narrowed down the focus of the accent on the tape to a mining town called Castletown, near Sunderland in Wearside, and as such the author of the letters and tape became known as 'Wearside Jack'. Both, however, felt that the West Yorkshire Police should not have been so adamant that the author of the letters and tape was the Yorkshire Ripper, and they believed that at that stage there was only a 50–50 chance.

Armed with this information, police decided to visit each of the 1,600 households in Castletown to find the person responsible. Twenty-five detectives knocked on doors and went through a detailed questionnaire with the occupants. This took ten days to complete, but it was estimated that to do the same with the entire north bank of the River Wear would take approximately eighteen months to complete – before that decision could be made, however, Sutcliffe struck again.

Chapter 29

Barbara Leach

On Sunday 2 September 1979, 20-year-old Barbara Janine Leach was murdered at around 01.00 in Ash Grove, Bradford – five months after the murder of Josephine Whitaker.

Barbara Leach was born on the 5 January 1959 in Kettering, Northamptonshire, to Beryl and David Leach. Beryl was a teacher at Henry Gotch Grammar School and David worked at Barclays Bank. She also had a brother, Graham, who was two years older than her.

Barbara excelled at Henry Gotch Grammar School and when she was old enough she got a Saturday job at a local branch of Boots. When she was 18 years old she went to Bradford University and began to study Social Psychology. At the time of her murder she was about to enter her third year. In her spare time she went to the university's horse riding club and would visit the stables at least twice a week. When she was on holiday between terms she would get a job as a casual worker at the local Prime Cut processing plant and at a handbag factory in nearby Desborough.

At the time of her death Barbara lived in a shared house with four men and two other girls on Grove Terrace, Bradford, which was just a short walk from her campus. She lived in an attic room and had recently returned from a holiday to Greece with a friend with whom she was planning to go to Crete the following year.

On the evening of Saturday 1 September 1979, Barbara had been for a meal and a drink with her friends Lynn Johnson 20, Paul Smith 21, and another 21-year-old male called Walter at the Mannville Arms pub on Great Horton Street. The pub closed at 23.00 but Barbara and her friends helped the landlord, Roy Evans, to collect the empty glasses and tidy up. He rewarded them, as personal guests, with a drink after the pub had closed. Barbara and her friends left the pub at around 00.25, but Barbara wanted to get some fresh air and go for a walk, despite it raining lightly. None of her friends wanted to go with her so she asked her flatmate, Paul Smith, to wait up for her as she didn't have her key and promised him that she wouldn't be too long. As she walked off she was wearing red high-heeled boots, jeans with a small badge which read 'best rump', and a beige long-sleeved blouse. She was carrying a cream coloured handbag.

When she didn't appear at home after a short time, Paul Smith put the door on the latch and went up to bed. He simply assumed that she had popped into one of the student parties that were always going on in the area.

Sutcliffe recalled:

> My urge to kill remained strong and was totally out of my control …
> I think I had been working on my car one Saturday night and I took it out
> for a run. I had the urge which was in me and I went to look for a victim.

It was late so I drove straight into town and then found myself going up by the university. When I reached the Mannville Arms, I had just passed it, when I saw a girl, who I later found out was Barbara Leach. She was walking up the road on my left.

I drove past her and turned left into a wide street. I just drove a few yards and stopped on the nearside. I was just going to get out of the car when Miss Leach turned the corner and walked towards the car. She was walking at a very slow pace. She was wearing jeans. She carried on walking past the car. I left the car and followed her for several yards. I had my hammer out and I think I had my big screwdriver with me. When she reached an entrance yard to a house, I hit her on the head with the hammer, she fell down. She was moaning.

I took hold of her by the wrists, or was it by the ankles, and dragged her up this entrance to the back of the house. She kept making moaning noises. There was like a dustbin area at the rear of the house. I remember that I stabbed Barbara with the screwdriver, the same one as Whitaker, and I remember that I put her in the dustbin area and covered her up with something, but I was acting like an automaton and I can't seem to remember the sequence of actions.

I think I was wearing my brown coat that night. When I left her, I went to my car and drove away and went straight home. I remember I later threw the big screwdriver away over the embankment near the lorry park on the westbound side of Hartshead Service Station.

When Barbara had not returned home by the Sunday night, her roommates called both her parents and the police, and a search immediately began.

It wasn't until 15.55 on Monday 3 September that PC Simon Greaves found Barbara Leach's body while he was searching Back Ashgrove, an alleyway that ran behind Ashgrove – just 200 yards from where she had left her friends to go for a walk.

When he was searching the rear of 13 Ashgrove, he saw something concealed beneath an old piece of carpet which had been weighed down by a number of stones. His attention had been drawn by a red boot sticking out from one corner and then he saw a part of someone's head at another. Professor Gee, the Home Office Pathologist, was immediately called for and when he removed the carpet he found Barbara's body, seated in a slumped position, propped against the angle where two stone walls of the recess met. It was obvious that a deliberate effort had been made to hide her. Her head was turned downwards and towards her right shoulder. Her left arm was lying across the front of her body and her right hand rested on the ground. Both of her legs were bent at the knees and twisted towards the right. Her blouse and bra were bloodstained and had been pushed upwards; the belt and zip of her jeans had been undone so that the lower part of her abdomen was exposed. She was still wearing her calf-length red boots and her bag was next to her body. Nothing appeared to have been taken.

Professor Gee then discovered blood on the wall near Barbara's head and also on the ground 2ft away. It appeared that she had either fallen over or been left lying briefly on her side before being pushed up against the wall and covered with the carpet. There was no sign of a struggle in that area so it was deduced that she had been attacked elsewhere and dragged down the side of the house into the recess.

There were clearly visible stab wounds on Barbara's body and blood soiled her brown hair and the exposed skin of her chest and abdomen. At the post-mortem, the pathologist found seven stab wounds to the front and sides of her abdomen and chest (a number of which were oval-shaped and triangular), a stab wound to her shoulder blade and a lacerated wound to the back of her scalp. A depressed fracture of her underlying skull was also clearly visible. In the tracks in some of these wounds, which had penetrated several vital organs, Professor Gee discovered some kind of streaky black material which he thought was a kind of grease – it turned out to be milling oil and the wounds had been caused by the bradawl Sutcliffe had fashioned and used previously on Josephine Whitaker. Once again, the stabbing instrument had not been fully withdrawn before being thrust back into the body.

Professor Gee came to the conclusion that Barbara Leach had been struck once from behind on the head with a hammer head just over an inch in diameter, and dragged up the alleyway. She was then stabbed and killed next to the recess, where her body was left bleeding, while he moved the bins out of the way. The eight penetrating wounds to the trunk had been made by an object with a three-sided blade at least five inches long. Her killer then put her in the recess, covered her with an old carpet and then weighed it down by putting some stones on top.

Detective Chief Superintendent Gilrain led this inquiry and he established an incident room at Bradford. Due to the wounds received it was immediately linked with the others in the Ripper series and Detective Superintendent Dick Holland was immediately informed. He had been on holiday in Scotland for just a matter of hours and immediately retuned to West Yorkshire to supervise the overall inquiry from the Major Incident Room in Millgarth Police Station.

Police inquiries quickly produced one suspect described as being a white male, early 30s, athletic build, short dark hair and a thin dark moustache. He was seen to put a 'bundle' into what was thought to be a green Hillman Avenger estate car that was parked close to the murder scene. In addition to this, a blue Datsun 160/180B saloon car was also seen in the area and a grey or light blue Morris Oxford was sought for elimination purposes. Computer print-outs were obtained of all green Hillman estates, of 'P' registered Datsuns in the 160 and 180B series owned by persons resident in West Yorkshire, Manchester and North-East England. Actions were raised for the owner/drivers to be traced and eliminated. Again, this is an indication of the wide and tenuous type of enquiry which had to be pursued because of the lack of any firm evidence which might identify the offender.

A left boot-print was found near the scene which was identical in shape, size and type to the boot-print found at the Whitaker murder scene.

Directly opposite where Barbara Leach had been attacked, police discovered that a house party had taken place and at the time she was attacked the windows were open and music was playing; unfortunately, nobody heard a noise.

At some point following the murder, Sutcliffe threw away the screwdriver he had fashioned into a bradawl near the Woolley Edge motorway service station on the M1, about eleven miles south of Leeds city centre (and not the Hartshead Services on the M62 as he originally claimed). It was retrieved by detectives from an embankment next to the

M1 motorway following his confession and was later described at the trial by Attorney General Sir Michael Havers as 'one of the most fiendish weapons you have ever seen'.

The Leach enquiry resulted in 4,950 vehicle enquiries being pursued, 36,344 individual actions were raised and 4,740 written statements obtained.

Barbara's murder prompted widespread press coverage, but this time the whole mood had changed. Instead of being supportive of police action, the press were highly critical – no doubt in retaliation to West Yorkshire's decision to release the details of the 'Wearside Jack' tape at a time that allowed the TV news to scoop them.

On 5 September, Detective Chief Superintendent Gilrain gave an interview to the press in which he seemed to put at least part of the blame for the murder on Barbara Leach herself: 'No woman in this part of the world should go out on her own at that time. These are extremely brutal attacks and he is now picking them at random, not just concentrating on prostitutes.'

Relevant Statistics

Incident Room set up	3 September 1979
House to House Enquiries	2,214
Actions	36,344
Statements	4,740
Vehicle Enquiries	4,950
Officers Engaged	239
Hours Worked (Not inc. Overtime)	223,761
Incident Room Closed	21 November 1980

On 13 September, an eighteen-page confidential report, entitled 'Murders And Assaults Upon Women In The North Of England' was circulated to the other police forces by the West Yorkshire Police. It detailed the sixteen known attacks and murders that they considered to have been perpetrated by the Yorkshire Ripper (including the Joan Harrison murder in Preston). It also included handwriting samples from the 'Wearside Jack' letters and the contents of the tape. The special notice included a 'points for elimination' section, where it stated that a person could be eliminated from the inquiries if:

a) Not born between 1924 and 1959
b) If he is an obvious coloured person
c) If his shoe size is nine or above
d) If his blood group is other than 'B'
e) If his accent is dissimilar to a North Eastern (Geordie) accent.

This criteria meant that now, without a shadow of a doubt, West Yorkshire Police believed that the writer of the letters and the sender of the tape, dubbed 'Wearside Jack', was the same person committing the attacks and the murders. Peter Sutcliffe was completely in the clear.

The following day 'Wearside Jack' contacted the police again. This contact was not released to the public at the time. The local incident room in Sunderland was being staffed by PC Keith Mount and a colleague. PC Mount had originally been one of the officers who had gone around Castletown playing the tape to the locals and asking if they knew who the voice could belong to. He knew the tape, and the voice, like the back of his hand. When that operation was over he was seconded to Sunderland to help with index filing and other paperwork in the incident room. There was an answerphone in the room so that people could call in and hear a copy of the tape, and every time someone called in the tape played aloud so PC Mount heard it over and over again.

At around 17.00 PC Mount was alone in the incident room as his colleague, a detective, had gone to get a sandwich from the canteen. The telephone rang on a specially installed number and when PC Mount answered it he grabbed a pen and was ready to take down any message. There was an intermittent tone which indicated the call was coming in from a payphone.

> **Mount:** I can't hear you, it's a bad line.
>
> **Caller:** Tell him it's a fake.
>
> **Mount:** What's a fake?
>
> **Caller:** The tape recording.
>
> **Mount:** What one is this? The one he's just received?
>
> **Caller:** The Ripper tape recording.
>
> **Mount:** How do you know that?
>
> **Caller:** Just tell him.
>
> **Mount:** Just tell him?
>
> **Caller:** The one in June.
>
> **Mount:** Pardon?
>
> **Caller:** The one in June.
>
> **Mount:** Sorry, it's a bad line, you're going to have to repeat it.

At that point the call ended. PC Mount had tried his hardest to keep the caller on the line and he immediately recognised the voice as the one on the 'Wearside Jack' tape. A tape of the call was instantly sent to the detectives in Sunderland and after listening to it they also had no doubt that it was from the person dubbed 'Wearside Jack'.

A few days later, and with no knowledge whatsoever of the telephone call, both Stanley Ellis and Jack Windsor Lewis, the linguistic experts brought in by Assistant Chief Constable Oldfield, wrote a letter to the Ripper Squad detectives telling them how they had reservations that the tape and letters had come from the Yorkshire Ripper and emphasised that they thought the police were placing too much importance on them.

Chapter 30

The Campaign

On 17 September, Mr R.E. Stockdale, a Principal Scientific Officer from the Wetherby Forensic Laboratory, was attached to the West Yorkshire Police as a resident scientific officer. He was joined on the 24 September by Mr R.A. Outteridge, Director of the Nottingham Forensic Science Laboratory. They were given accommodation in the Western Area HQ at Bradford and their role was one of 'liaison and coordination', and Chief Constable Ronald Gregory wanted them to be available to the Ripper inquiry on a daily basis.

They reviewed the forensic evidence available so far in all of the cases considered to have been committed by the Ripper and they were able to suggest a number of new lines of inquiry to detectives. The two scientists stayed with the investigation until January 1980.

A dossier drawn up by the West Yorkshire Police for the Forensic Science Service stated that 'All the victims are usually either known prostitutes or of questionable moral standing (thirteen of the sixteen incidents listed in Appendix 1 involves women in this category).'

In the same dossier, under the heading 'Wounds and Marks', it is stated:

> In the most recent murder traces of silicon carbide and mineral oil have been identified in debris recovered from the stab wounds. Each wound should be carefully examined for evidence of debris carried into the tissues by the stabbing weapon. There may be indistinct marks associated with the stab wounds which suggest an instrument with a handle. Two cases to date exhibit such marks.

Interestingly, the confidential dossier then claims: 'A "Marigold" patterned rubber glove impression in blood was found on the skin surface of one of the victims. Glove prints or even fingerprints in blood or mud are a distinct possibility in future cases.'

On 25 September 1979, following on from the phone call to the Sunderland incident room, Detective Inspector David Zackrisson of the Northumbria Police wrote a nine-page report entitled: 'Commentary on the "Ripper" Letters and Tape' for his superiors. He pointed out the errors in the letters and tape regarding the number of victims and he showed how the writer of the letters had clearly copied parts from the original 'Jack the Ripper' letters written in 1888. He was also able to show how the writer of the letters could have got the information that senior detectives investigating the 'Ripper' crimes thought only the killer would know – such as the murder of Joan Harrison and the fact that Vera Millward had been in hospital – from newspapers. He also pointed out how, at a conference of top detectives in Bradford two weeks previously, Jack Ridgeway had informed colleagues that he himself had told the press how Vera Millward had received medical treatment in order to 'generate some public sympathy'. DI Zackrisson was adamant that the writer of the letters and sender of the tape was a hoaxer, and he later said:

> West Yorkshire had the pressure of the murders. George Oldfield himself was under a terrific amount of pressure. At least I had the luxury to be able to sit back and examine [the letters/tape] for what they were, because after all that was the only connection with Sunderland ... My intention was to say, 'Let's be cautious about this.' I had the greatest admiration for what the officers in West Yorkshire were doing. They were the ones directly in the firing line, they were the ones who had accumulated huge amounts of information. We were dealing with a random killer and there was no connection between the culprit and the victim. He didn't leave anything at the scene. I was seriously concerned.

Further warnings about the letters and tape were sent to the 'Ripper Squad' the day after DI Zackrisson submitted his report. The two scientific officers at Wetherby had been analysing the evidence from the Joan Harrison murder in Preston, and while they acknowledged that there were some similarities with some of the other murders, there were aspects of the killing which were different and therefore 'the certainty of Harrison having been murdered by the Ripper is diminished'. The report continued:

> It may therefore be unsafe to place too much reliance on the B grouping result of the semen found, which is itself one of the atypical features ... again the authenticity of the letters and tape as being communications from the murderer must be regarded as doubtful, even though the degree of doubt may be small, for a number of reasons which include the paucity of verifiable information which they contain.

Unfortunately, Chief Constable Ronald Gregory insisted otherwise and in October he decided on a media blitz in order to find the Yorkshire Ripper – despite opposition from some of his own senior officers, including George Oldfield who was still on sick leave. It was called 'Project R'.

He achieved his own personal aim of making a 'dramatic impact', and a 'Flush out the Ripper' campaign began, which included putting billboards in more than 600 locations, posting posters, and printing a special four-page newspaper that was delivered to every home in Yorkshire, Lancashire and the North-East. The tape was played on local radio stations and messages from the police and the tape were also played in pubs, working-men's clubs and even at football grounds.

The incoming information completely overran the incident rooms, and by mid-November the list of possible suspects had shot up to approximately 17,000. The investigation of murders committed up to eighteen months before were pushed even further back due to the campaign.

Meanwhile, the investigation on Wearside was ongoing and an attempt was made to track down every male born in the area via school and birth records, and DHSS computer records. This included 60,000 interviews, 16,000 vehicle checks, 11,000 company indexes, 7,000 handwriting specimens and 5,500 telephone tips.

There was, however, a marked difference between the search conducted by the West Yorkshire Police and their counterparts in the North-East. While the West Yorkshire Police posters declared: 'The Ripper would like you to ignore this', the Northumbria Police posters took a more cautious and sensible approach with the message 'The writer, who signs it Jack the Ripper, claims to be connected with the murders.' Northumbria's Police Assistant Chief Constable later stated: 'Let's say we weren't as convinced as Mr Oldfield, and we took certain actions to establish our point of view.'

The Byford Report found:

> A massive publicity campaign aimed at detecting the series of crimes by identifying the author of the 'Sunderland' tape and letters was launched throughout the North and the North-East of England. The cost of this campaign (estimated at around £1 million) was met by contributions from local industry and commerce with a relatively modest contribution by the Police Authority.
>
> The effort was so effective that the public response swamped the Major Incident Room with low grade information, a situation which ought to have been foreseen by the Chief Constable and his senior officers. It is now clear that the objectives of this campaign should have been specified more exactly and that proper provision should have been made within the Major Incident Room or elsewhere for adequate staff to be available to handle the response which the campaign was intended to promote from the general public.
>
> In the event, of course, this additional publicity further brainwashed police and public alike into accepting the validity of the North Eastern connection.'

As well as the information coming in from the advertising campaign, the £5 note investigation was also now restarted. With the full cooperation of the Bank of England and the Midland Bank detectives were able, by experiment, to eliminate several firms as possible recipients of the £5 note.

The total number of employees to be seen was now at a manageable 241. Peter Sutcliffe was number seventy-six on that list, being forty-four of forty-nine employees from T. & W.H. Clark Ltd.

Before the people on the list were seen their names were searched against the nominal index in the Millgarth Major Incident Room to see whether they had been previously involved, other than in connection with the original £5 note inquiry. For some reason, which has never been discovered, Sutcliffe's name was marked 'N/T', meaning 'No Trace'.

Sutcliffe, knowing that the police and public were looking for someone with a North-Eastern accent and for someone whose handwriting didn't match his, was confident that no one would be looking at him. It was safe for him to go looking for another victim.

Chapter 31

Yvonne Mysliwiec

On Thursday 11 October 1979, 21-year-old Yvonne Jane Mysliwiec was attacked at around 20.55 in Ilkley, a little way north of Bradford – just over five weeks after the murder of Barbara Leach.

Yvonne, who was of Polish decent and dating an Iranian student, worked as a reporter for the *Ilkley Gazette* and had recently completed her four-year training. Earlier in the year she had featured in an article in her own newspaper after being chosen as one of the six finalists in a Miss Bradford World personality contest. She lived with her parents Jan and Ellen, and her two sisters, Suzanne and Janette, in Tivoli Place, and on Thursday nights she worked as a barmaid at 'Il Tovatore'. She was attacked as she crossed over a footbridge that went over Ilkley Railway Station.

The attack was investigated by Detective Chief Superintendent John Stainthorpe and he told the press:

> The young lady left her home in the centre of Ilkley and as she was coming into Springs Lane she noticed a man. She just thought he was waiting for someone and carried on towards her place of work.
>
> She continued over the railway footbridge. As she was near the far end of the footbridge she heard footsteps behind her.
>
> She was attacked from behind by a man wielding a ball pein hammer and she was given a massive blow to the back of the head and she's very lucky to be alive.
>
> The only reason she is alive was the arrival of another person on the scene who had just alighted from a train and he disturbed the attacker. Had it not been for his arrival, he would have attacked her further with the hammer and left her a corpse.
>
> We have a very good eye witness – the assailant had passed him directly under a lighted street lamp so the witness had a very good look at him indeed. He said he was a man in his 30s with dark crinkly hair, a swarthy complexion, 5ft 8in, a square face.

The 'very good eye witness' was 16-year-old Bryan Copping. He later recalled how he had stopped on the bridge over the train tracks and had actually spoken to Yvonne, whom he knew, and when they parted he noticed a man walking towards him, trying to hide his face. He was approximately 5 yards behind Yvonne. He later said: 'We both made quick eye contact. He immediately turned his face downwards. I proceeded over the bridge and he proceeded down the steps not far behind Yvonne ... Peter Sutcliffe is the man that attacked Yvonne 100 per cent on the night of October 11, 1979.'

When Yvonne reached the bottom of the stairs she was out of sight because of the high walls at the exit onto Railway Road and it was then that she was attacked.

Bryan Copping remembered that the same man later ran back past him: 'I turned round and looked over my shoulder to see the same man I had just seen on the footbridge.' The man ran to a flat-bed style lorry and drove off.

Bryan Copping also stated that he believed he had seen the same man six weeks earlier when he and his friends had been drinking in a local park. He had gone over to some bushes to urinate and the man ran out.

Jonathan Davies, his girlfriend and her brother, 20-year-old laboratory technician Adrian Roe, were walking down Golden Butts Road, making their way to the pub when they inadvertently disturbed the attack. They found Yvonne at the foot of the steps in a pool of her own blood. They quickly ran to 'Darbyshire's' shop and called for an ambulance, but at first had just assumed that she had fallen down the stairs.

The owner of the shop, Betty Darbyshire, ran out to see if she could help and recalled:

> She was in an awful state. In fact, I thought she was dead. We heard nothing before Yvonne was found. It is an awful thing to happen. She is such a lovely girl. The footbridge is very dark and scary at night. I have used it myself and it is very frightening if you meet someone on the bridge.

Yvonne was rushed to Chapel Allerton Hospital where she spent some significant time recuperating from the injuries sustained in the attack. She underwent a three-hour operation and stayed on the neurosurgical ward of the hospital for five weeks.

Her mother, Helen, recalled:

> It was her second week as a barmaid at Il Trovatore ... she usually went in her father's car but she walked last night because her father was repairing the brakes.
>
> It was a savage attack. Yvonne's face is badly puffed up and her eyes are black. She remembers someone hitting her. I only got about three words out of her. When I ask her a question she only nods her head.
>
> Before she left, her father, John, and I told her to stick to the main road and keep to the light – but she obviously took a short cut.

The following day, Detective Chief Superintendent Peter Gilrain told journalists: 'Because I am investigating one of the Ripper murders my interest was whether this was connected with the Ripper. There are many dissimilarities and at the moment I am not connecting this attack with the Ripper.'

Because the Major Incident Room was totally overwhelmed by the response from Chief Constable Ronald Gregory's advertising campaign, Detective Superintendent Stainthorpe was told that the Ripper was not responsible for the attack and that it did not bear his hallmark. They told him that it was probably a local man looking to imitate the Ripper, but DS Stainthorpe thought otherwise.

> It was clearly, in my view, another Ripper attack – stalking the victim from behind, using a ball pein hammer. Certainly all my team, and I had about 60 officers there, I left them in no doubt, and said if we find this man then we find the Ripper.
>
> But senior officers from the Ripper Squad didn't think this was another Ripper attack and I was given the job of investigating it as a non-Ripper attempted murder, and I can well understand the reason for trying to placate the public and saying this is unlikely to be the Ripper, because all it would have done would be to create more pressure, and we were a sinking ship, believe you me, we were in very deep trouble at that time.

Years later, he stated that the facts were covered up:

> That clearly was a Ripper attempt right from the word go. A ball pein hammer had been used and I was told to take charge of the investigation and when I attended the first press conference I was told not to put it down as a Ripper attempt and I was bound to obey. I did this, of course, I can understand the logic behind the request – they wanted to keep the pressure down but in doing so I was conducting an investigation really with one hand tied behind my back.

Had Yvonne's and Bryan's accounts and descriptions been linked with the Ripper series, then the police would have added to what they already knew about the killer with his occupation – a lorry driver. Surely this would have pointed the finger closer towards Sutcliffe?

A week later, on 19 October, Sutcliffe may well have struck again. Just 100 yards from Keighley Police Station, on Albert Street, a 22-year-old blonde woman was attacked from behind at around 20.00. She asked to remain anonymous for fear of a repeat attack.

She described her attacker as aged 23–25, about 5ft 7in tall, wore a coat with the hood pulled down over his face and during the attack he pulled an object from his pocket and raised it above his head as if to strike her.

She recalled:

> The street seemed deserted, but I sensed someone was behind me. Then I heard footsteps and this man seemed to come from nowhere. It was raining and I had my umbrella up. I think the man rubbed against it. I heard him say, 'Do you want…' but I couldn't catch the rest of the sentence. I know I told him 'no' to whatever he said. Then I ran to the side of the road and he followed me, but a car turned into the street and he stopped to hide his face. Then the car went past and he chased me again. He was coming at me. I started to run and saw two young lads. I asked them for help, but he saw them too and began to get away.

She recalled that the next few minutes were a blur, but 'I went straight away to the police station – I was hysterical with fear.'

Twelve days on from the attack on Yvonne Mysliwiec, (and four days on from the possible attack in Albert Street) on 23 October 1979, Peter Sutcliffe was interviewed for the sixth time.

On 9 October 1979 an Inspector in the Incident Room, checking the backlog of uncompleted actions, dealt with the report dated 23 November 1978, which related to the fourth interview, and directed it to the Bradford team of detectives for attention by raising a new action form, as he considered the elimination and alibi provided by Sutcliffe's wife as unsatisfactory. He instructed that Sutcliffe be interviewed again for the most recent murders, Whitaker (April 1979) and Leach (September 1979).

DC Vickerman and DC Eland were dispatched to re-interview Sutcliffe. When the detectives went to the house Sonia answered the door and the detectives explained the reason for their visit. Sonia replied: "Oh, not again." She later explained this remark by telling the officers that her husband had been seen three times previously. Sutcliffe was not at home and so the officers arranged to see him that evening. When the officers returned Sutcliffe was there and during the course of the interview he said that he had previously given a sample of his handwriting. Sutcliffe agreed to provide a full handwriting sample and whilst this was being done Sonia remarked that her husband was not the Ripper. Detective Constable Eland, in an attempt to induce some positive reaction from Sutcliffe and his wife replied. "I think he is." Sutcliffe stopped writing and looked at Constable Eland, but showed no other reaction and continued writing. The detectives also noted that Sutcliffe wore size 8 shoes and had a gap in his front teeth.

Before the end of the interview the officers told Sutcliffe and his wife that as they had been unable to supply any satisfactory alibi there was every possibility that they would be interviewed again should further murders occur. Neither officer considered Sutcliffe to be a strong suspect but they described the couple as "strange" and were unhappy about their inability to eliminate him from the investigation. They were, however, convinced at that time that the "Sunderland" letter writer was the murderer and believed that the handwriting sample which they had obtained would either incriminate or eliminate Sutcliffe.

After the interview the officers completed their actions sheet to the effect that Sutcliffe maintained a constant alibi (that he was at home with his wife and she confirmed this) and added that as he was a long distance lorry driver he spent most of the week away from home and devoted his weekends to his wife and to the improvements of his home. They also mentioned that Sutcliffe was slightly unusual in that although he had been interviewed previously he had not made a mental note of his whereabouts on the dates of the last two murders in the series. Inquiry officers had found that it was common practice amongst people who had been interviewed on a number of occasions to have taken positive steps to identify their whereabouts at the time of each new murder.

The Byford Report stated:

> Sutcliffe was interviewed again, on this occasion by Detective Constables Vickerman and Eland who were investigating the murder of Barbara Leach. This interview resulted from a resurrection of the inquiries made by Detective Constable Smith who had seen Sutcliffe in August and November 1978 in connection with the sighting of the red Corsair motor car in the prostitute areas of Leeds and Bradford.

The officers were told that Sutcliffe's alibi for the Jordan murder was inadequate and they were asked to check his movements in relation to the murder of Barbara Leach.

Unfortunately, they were unaware of the previous interview of Sutcliffe by Detective Constables Laptew and Greenwood and of their reservations about him.

When the officers spoke to him, Sutcliffe quickly volunteered the information that he had been interviewed before (3 times) but he also said that on the night of Barbara Leach's murder he had been at home working on improvements to the house. This was confirmed by his wife as in previous interviews.

A further handwriting sample was obtained and this was subsequently used to eliminate him from the inquiry again.

The 1983 'Report into the Investigation of the Series of Murders and Assaults on Women in the North of England between 1975 and 1980' found:

These officers in their report mentioned that because of the previous police interest in Sutcliffe they found it surprising that neither Mr nor Mrs Sutcliffe had made a mental note of their movements on the subsequent murders.

The detectives reported that Sutcliffe owned a Rover motor car, had size 8 shoes, had a gap in his teeth and that his blood group was not known. It was reported by them that Sutcliffe still came up with the same alibi, 'being at home with his wife', which she verified.

They concluded that every possible avenue had been explored and it really came down in the end 'to a comparison of the handwriting'.

They drew attention to the fact that Sutcliffe claimed he had provided handwriting samples on his last interview but there was no record of any officer interviewing him that year (1979).

The sample was examined by handwriting experts, who eliminated it, and accordingly a Detective Superintendent marked the report 'file'. The papers were filed towards the end of November 1979. It was not linked with the fifth interview report which, in all probability, was still pending waiting for the handwriting samples to be returned.

Imagine what might have happened had the detectives had the description of Yvonne Mysliwiec's attacker to hand? They might have been able to put the description together with the fact that her attacker had escaped in a lorry, that Sutcliffe was a lorry driver, and at the very least asked more questions.

By now, some of the press and public began calling for officers from Scotland Yard to be involved, and when this reached the incident room it was met with hostility, with one detective even commenting 'they haven't even caught their Ripper yet!' However, on 21 November 1979, Commander Nevill and Detective Superintendent Bolton from the London Metropolitan Police visited West Yorkshire at the invitation of Chief Constable Ronald Gregory to examine and report on the overall Ripper investigation up to that point. The two officers held discussions with the investigating officers from all forces involved and also examined the incident room systems and records then in use.

They wrote a report to the Chief Constable on 8 January 1980 and Commander Nevill stated: 'The following lines of inquiries were agreed as viable and could be completed in a reasonably short period:

a) Persons born and/or educated in Wearside to be located and interviewed.
b) An inquiry throughout England to trace all owners of Avenger estate cars and Datsun 160/180 saloon cars. Positive sightings of vehicles of these descriptions were seen near the venue of the Leach murder.
c) To trace the history of a £5 note issued at or near Bingley and found in possession of the murdered prostitute at Manchester.
d) Inquiries at speech therapists. (Prompted by the suggestion by a linguistic expert that the author of the letters and tape suffered from a stammer for which he had probably received speech therapy.)
e) Inquiries at all banks to attempt to identify handwriting through counter staff.

It would seem, therefore, that Commander Nevill accepted the letters and tape connection, but he did introduce a point later in his report:

During the years of the inquiries many persons were eliminated only on the facts known at the time. It may well be prudent to re-evaluate these in the light of all the facts known today. For instance, many have been cleared purely on dialect or handwriting. While it is agreed that the author of the letters and tape is probably the murderer it is not a complete certainty.

Commander Nevill made recommendations for streamlining the Major Incident Room with a view to the accurate monitoring of outstanding and completed actions, and to the filtering of information reaching incident officers.

He commented on the absence of forensic evidence and the lack of dialogue between scientists and investigating officers, and finally warned that other assaults on women already committed in West Yorkshire might well prove to be part of the series of crimes.

Unfortunately, there is no evidence whatsoever that Commander Nevill's more important recommendations were ever implemented by the West Yorkshire Police.

On 20 December 1979, Chief Superintendent Gilrain was placed in overall charge of the Ripper inquiry. The Byford report found:

It was then clearly inconsistent that a Chief Superintendent should be in charge of an individual murder while a Superintendent was in charge of the whole series and this situation was remedied on the 20 December 1979 when Chief Superintendent Gilrain was placed in overall command of the Ripper series, with Superintendent Holland as his deputy.

Although I have not been able to clarify the situation fully, there is an inference that during the period between 6 August 1979 when Mr Oldfield started his period of sick leave, and the 20 December 1979 when Chief Superintendent Gilrain was formally placed in charge of the Ripper series, Mr Oldfield continued to direct the Ripper inquiry from his sick-bed using Superintendent Holland as his intermediary. This was clearly most unsatisfactory and it is perhaps not surprising that it was during this period that the all important 'Special Notice' authorising elimination on accent and blood group was prepared and issued to all forces on Superintendent Holland's authority.

Chief Superintendent Gilrain's early attempts to qualify the categoric authority for elimination demonstrate quite clearly that although he was the senior investigating officer of the most recent murder, he was not consulted about the 'Special Notes' in advance of the publication of it.

At the end of the year, 31 December, the 'Triple Area Sighting' exercise, which had been 'decaying into misuse' according to one former West Yorkshire officer, was stopped and instead a system of mobile observation points was started.

South Yorkshire Police then withdrew from the exercise completely but West Yorkshire's mobile observations continued and were still running when Sutcliffe was finally arrested over a year later. However, the emphasis was shifted to record only those vehicles containing a single white male with or without a female.

Assistant Chief Constable Oldfield returned to work on 6 January 1980, and a week later Sutcliffe was interviewed for the seventh time when detectives from Manchester returned to Bradford in an attempt to trace the owner of the £5 note left at the scene of Jean Jordan's murder.

The enquiry had reopened following further information which specifically linked the source of the suspect bank note to the Shipley branch of the Midland Bank. While tending to eliminate a proportion of individuals and companies who had featured in the original enquiry, this was by no means conclusive and, despite intensive enquiries, the note was never specifically linked to Sutcliffe or indeed his place of employment.

He was interviewed at home by DC Bell from the Greater Manchester Police and DS Boot of the West Yorkshire Police. They questioned Sutcliffe in regard to his work and social life, and Sutcliffe told them that when he was not working he spent all of his spare time with his wife working on their house and that he did not go out in the evenings without her. Sonia, who was present, again backed up his statement. The detectives also asked him for an alibi for the night of the murder of Barbara Leach, but he was unable to provide one as it was four months previous. The detectives satisfied themselves that Sutcliffe had not visited Sunderland on any of the dates relevant to the letters and tape, nor had he any connections with the North East, other than the occasional visit to deliver to a particular firm in Sunderland. The detectives then searched Sutcliffe's house and examined the tools in his garage; unfortunately they did not do a thorough enough job and failed to find his wellington boots which were in a wardrobe. These boots were the ones the police were looking for and would have linked him to the scene of the murders of Emily Jackson, Patricia Atkinson and Josephine Whitaker. They did, however, find other boots – but they were 'not of the type sought'.

They made reference to his current vehicle, recording tyre details and mentioned his previous ownership of a Sunbeam Rapier and the red Corsair.

Due to the catastrophic failures in the Major Incident Room, these two detectives were unaware of Sutcliffe's fifth interview and were only aware of his interviews regarding the previous £5 note inquiry and the last interview. Sutcliffe told them that he had already provided a handwriting sample – which surprised them – and that he had already been seen by detectives in connection with sightings of his motor car. When they rechecked the index in the Major Incident Room they discovered some documents relating to interviews conducted during the monitoring of red light districts in relation to his red Ford Corsair, but the documents in relation to his black Sunbeam Rapier (which referred to the Manchester sighting) were not there because they were attached to documents waiting to be returned to his employers.

The two detectives knew that Sutcliffe had been eliminated on handwriting but, being suspicious about him, they recommended that another inquiry team should interview him to see whether they too might share similar reservations. It was a shame that DC Laptew's report was also still missing.

The 'Report into the Investigation of the Series of Murders and Assaults on Women in the North of England between 1975 and 1980' states:

> In an obvious reference to the Sixth Interview report, the officers stated Sutcliffe had been seen previously and eliminated on handwriting and their report was endorsed at the Manchester Incident Room, requesting a full file of the West Yorkshire papers to be attached. It appears now that the papers which were supplied to the Greater Manchester Police did not include the Fifth Interview report which, at that time, had still not been filed at the Leeds Incident Room.
>
> On receiving the West Yorkshire papers a Detective Inspector from Greater Manchester Police directed further enquiries to be made, which led to Sutcliffe being interviewed again.

Of the 241 suspects that were interviewed during the original £5 note investigation, only seven had been flagged as having any additional information in the index. It was later discovered that Sutcliffe was one of eighteen others who should have fallen into this category, but who had been missed in the initial search of the index.

The follow-up interview with Sutcliffe was conducted on 30 January 1980 at Kirkstall Forge Engineering Works – just around the corner from where Debra Schlesinger had been murdered. Sutcliffe was busy loading his lorry, but was asked by DS McAlister of Greater Manchester Police and DC McCrone of West Yorkshire Police to explain his car's movements through red light districts and was again asked to account for his movements on the night of the Barbara Leach murder. Sutcliffe stuck to his previous story and said that his wife could back him up. He again denied any access to a tape recorder.

The 'Report into the Investigation of the Series of Murders and Assaults on Women in the North of England between 1975 and 1980' stated: 'Some idea of the difficulties facing the detectives can be imagined in that they were having to ask him about his wages for the week ending 30 September 1977 and, not unnaturally, his explanation had to be accepted.'

The two officers then searched the cab of Sutcliffe's lorry, but falsely claimed that they went to search Sutcliffe's home and car. They knew at the time that Sutcliffe's house had been searched in the previous interview so did not bother to search it.

Sutcliffe would later claim that during this interview the detectives had a photograph of his boot print with them and that he was actually wearing those exact same boots. He recalled:

> I stayed dead calm, and as I got into the wagon I realised I was standing on the steps, which were mesh, and they could look up and see for themselves that I was wearing those boots. But they didn't. They couldn't see what were in front of their own eyes.

Sutcliffe's ninth and final interview followed a week later on 7 February 1980 at Clark's Transport. Because the Major Incident Room inspector was not satisfied with the outcome of the previous interview, he sent DC Jackson of Greater Manchester Police and DC Harrison of West Yorkshire Police to carry out a more in-depth interview with Sutcliffe – again at his workplace. The two detectives were unaware of the sightings of Sutcliffe's Sunbeam Rapier in Bradford, Manchester and Leeds – and also of DC Laptew's report, which was still missing.

Sutcliffe recalled:

> They questioned me at work and at home. One of them said he knew it was me and that he had no doubts at all, but he did go away. He must have had doubts. Another officer said that he knew it was me and he had a picture in front of him with my boot print on it. He had been in my car accusing me of being the Yorkshire Ripper.

The 'Report into the Investigation of the Series of Murders and Assaults on Women in the North of England between 1975 and 1980' states:

> The reason was apparently another attempt to establish the reason for the Leeds 'sightings' which had been in a red light area. His explanation was that both he and his wife occasionally visited a club and a public house in Kirkstall. He even described how they had met a couple, called Paul and Wendy, at the pub and had given them a lift to a street near a public house.
>
> The officers checked this and ascertained that there had been a police observation point nearby, which would explain the sighting.
>
> The officers interviewed Sonia Sutcliffe, who claimed she recalled meeting the couple and giving them a lift but was unable to say where she and her husband dropped them off.
>
> The officers reported they had checked Sutcliffe's explanation as to the disposal of his white Ford Corsair by examining the incoming scrap ledger of the purchasing firm but could not locate the transaction in those records. (An examination of that company's records, however, on 9 January 1981, revealed a record of the Ford Corsair concerned coming into the possession of that company on 3 September 1977).
>
> The Greater Manchester Detective Constable concluded his report by stating that he was continuing the enquiry as Sutcliffe had never been fully eliminated from any of the murders. He intended to verify Sutcliffe's

whereabouts on the date of the Whitaker murder by checking Sutcliffe's log books held by his employer.

On 20 February 1980 the same Detective reported the outcome of his enquiry. On 4 April 1979 the vehicle log book showed Sutcliffe as working from the Bradford depot and having travelled 260 miles but there were no details of where he had visited or what time he finished work. His employers were certain he would have finished at Bradford between 5pm and 5.30pm.

The officer concluded the report with the comment that his further enquiries did not assist in eliminating Sutcliffe and considered the only alternative as 'to start afresh on any subsequent murder in the series'.

His immediate supervisor prepared a report dated 10 March (1980) addressed to his SIO at Manchester. He summarised the enquiries carried out and made certain points which can be summarised as follows:-

a) The Detective Constable was suspicious of Sutcliffe but did not consider he was the man responsible.
b) Sutcliffe was not the author of the tape and letters; handwriting experts had eliminated that possibility.
c) If Sutcliffe's claim of disposing of his Ford Corsair in February 1978 was true, then his vehicle could not have left the suspect tyre tracks at the Millward murder (May 1978).
d) Mrs Sutcliffe alibied her husband for the Leach murder but, even more persuasive, was the alibi for the night of Sunday 9 October 1977, when a house-warming party was held (the same date as Jordan's body had been mutilated).
e) None of Sutcliffe's work journeys coincided with a letter or tape-posting date.

He concluded his summary by saying that, in his view, Sutcliffe was not the man, there was nothing of significance to single him out as a priority suspect and suggested no further action. On 10 April 1980 the SIO marked the report 'File' and signed it.

Detective Constable Jackson decided that he was unable to eliminate Sutcliffe but, following a discussion with his senior officers, it was concluded that as he had been alibied by his wife and mother for the night of the 9/10 October 1977, when Jean Jordan's body had been moved and mutilated, he could be eliminated from the inquiry.

Knowing it wouldn't be long before he would be questioned about his Rover being sighted in red light areas, Sutcliffe bought a second-hand red Mini saloon, registration 372 SRR, on 23 March, which he would use on occasions and he registered it in Sonia's name. He then sold it on 1 November 1980.

This was quite a long period of inactivity in regard to Sutcliffe's attacks, and a possible reason for this (other than the three police interviews in quick succession) could be because he was having an affair with a woman he had met on one of his regular trips up to Scotland for work in late 1979. He had met 35-year-old mother of two Theresa Douglas in the Crown Bar in the village of Holytown, near Motherwell, when he was on a delivery to the local General Motors plant and he would stay with her when he was on an overnight run, telling her that his wife had died ten years previously. He made such a good impression on her that he was soon introduced to her family. They would write each other steamy love letters which Sutcliffe would have delivered to his father's house under the name of 'Peter Logan'. He ended the relationship in the summer of 1980 when it became clear that she wanted to come to Yorkshire to see him. Brian Hannam, who worked with Sutcliffe, recalled: 'Pete asked the boss at our firm to tell any woman who rang or called that he had left the firm and gone to another part of the country.'

Sutcliffe's brother Mick also recalled going to London with him on one occasion in the early summer of 1980, to house-sit for Sonia's sister Marianne for a week. On the second day Sonia and Marianne's father, Bohdan, arrived too. Mick recalled that he (Mick) and Peter went to Soho every day and night and would get drunk. They would then attract the attentions of a couple of women and drive them to a park near Alperton before engaging in sexual activities, and would then drop the women off closer to London.

Sutcliffe was angry that he had to break off the relationship with Theresa Douglas and things at home had turned sour too. So much so that he had twice packed his bags to leave. According to Peter's brothers, Sonia was constantly 'nagging' at him, and Carl Sutcliffe actually thought that Sonia was 'cracking up'. She had become extremely obsessive regarding cleaning, and even when she was out she would take a couple of minutes cleaning a chair before she would sit on it.

On one occasion Sonia had invited Carl and his partner Sue over for dinner and then the four of them were to go on to watch a film at the local cinema. When Carl and Sue turned up however, Sonia stormed off into the dining room without saying a word while Peter invited the couple in and showed them into the living room. Peter went to see what was wrong with Sonia, who hadn't even said hello, and she began shouting at him saying that she wished they would give her warning if they wanted to come over, rather than just turn up at the door. She had absolutely no recollection of inviting them over. Carl and Sue never went back to the house again.

Sutcliffe was starting to become reckless, and on 25 June 1980 he was arrested for drink driving. He had spent the evening drinking alone in the Royal Standard pub in Bradford and was spotted driving erratically and at speed by Constables Doran and Melia, who were keeping mobile observations in Manningham Road at around 22.30. They gave chase, reaching speeds of 80mph, but were unable to stop the car until it reached 6 Garden Lane, Heaton – Sutcliffe's home address, where he was arrested.

Neighbours recalled a shouting match between Sutcliffe and the officers, and when they wanted to breathalyse him he tried to escape.

The officers did, as a matter of routine, check with the Incident Room at Millgarth Police Station to enquire whether this man was known and, when told that he had been interviewed and eliminated, they naturally accepted that. The information given was based on elimination by handwriting, stemming from November 1979, and endorsed on Sutcliffe's index card.

Sutcliffe was duly charged with driving while under the influence of alcohol and was summoned to appear before Bradford Magistrates' Court on 14 January 1981. Knowing that a conviction would mean him losing his job, and possibly his licence, this made him even angrier and it wasn't long before he decided to release that pressure.

Chapter 32

Marguerite Walls

On Wednesday 20 August 1980, 47-year-old Marguerite Walls was murdered at around 22.45 in Farsley, Leeds – almost ten months after the attack on Yvonne Mysliwiec.

Marguerite was born in Dunston, Lincolnshire, on 17 December 1932 and had a younger brother and sister. In 1948 Marguerite's family moved to Londonderry, Northern Ireland, where she continued her education at a business college where she took a course in shorthand and typing. When she left, Marguerite got a job as an office clerk in Londonderry, where she remained from January 1949 to May 1951. From June 1951 to April 1953 she worked as a shop assistant in Londonderry before she joined the Women's Royal Army Corps as a clerk in May 1955 and reached the rank of sergeant. She was discharged from the Army on 23 April 1959, with a character assessed as 'very good'. On being discharged from the Army she joined the Civil Service as a clerk with the Ministry of Labour in Northern Ireland.

In October 1960, she transferred to the Ulster Office in Regent Street, London, and took up residence in a flat in Tooting Bec. She left this job in April 1961 and then worked as a receptionist/clerk at St Thomas' Hospital, London, until March 1963. She then worked for a short period as a receptionist at a holiday camp in Weymouth and from November 1963 to January 1964, as a Clerk/Typist in an office in London. From January to December 1964 she worked as a receptionist at St Stephen's Hospital, London, and from then until March 1965, as an agency typist. She was then employed for a short period as a shop assistant.

In November 1965, she commenced employment with the Civil Service as a clerical officer at the Department of Employment, Red Lion Square, London. Later, in December 1967, she transferred to the Civil Service Commission at Basingstoke as a clerical officer. She was promoted to executive officer in March 1972. It was also around this time that Marguerite was a victim of an attempted sexual attack.

At the commencement of the VAT system in June 1972, she transferred to the Customs and Excise Office at Leicester. She worked as an executive officer and bought her own house at 10, Grendon Close, Wigston Magna, Leicester.

She then had a long-standing relationship with a local man, but when that relationship ended in 1978 she transferred to Pudsey, near Leeds, on 16 March 1978, and worked as an executive officer in the Civil Service, employed as a supervisor at the offices of the Department of Education and Science in Richardshaw Lane.

For the first six weeks in the job she stayed in various hotels in Leeds, after which she moved to a bedsit at 13 Claremont Drive, Headingley, Leeds. In July 1978 she sold her house at Wigston Magna and decided to purchase a new house at 7, New Park Croft, Farsley, which was an estate then under construction. She moved into the three-bedroom detached house in January 1979.

Marguerite Walls

She liked to keep herself fit and was a member of the Leeds and Bradford Fell Walking Club. She also walked to and from work every day.

On the evening of 20 August 1980, Marguerite was working late as she was going on holiday to the Lake District following a funeral in Newcastle the following day. She had ordered a Chinese takeaway, which she ate at her desk, and then left the office between 21.30 and 22.30 to walk the half a mile to her home.

When Sutcliffe was originally questioned about this murder following his eventual arrest he claimed: 'No, that wasn't me. You have a mystery on your hands with that one.' He did subsequently admit to it on 25 January 1981 and stated:

> I was on my way to Leeds, with a view to killing a prostitute, when I saw that this woman was walking towards me at a distance of about sixty yards. She disappeared around a corner on my left, so I slowed down and turned into this particular road. I was already in some kind of a rage and it was just unfortunate for her that she was where she was at the time, 'cos I parked the car and got out and followed her along the road.
>
> Having caught up with her over a distance of three or four hundred yards, I let her have it with a hammer, I hit her on the head, it seems as though there was a voice inside my head saying, 'Kill, kill, kill', and as I hit her I shouted, 'You filthy prostitute.'
>
> There was nobody else about, but as she was on the pavement, I dragged her inside a gateway quite a few yards, in what appeared to be someone's garden. Round about this time somebody walked past the entrance, I don't know whether they had seen me or not, because they appeared to look in.
>
> I didn't have a knife on me this time, but I had a length of cord which I strangled her with. I removed her clothes and I was going to leave her in an obvious position for people to see, but round about this time the road outside started to be quite busy with pedestrians going back and forth. I changed my mind and covered her up with some straw instead.

He may well have decided to use strangulation as a killing method as a way of prolonging his sexual release.

He was then asked where he had left her body:

> In the far corner of the garden near a wall. I was very upset again after this time, I knew I couldn't do anything to prevent myself carrying on killing. The inner torment was unimaginable, because, as strange as it may seem, I never wanted to kill anybody at all, I just had to get rid of all the prostitutes whether I liked it or not.

He said that he had initially denied responsibility for the attack,

> Because when I was questioned initially I knew I was in such deep water through killing through the method I normally use, that this would possibly open complete new lines of enquiry into other murders which could have been committed and which I knew I hadn't done.

> I thought that maybe it would be better to sort this out at a later date, when I had cleared up all the other matters, and having denied it first, it would have made matters worse at the time if I had changed my mind again. Nothing I would have said could have been taken seriously, this is why I'm making a true account of everything and every detail.

He was then asked why he had changed his killing method and strangled Marguerite. He replied:

> Because the press and the media had attached a stigma to me, I had been known for some time as the Yorkshire Ripper, which to my mind, didn't ring true at all. It was just my way of killing them, but actually I found that the method of strangulation was even more horrible and took longer.

Marguerite's body was found just before 09.00 the following day in the garden of a detached house in New Street, the home of Peter Hainsworth, chairman of Pudsey magistrates, by two gardeners. When they turned up they saw a pair of shoes on the driveway and as they went further down the pathway towards the house they noticed a violet-coloured skirt, a large leather shopping bag and a chequebook near a rockery. Finding this extremely odd, they dialled 999.

When the police arrived they quickly found Marguerite's body, which was lying face down and was practically naked. She was covered by a tartan-lined blue Macintosh and some grass cuttings. Close by the body were a purple woollen cardigan and a purple blouse with strings at the back, also covered by lawn clippings.

Detective Chief Superintendent Jim Hobson was put in charge of the investigation and he set up an incident room at Pudsey Police Station. The police quickly detected some bloodstains near to the gateway which suggested that she had first been attacked there. It was believed that after she had been struck twice on the head, the ligature was immediately put over her head and around her neck, at which point she put up a fight, as indicated by bruises to her knuckles, but she was overpowered and, according to the Attorney General at the later trial: 'She was then dragged up the driveway, across the rockery, and into the wooded area to the left of the drive. There she was murdered by strangulation. She was stripped completely naked, apart from her tights, and then moved to the position by the garage.'

A ligature mark was clearly visible around her neck and a post-mortem showed that she was covered with bruises and abrasions. There were two clear lacerations to her head – one V-shaped, the other curved. Three of her ribs on the left side were fractured where her killer had knelt on her chest while strangling her and there was also clear evidence of some kind of sexual interference with three tiny scratches, probably caused by fingernails, on the external walls of her vagina.

Due to the lack of stab wounds, Detective Chief Superintendent Jim Hobson told the gathered press:

> We do not believe this is the work of the Yorkshire Ripper ... This was a savage killing – a great deal of strength and violence was used to murder this innocent and respectable woman. It appears the motive for the attack

was sexual. Miss Walls put up quite a struggle, but her clothes were torn from her. Her attacker must be of a heavy physique because he dragged her, this fit lady, or carried her, a fairly long way. I believe he may be injured and heavily bloodstained.

My feelings are that it is a local man who did this murder. I have a team of detectives at Miss Walls' house, looking for addresses of male and female friends. She had boyfriends in the past but that was about twenty years ago. She was a very private person who would always go home after finishing work.

Police collected descriptions of men who had been seen in the vicinity at the time of the murder but none of these proved useful and they instead focused their attention on a number of men living in the area who had previous convictions for serious sexual offences.

Kathleen Milne, Marguerite's cousin, described her as:

> a very nice and pleasant person ... I can't for the life of me see why anyone should wish to harm her. She was an exceptional person and extremely well-liked. I can't think of anyone who would have any ill feelings towards her. Margo was very, very reserved, but she was a fantastic person – and dedicated to her job.

Six days after Marguerite's murder, and despite stating that this murder was not Ripper related, the West Yorkshire Police discontinued the vehicle observations in all red light areas because they believed that the Ripper was now operating outside of 'prostitute areas'. A total of 1,223 vehicles had been printed out as 'Triple Area Sightings'.

The following day Sonia Sutcliffe's grandmother arrived in Yorkshire for a holiday from Czechoslovakia and a week later Sonia, her mother Maria and her grandmother, all went for a holiday to Morecambe. Sutcliffe then joined them later, but he was annoyed that the latest murder wasn't being attributed to him. He soon set out to put that right and went back to his new favourite hunting grounds – university areas.

Relevant Statistics

Incident Room set up	21 August 1980
House to House Enquiries	1,826
Actions	1,853
Statements	1,202
Vehicle Enquiries	850
Officers Engaged	58
Hours Worked (Not inc. Overtime)	24,756
Incident Room Closed	2 December 1980

Chapter 33

Uphadya Bandara

On Wednesday 24 September 1980, 34-year-old doctor Uphadya Anadavathy Bandara was attacked at around 22.30 in Headingley, Leeds – a month after the murder of Marguerite Walls.

Uphadya, who had seven older sisters and three older brothers, graduated from the University of Singapore in 1967 and worked with the Ministry of Health in Singapore. She was visiting Leeds University to attend a course at the Nuffield Centre, having won a scholarship from the World Health Organisation and had got quite used to walking home alone to St Michael's Villas over the previous eleven months.

On the evening she was attacked she had been visiting friends and, after leaving them, walked down Otley Road, near the Arndale Centre. As she passed a Kentucky Fried Chicken shop she noticed a man inside staring at her. She continued on her way and turned into a dimly-lit cobbled street called Chapel Lane which was essentially an alleyway which cut through to Cardigan Road. It was just a two-minute walk from Headingley cricket ground.

It was now around 22.30 and as she walked down Chapel Lane she heard someone behind her and moved off to the side to allow them to pass. She was then hit over the head twice and had a length of rope looped around her neck before losing consciousness.

As Sutcliffe dragged her along the cobbles, her shoes made a loud scraping noise so he took them off and threw them over a wall, along with her handbag.

At that moment Mrs Valerie Nicholas, whose house backed onto the spot where Uphadya was being attacked (number 13), heard metal bins being knocked over and went out of her back door to investigate. Sutcliffe, having knocked one over accidentally as he was looking for a place to hide Uphadya's body, had run off.

Mrs Nicholas found Uphadya lying 'face down with blood all around her head'. Her beige cardigan had been pulled around her head and there were bloodstains on her brown trousers and red shirt, and bloody drag marks on the cobbles. Mrs Nicholas ran in to call for the emergency services.

The police were there within seconds and as Uphadya began to regain consciousness she found a policeman standing over her. As she was being loaded into the back of the ambulance, Mrs Nicholas recalled: 'She was concussed and when she came to in the ambulance she had no idea who she was or what had happened to her.'

Detective Superintendent Tom Newton took charge of the investigation which was supervised from a Major Incident Room in Pudsey Police Station. Because there were no stab wounds and the attacker had used a ligature it was not linked to the other Ripper attacks – but it was linked to the attack on Marguerite Walls and the police began to believe that they had another killer to contend with.

Examination of her neck revealed that a plaited ligature had been applied. There was also an arc-shaped laceration to the back of the head with an underlying fracture. Police were unsure as to whether the head injury had been caused by a weapon or by her falling down against the pavement edge.

Uphadya was able to tell detectives that the man who had attacked her was the same man she had seen in the KFC shop staring at her. Before he hit her, she caught sight of him again and described him as white, about 25 years old, 5ft 4in tall, black hair and with a full beard and moustache.

At the hospital it was discovered that Uphadya had injuries to her face and the back of her head, in particular an 'arc-shaped' laceration one and a quarter inches long, which was stitched. There was another mark on the back of her head where she appeared to have been kicked. She also had a clear ligature mark around her neck and abrasions to her hands and fingers where she had tried to prise the rope loose.

Sutcliffe, who had driven his wife Sonia to her evening job at the nursing home earlier that evening, recalled in the interview following his arrest:

> I used it [a blue and pink cord] on that girl at Headingley not so long ago. She was walking slow like a prostitute, I followed her down the narrow road. I hit her on the head with a hammer. I didn't have any tools on me to finish her, so I used that rope to strangle her, but I was overcome with remorse, so I didn't finish her off. I apologised to her and left her there.

While he confessed to the attack, it did not get included in his 4/5 January 1981 confession statement. It is not clear why he admitted to this attack straight away but not the attack on Marguerite Walls.

When he was going over his statements again on 26 January 1981 and confessed to the murder of Marguerite Walls, he was talking about using the rope and said: 'This is when I decided I couldn't kill people like this. I couldn't bear to go through with it again, as there was something deep inside preventing me.' The truth is that had he used a knife instead of the rope, he would have fulfilled his intention to kill her.

Uphadya was discharged from hospital within a week and cancelled the European trip she was due to go on, agreeing to take part in a reconstruction aimed at jogging people's memories. She dressed in the same outfit she had worn on the night of the attack and retraced the entire journey from Cottage Road to Chapel Lane.

Detective Superintendent Newton told reporters: 'It was an ordeal for her to go through – but nevertheless she went through it to help us. The operation has resulted in lots of useful information being brought to light.'

In early October Uphadya flew back to Singapore and only told her family what had happened following Sutcliffe's arrest. She refused all requests for interviews from the media and never spoke publicly about the attack. She continued to work at a government outpatient dispensary and passed away in 2006, aged 60.

Sutcliffe, annoyed that he had failed to kill, went on the prowl looking for another victim – and again students were his targets.

Relevant Statistics

Incident Room set up	25 September 1980
House to House Enquiries	529
Actions	695
Statements	277
Vehicle Enquiries	310
Officers Engaged	37
Hours Worked (Not inc. Overtime)	N/A
Incident Room Closed	15 October 1980

Chapter 34

Mo Lea

On Saturday 25 October 1980, 20-year-old Mo Lea was attacked at around 22.50 on Hillary Place, in the grounds of Leeds University – a month on from the attack on Uphadya Bandara.

Maureen 'Mo' Lea was born on 28 October 1959 in Liverpool, and three days before her 21st birthday, the art student had spent the evening with her friends in a pub called the 'Little Park' near Headingley and decided to head home to the flat she shared with her boyfriend in Chapeltown. She recalled:

> After leaving the pub I headed through the university grounds. I thought I'll take this shortcut. It'll get me to the bus stop quicker and I'll be home safe ... I remember hesitating because the road was so poorly lit – a streetlight was out – but I thought that as no one would be able to see me, I'd be fine.
>
> After going a few yards, I was aware that there was a figure watching me. I heard footsteps and someone came out from the right-hand side of the road and shouted 'Oi' or 'Hey, don't I know you?' [Sutcliffe was standing behind a tall front garden hedge on the other side of the road.]
>
> I'd never seen him before – he had a swarthy complexion and dark, dark hair ... olive skin and bright eyes.

She recalled that he was wearing jeans and a bulging bomber jacket, which he was hugging with one arm folded across it.

As he approached Mo, she became very nervous and was certain that he was hiding something underneath his jacket. She began to run towards the streetlights, but Sutcliffe was quicker and the next thing Mo remembered was a crack on the top of her head and then she fell, hitting the side of her face on a low wall and then losing consciousness as she hit the ground.

At the same time Lorna Smith and her friend Michael were returning home after meeting friends, and as she reached Hillary Place she recalled:

> As we turned towards the university I was aware of a struggle and I do distinctly remember seeing a man's arm raised – I don't remember if it was the right arm or the left arm – but I remember seeing a man's arm raised and I could hear shouts.

> As we got slightly closer I remember seeing this man running off and then we realised there was somebody lying in the gutter and when I got even closer I saw her and just how much blood was there ... so much blood.

Mo Lea recalled:

> It must have been a real shock to the people who came to my rescue. If they hadn't have found me, I wouldn't be here now. I think he was ready for his final blow.
>
> My jaw was broken, I had a large dent in the top of my head, my skull and cheekbone were fractured. The doctor said these were similar wounds to some of the Ripper victims.

Mo was taken to St James' Hospital where it was discovered that she had been beaten around the head with a hammer and her skull and cheekbone were fractured in several places. Her jaw had been shattered and she had been stabbed twice in the base of her skull by a screwdriver, narrowly missing her spinal cord.

Lorna Smith recalled:

> What I do remember is the officer saying, 'If we decide to take this incident seriously we may want to question you again.' And that phrase 'If we decided to take this seriously' just echoed in my head and took my breath away. I just thought 'What state do you have to be in for them to take it seriously?' I just found it an extraordinary statement.

This was because the police were afraid of adding other attacks to their ever mounting mountain of work.

Mo was able to describe her attacker as male, white, around 25 years old, 5ft 9in, with medium length dark hair. Being an artist, she offered to draw an identikit and knew his face but, for reasons best known to themselves, the police declined her offer.

When Sutcliffe was arrested and his face appeared on the TV, she recalled:

> I recognised him. It floored me. I knew it was him. The police said they weren't sure because I hadn't included a beard in my description of him, but that was because he had his bloody collar turned up, not because my attacker didn't have a beard! But then I felt this other thing – I didn't want to be known as a victim of the Yorkshire Ripper. Or a survivor – I didn't want that connection made because the way everyone judged the women he attacked. There was no justice for them, not in the way they were discussed. I didn't want that attitude coming back on me.

What she meant was that because of the police language of 'innocent' and 'respectable' women, being attacked by 'mistake', they were still subconsciously telling the public that most of the women attacked by the Ripper were 'prostitutes' or 'women of loose moral character', and she did not want to be tarred with the same brush.

The attack was not treated as part of the Ripper series at the time, probably because the man did not speak in a 'Geordie' accent, but also because the Major Incident Room was in total chaos and they were trying to play down the amount of attacks being committed by the Ripper.

Sutcliffe denied all knowledge of the attack but, in 2002, after the Law Lords found against the Home Secretary being able to increase the minimum life sentencing tariff recommended by the judiciary, there came the possibility that police would lay new charges against some murderers to keep them from being considered for release. *The Sunday Telegraph* newspaper reported that West Yorkshire Police were confident they could bring new charges against Sutcliffe in regard to the murder of Debra Schlesinger and the attempted murder of Mo Lea.

Chapter 35

Theresa Sykes

On Wednesday 5 November 1980, 16-year-old Theresa Simone Sykes was attacked at around 20.00 in Willwood Avenue, Huddersfield – eleven days after the attack on Mo Lea.

Theresa had lived with her parents, Raymond and Margaret Sykes, at The Minstrel pub on Cross Church Street, Huddersfield, but in September 1979 she became pregnant, left school at Deighton High and set up home with her boyfriend, Jim Furey, at 39 Willwood Avenue. She then gave birth to their son, Anthony.

The evening of 5 November was bonfire night and after watching *Coronation Street*, Theresa had an argument with her boyfriend, a Millworker, over who should go to the local shop to buy some cigarettes. Theresa stormed out and went to buy the cigarettes and on the way, as she passed a telephone box on the A640 New Hey Road opposite the Bay Horse pub, she noticed a man inside watching her and that, oddly, he was not using the telephone.

After buying the cigarettes she walked the same route home and noticed that the same man was still in the telephone box. He then followed her along the New Hey Road and as she turned left past the petrol station (down the concrete pathway with houses to her left and a park to her right) she first became aware of someone behind her.

Theresa recalled:

> Once he got under the light I turned around and he was behind me and I looked at him and he looked at me, and it was a couple of seconds and he walked off down the path [towards Raynor Close] and then obviously I thought I was alright – he'd gone, and I carried on walking ... I got just past the second light and noticed a shadow on the floor – didn't hear anything – just the shadow, so I knew he was there, but I still got the feeling that there was somebody behind me and when I saw the shadow that's what really frightened me.
>
> I couldn't run, I couldn't do half the things you think you can do and I couldn't do it. So I grabbed hold of the gate and that is when he hit me.
>
> I still didn't realise I was really hurt until I actually got in and saw blood.

That evening Sutcliffe finished work and clocked off at Clark's Yard on Hillam Road at 17.03, but he phoned Sonia at home and told her he would be late. He arrived in Huddersfield around three hours later and parked in the car park of the Bay Horse pub on Acre Street, which was effectively a space on the pavement in front of the pub which gave easy access straight onto the A640 New Hey Road. He then recalled during his confession interview: 'I saw her walking along the road and followed her down this footpath and hit her a couple of times and knocked her down. But someone started shouting and I ran away and hid in a garden.'

In a statement to police read out to court during his trial, Sutcliffe stated: 'I attacked her because she was the first person I saw that night ... I think something clicked because she had on a straight skirt with a slit in it.'

After the first strike with the hammer, and as she was falling, Theresa managed to grab the hammer, but after a struggle Sutcliffe regained possession and hit her twice more on the head, the second blow hitting her high on the forehead and leaving a half-moon-shaped scar. Theresa recalled her attacker then began to walk away before turning around and coming back towards her and with all her might she managed to let out a scream.

Her screams were heard by her neighbours Stephen Humphreys and his wife. Stephen recalled: 'We heard this firework go off and then there was this screaming. The wife put the milk bottles out and there was somebody shouting for help.' Theresa's boyfriend, Jim Furey, had been watching the fireworks out of the window when he noticed what he thought was an altercation and heard a scream. He ran out of the house to investigate and it was only as he got closer he realised that the figure on the ground was Theresa.

As he shouted out her name, her attacker began to run off and Jim gave chase. He ran straight past Theresa, who was lying on the ground, and chased her attacker into Millfield Close, shouting 'I'll fucking kill you!' He chased Sutcliffe the length of Millfield Close, and turned right into Reinwood Road and then diagonally left into Adelphi Road. At this point, Jim lost sight of Sutcliffe and returned to Theresa, while Sutcliffe had turned right into an alleyway around 15 metres down Adelphi Road and hid under a hedge for a while until he felt it was safe to leave.

Detective Superintendent Dick Holland lived just a mile from the scene of the attack and was there within minutes of it being reported. Police tracker dogs were brought in and they were able to pick up Sutcliffe's scent from the scene of the attack all the way to the alleyway that ran behind Holland's daughter's house on Adelphi Road. They had missed him by minutes.

Theresa was carried home by her neighbours and when she sat down she then realised that she was covered in blood. An ambulance took her to Huddersfield Royal Infirmary and then on to the specialist neurosurgical unit at Chapel Allerton Hospital in Leeds. The blows to her head had caused lacerations and compound fractures to her skull. She required surgery to remove the pressure from her brain and it was another five weeks before she was released from hospital. She had a further operation at Pinderfields Hospital, Wakefield, on 1 December for a hole the size of a 50p piece in the centre of her skull.

The attack was investigated by Detective Superintendent Hickley and an incident room was set up at Huddersfield, but it was not immediately linked with those in the Ripper series. The 1983 'Report into the Investigation of the Series of Murders and Assaults on Women in the North of England between 1975 and 1980' found:

> Senior investigating officers were of the opinion that the attacker was the person responsible for the other murders and assaults in the series. This was based on medical evidence that the victim had received two severe

blows to the head which were consistent with having been caused by a hammer. The attack was not, however, linked publicly with the series but was, nevertheless, treated as a major investigation.

Theresa was able to describe her attacker as having black hair, a beard and a moustache.

Again, this was another attack that police were reluctant to attribute to the Ripper because they were overwhelmed with investigations into the crimes already committed by him. They had by now decided they would only add attacks that resulted in a murder to the series.

The Byford Report stated that the denial that the attempted murder of Theresa Sykes was connected with the Ripper series wasn't easy to explain in retrospect.

> It is now apparent that although denial of the connection between this assault and the remainder of the series was categoric, a number of senior detectives were convinced that it was a Ripper crime. The denial given to the press may therefore have been little more than an attempt to reduce the public, media and Parliamentary pressure to which the force was being increasingly exposed.

Theresa later moved back to live with her parents and commented:

> I used to go to the bedroom of a night, put the wardrobe behind the door, put the dressing table behind the door and I'd sleep with a knife under my pillow – which my mum used to go barmy about, but that was the only thing that made me feel that bit safer.

Relevant Statistics

Incident Room set up	6 November 1980
House to House Enquiries	2,137
Actions	285
Statements	122
Vehicle Enquiries	407
Officers Engaged	80
Hours Worked (Not inc. Overtime)	6,417 ¾
Incident Room Closed	24 January 1981

Chapter 36

Jacqueline Hill

On Monday 17 November 1980, 20-year-old Jacqueline Hill was murdered at around 21.25 on Alma Road, Headingley, Leeds – twelve days on from the attack on Theresa Sykes.

Jacqueline was born on 22 May 1960 to Jack and Doreen Hill and grew up on Lealhom Crescent in Ormesby, near Middlesbrough. She had a younger brother, Adrian and a younger sister, Vivienne.

She attended Gillbrook Comprehensive School until June 1976 when she transferred to South Park Sixth Form College where she remained until going to Leeds University in October 1978. She had gained eight GCE 'O' Level passes and three GCE 'A' Level passes and went to university with a view to taking a Bachelor of Arts Degree in English Literature.

Jacqueline was in the third year of her English degree at Leeds University and she had plans to start a career in the Probation Service. During her holidays she taught at a Sunday School near her home in Ormesby and she spent time planning for her wedding to long-term boyfriend Ian Tanfield, who was a junior technician at RAF Kinloss in Scotland. A friend of hers recalled, 'She was a decent, beautiful sort of girl that many people do not imagine exists any more. She was a model student who worked hard and got on with her studies.'

During her first year she lived in Hall of Residence accommodation at Lupton Flats, Alma Road, in Leeds. Due to a shortage of accommodation it was common practice for students in their second year to move out of Halls of Residence and into alternative living quarters. In Jacqueline's case, she opted to rent a house with four other female students close to the university.

However, because of the attacks by Sutcliffe in and around Leeds and thinking it would be safer, her mother wanted her to move back to the Halls of Residence, so this she did for her final year. In October 1980 she moved back into Lupton Flats and took a flat on the second floor of 'L' block.

Since May 1980 Jacqueline had become interested and involved in Social and Voluntary work and to that end she attended monthly volunteer Probation Officers meetings at the West Yorkshire Probation Office in Cookridge Street in Leeds City Centre.

On the evening of 17 November 1980, Jacqueline had been at one of these seminars and had caught a bus in Cookridge Street at 21.00 before getting off at a stop along the main Leeds-Otley road across from the Arndale Shopping Centre at 21.23. She crossed the road in the rain and turned up Alma Road. She was approximately just 100 yards from her residence.

Sutcliffe had made a delivery to Kirkstall Forge earlier in the day and clocked off work at 19.00 that evening. He telephoned Sonia and told her that he was in Gloucester making a delivery and wouldn't be home until very late.

He recalled:

> The last one I did was Jacqueline Hill up at Headingley. This was on a Monday night. I drove to Leeds on Leeds-Bradford Road, straight through the traffic lights at Kirkstall, up the hill to Headingley. I was in my Rover.
>
> I saw a Kentucky Fried Chicken place. I parked up outside it and went in and bought some Fried Chicken I took back to the car and ate it in the car. [This was the same KFC shop he had been in when he first noticed Uphadya Bandara].
>
> I had parked in a car park at the back of the Kentucky Fried Chicken place. When I'd had this, I drove out to the traffic lights, intending to turn right at the main road, but I found it was a no right turn, so I carried straight on through the lights. I turned right into a road, right again, and came back to the main road, it was just a junction with no traffic lights.
>
> I turned left on the main road [Otley Road]. I was driving slowly when I saw Miss Hill walking on the pavement to my right towards the road I now know is Alma Road. I decided she was a likely victim.
>
> I drove just past her, turned right into Alma Road, and parked in the near side about five-six yards up and waited for her to pass. I saw her walk up the right hand side of the road. I got out of the car and followed about 3 yards behind her.

It would appear that Sutcliffe was parked there for some time, rather than just the minute or two he implies, as during the early stages of the inquiry a number of witnesses were traced who recall seeing a vehicle parked in this position at the time. Apart from two of these witnesses, the remainder – while recalling a car parked on the nearside of Alma Road as described – are at variance with regard to colour and makes of the car.

Sutcliffe continued:

> As she drew level with an opening on the right hand side, I took my hammer out of my pocket and struck her a blow on the head. She fell down. She was making a noise. By this time I was again in a world of my own, out of touch with reality. I dragged her, I cannot remember whether by the feet or the hands, into the entrance to the spare land.
>
> Just as I got there a car drove down into Alma Road from Otley Road with its headlights on. I threw myself to the ground so I wouldn't be seen.
>
> By now, Miss Hill was moving about and I think I hit her once again, or maybe twice, on the head. Then I dragged her further onto the spare land out of sight of the road. As I was doing this a girl walked past the entrance, I think she was walking up the road from Otley Road. I just stopped dead and waited for her to pass.

The girl, Andree Proctor, began walking down the same road and Sutcliffe dragged Jacqueline approximately 30 yards further onto the wasteland. Something caught Andree's eye about 50ft in front of her, but the road was poorly lit and she couldn't make out what she had seen. It moved off the footpath quickly and into the shadows on her right-hand side. She later recalled: 'I just did not realise what I had seen. I knew it was suspicious ... It was creepy, I had to do a double-take and saw something move.'

As she got to the area she moved over and walked into the middle of the road, keeping an eye on the piece of wasteland, but because it was so dark she failed to see anything.

Sutcliffe continued:

> I pulled Miss Hill's clothes off, most of them. I had a screwdriver on me, I think it had a yellow handle and a bent blade. I stabbed her in the lungs. Her eyes were wide open and she seemed to be looking at me with an accusing stare. This shook me up a bit, I jabbed the screwdriver into her eye but they stayed open, and I felt worse than ever. I left her lying on her back with her feet towards the entrance. I think she was dead when I left.
>
> I went to my car and drove up Alma Road to the top and turned round and drove back down to Otley Road. I remember that when I reached about halfway down someone walking indicated to me that I was obviously going the wrong way down a one way street but I carried on into Otley Road and turned left, I turned right at the lights and drove home.
>
> The hammer I used on Hill was the one I dumped at Sheffield with the knife I've told you about before.

Shockingly, he later told detective Keith Hellawell why he had stabbed her in the eye: 'I couldn't stand her looking at me. I was surprised how easy it was until it reached the back of her skull. There was no blood – only pus.'

Around half an hour later, at 22.00, 31-year-old Iraqi student Amin Moosa Hussain was walking along Alma Road from Otley Road when he found a handbag on the footpath opposite an occupied house called 'Oakfield'. He opened it and found that it contained a Barclaycard and a small amount of cash.

He intended to take the handbag to the site office at Lupton Flats where he also resided, but the office was closed so he took the handbag to the shared kitchen of the block where he lived and discussed it with two other students.

He couldn't speak English very well but one of the other students, Thomas Curtis, said that he would deal with the bag in the morning. Curtis intended to check with the site office again the following morning and to report the matter to the police in the event of the bag being reported as lost.

Shortly before midnight Amin Hussain returned to the kitchen (where the handbag had been left) to prepare some food. He looked over the bag and for the first time noticed that there were spots of blood on it.

Just then two other students came into the kitchen and after Hussain had showed the handbag to them, one of them volunteered to take it to the 'duty student'. The men then discussed what to do and another student, Anthony Godsen, who had previous service as a Colonial police officer, became involved. He said that because there was blood involved, the police should be called immediately.

The West Yorkshire Eastern Area control room in Leeds received the call at 00.03 and the details of the call were recorded on a message form under the heading 'Found handbag with blood on it.' The message was immediately referred to Ireland Wood Police Station where it was received by Policewoman Denham, who made out a message form under the heading 'Found handbag covered in blood.' She then passed the information by radio to Constables Hardisty and Burrough who were working in an incident car. The two constables arrived at Lupton Flats at 00.12. At about this time Sergeant Ward read the message form in the Ireland Wood control room and stated: 'This will be the Ripper's 13th victim.' He took no further action in connection with the message.

On their arrival at Lupton Flats Constables Hardisty and Burrough went to the kitchen where the handbag had been left and examined it. Hussain, who had been sent for, explained where and how he had found it. He was then given a receipt for it. There was a discussion between the students and the police officers and at some stage the suggestion was made that the owner of the handbag could be traced by calling the telephone number on the Barclaycard, as one of the students had worked there previously. The officers declined to act on this suggestion. Constable Hardisty then went with one of the students to the site agent's office to check student records but they were unable to gain entry.

While this was happening Constable Burrough had been shown where the handbag had been found and when he was joined by Constable Hardisty the two officers searched the grounds of 'Oakfield', otherwise referred to as No. 7 Alma Road. They spent a grand total of three minutes searching with their flashlights. The officers later said that the reason for searching this area was that they were aware that in the murder of Marguerite Walls at Pudsey the body had been concealed in the grounds of a large house. The body of Jacqueline Hill lay on the other side of the road.

At 00.30 the officers were called on radio and instructed to deal with a burglar alarm call. They were engaged on various calls throughout the night and went off duty at 06.10 on 18 November, having arrived at the Police Station too late for the ordinary debriefing parade.

Constable Burrough completed a 'found property' report in connection with the handbag but omitted to mention that there were bloodstains on it. The bag was thus dealt with as found property and no special significance was attached to it.

At 09.00, close to where the handbag had been found on Alma Road, pedestrians walking past noticed a Fair Isle mitten and a pair of spectacles on the ground. Somehow, these had been missed by the two constables. An hour later the body of Jacqueline Hill was found by Donald Court, a manager of a shop at the Arndale Shopping Centre, who, while walking up a ramp leading to the car park, just happened to glance over the wall and see her body.

An incident post was set up on Alma Road and Amin Hussain reported the finding of the handbag to them. Detective Superintendent Finlay, who was dealing with the murder, obtained the handbag from Ireland Wood Police Station and subsequently identified it as the property of Jacqueline Hill. He set up an incident room at Belle Vue, Leeds.

When Professor Gee arrived he discovered Jacqueline Hill lying on her back with her jeans pulled down to her ankles, covering her feet. A bunch of keys was still clipped to the waistband of her jeans. She was still wearing her blue woollen knee-length socks and her body was partially covered by her check-patterned coat.

Her bra had been pulled up, exposing her breasts and a silver heart-shaped locket and chain were entangled in her hair which was matted with blood.

He could see a severe wound in the region of her left breast, along with five lacerations to the top and back of her head. There was also a puncture injury to her right eye.

As a result of the post-mortem the professor was able to say that the principal injuries sustained were four depressed fractures to the skull, including one circular fracture almost 1½ inches in diameter depressed below the surrounding skull by approximately 3/16 of an inch. In addition to the four fractures there was a rectangular hole 3/8 of an inch by ⅛ of an inch through the back of the right eye socket resulting from a stab wound through her eye. There was bruising and a laceration on the brain surface in consequence of the bone injuries. Jacqueline Hill had also been stabbed on the left side on the front of the chest, the wound being 4½in deep. There were also numerous bruises and abrasions on her body.

The cause of death was a combination of the head injuries and two of the stab wounds. Professor Gee believed that the head injuries played a major part, but that the stab wound of the chest which caused a collapse of the lung and bleeding into the chest cavity was a contributory cause. The professor concluded that although the injuries were severe they might not have proved immediately fatal, and that death probably occurred around midnight – meaning that she was unconscious and lay slowly dying for two-and-a-half hours.

Professor Gee believed that, had she been found immediately after the attack, there was a possibility that she might have survived since her injuries were not much more serious than those inflicted on Maureen Long, who had survived.

He also believed that by the time the 999 call was made for police assistance regarding the found handbag, the probability is that Jacqueline Hill was either dead or at least very close to death. Professor Gee concluded that had the officers continued their search and found her body at about 00.15 there was no likelihood that even if still alive, she could then have survived.

The Byford Report found that:

> I consider that on the facts disclosed the police officers who dealt with this incident, which was at a time when the local police believed there were two separate undetected series of murders (the Ripper series and the Walls/ Bandara crimes), did not display the standards of professionalism which the public is entitled to expect even in a city such as Leeds where the work of incident car crews can be extremely busy and demanding. Although the bloodstains on the handbag are small, the officers appear to have treated the call as one which related to found property rather than to the possibility of a serious crime. Although they did search the grounds of 'Oakfield', this search must have been fairly hurried since they were not at the scene for more than 18 minutes in all.

Following an internal inquiry by the West Yorkshire Metropolitan Police after Sutcliffe had been arrested, Constables Hardisty and Burrough were seen by the Deputy Chief Constable and given advice about their handling of the case. Sergeant Ward was also seen and officially admonished for his failure to take effective action.

The murder was officially linked with the Ripper series and circulated to all forces in an edition of 'Police Reports' published on 19 November. No details of her injuries were released to the press as they could use the fact of her attacker stabbing her in the eye to eliminate anyone falsely claiming to be the Ripper.

A number of suspects had been sighted in the area and the person who Sutcliffe saw when driving the wrong way as he left the scene of the crime came forward, but unfortunately he could only describe the car as 'squarish'.

In response to this murder a number of newspaper offices in the area agreed to add £30,000 to the reward being offered by the Police Authority for information, bringing the total amount now on offer to £50,000.

Relevant Statistics

Incident Room set up	18 November 1980
House to House Enquiries	3,063
Actions	11,348
Statements	1,785
Vehicle Enquiries	4,400
Officers Engaged	136
Hours Worked (Not inc. Overtime)	47,530
Incident Room Closed	24 January 1981

On 22 November there was a demonstration by women in Leeds which resulted in some violence. The group 'Women Against Violence Against Women' protested on the streets for several days, angered by the lack of progress in the investigation by the police and also angered by being told not to go out alone at night. They felt that it should be men who were not allowed out at night, as the Ripper was, after all, a man.

Another woman who had become incensed that the Ripper was still on the loose was the Prime Minister, Margaret Thatcher. She had become so angry by the lack of progress that she insisted on going to Leeds that weekend to take personal control of the whole investigation.

It was the Home Secretary, William Whitelaw, who finally managed to persuade her that her presence in Leeds would actually distract the police effort and would be seen by the public as an overreaction. 'Above all it would gratuitously associate the government with the failures of the West Yorkshire Police and, if the Ripper was not caught, immediately make people think ministers were responsible for the next murder.'

The following day, in response to calls from the press that Scotland Yard be brought in to help on the case (they wanted a team of detectives and senior officers to come up from London and take charge), Chief Constable Ronald Gregory categorically stated that there would be no outside involvement with the investigation.

At the request of the Home Secretary, HM Inspector of Constabulary, Lawrence Byford (author of the later 'Byford Report'), spent the 24 and 25 November in the West Yorkshire Police area in order to get an up-to-date picture of the latest murder inquiry and also to advise the Chief Constable and other senior officers about possible innovations in the investigation.

Lawrence Byford recalled that he immediately went to the Police Headquarters and held a long discussion with Chief Constable Ronald Gregory, in which it was strongly 'suggested' that Assistant Chief Constable George Oldfield be relieved of his command of the Ripper Inquiry team. This happened immediately and Detective Chief Superintendent Jim Hobson was appointed in his place with authority sought to upgrade him to the temporary rank of Assistant Chief Constable.

There were also a number of other changes in the Ripper Inquiry command team, and despite Ronald Gregory stating less than twenty-four hours earlier that no outside involvement would be necessary, he had no choice but to agree to an expert team of specially selected police officers from across the country being appointed to advise and assist the local investigations. The officers were:

- Leslie Emmet (Deputy Chief Constable of Thames Valley)
- David Gerty (Assistant Chief Constable of West Midlands)
- Andrew Sloan (National Coordinator of Regional Crime Squads)
- Ronald Harvey (Commander, Metropolitan Police and crime advisor to HM Chief Inspector of Constabulary)

They were supported by Stuart Kind, the Director of the Home Office Central Research Establishment.

Chief Constable Ronald Gregory now told the press that he was pleased to welcome some of the 'best brains in the police service'.

There was also a small team of West Yorkshire police officers set up to report directly to the new team who were to conduct a reappraisal of the investigation carried out so far. The senior officers involved were Superintendent Alan Charlesworth, Superintendent Jim Bass, and Superintendent Frank Morritt. Superintendent Morritt had particular responsibility for dealing with the press and public relations aspects of the case.

West Yorkshire Police set up two separate incident rooms, one dealing with the latest murder, that of Jacqueline Hill, and the other dealing with the series of murders as a whole. In the first of these, the officer in charge was Detective Superintendent Alf Finlay, and his Deputy was DCI Peter McKay. The Incident Room dealing with the series of murders was headed by Detective Chief Superintendent Peter Howard and his deputy, Detective Superintendent Dick Holland. The press speculation that the attack on Theresa Sykes was carried out by the Ripper meant that it, together with other unsolved attacks, was being reviewed by the new team as part of the reappraisal process.

At this point there were 188 police officers working full time on the case in the force area, and a further 101 officers elsewhere, plus the Regional Crime Squad's commitment. Byford was able to see the dedication of the officers involved, but felt that there was 'a need for more imagination at the top'.

On 25 November 1980, Chief Constable Ronald Gregory gave a statement to the Police Authority and spoke first of the murder of Jacqueline Hill:

First of all the handbag handed to the Police.

> There was a delay of two hours before the handbag was reported to the Police. Investigation has since disclosed that the officers could have found

the body if they had widened the search. They obviously did not imagine that small bloodstains on a found handbag was evidence of murder. But after the handbag had been handed to them they could have made further enquiries to trace the owner. The fact Miss Hill was not in her room or did not appear in her room that night was not conclusive, but her address could have been found. With hindsight the officers might have used more initiative and they will be censured. A supervisory officer will also be censured for lack of appreciation.

The initial two hours was the most crucial time in this investigation. It is regrettable there was delay but it would be no more than conjecture to say to what extent that delay has impaired the investigation.

The constables can be criticised, but they will not be pilloried for the failure of police to detect the Ripper.

The murder of Jacqueline Hill is a tragedy which saddened me greatly. It was a possibility which all officers engaged on this investigation had feared and it happened despite the efforts of a large number of policemen to prevent it. They are all dedicated to finding the so called 'Yorkshire Ripper' and have made unstinted efforts to bring an end to these murders. We have asked the public for their help and the response has been tremendous.

It is our belief that someone either knows or strongly suspects who this man might be and I do implore them to tell us. The cooperation of the public is vital, but I am also anxious that the police effort is at a maximum.

Last year officers from the London Metropolitan Police came to our assistance. They made several suggestions which were adopted, but in general they were satisfied we were doing all that was possible. I quote from their report:-

'In any investigation of this nature one would expect to find a 'tailing off' of enthusiasm over so long a period. This was not so and we were both impressed by the standard of morale and dedication displayed by the numerous junior officers we spoke to,' and '... it is unfortunately apparent that despite the unstinting efforts of the officers involved and the numerous arduous lines of enquiry that have been undertaken, very little actual evidence has come to light to connect any particular person with these crimes. However, we feel we must state very clearly that this in no way impinges on the investigative abilities of the officers involved who have shown great patience and tenacity in a difficult and complex investigation.'

Senior officers from West Yorkshire, Greater Manchester, Lancashire, Forces in the North East and senior detective officers from other parts of the country have been briefed and frequently joined together to contribute their experience.

There has been a nationwide interest and several schemes including a massive publicity campaign have sought to produce that vital piece of information which will identify the murderer.

Two MPs have demanded that we should call in Scotland Yard, as if 'calling in the Yard' is the panacea. When there were small forces which did not have the resources or experience of homicide investigation it was appropriate to seek the assistance of the largest police force in the country, but with the amalgamation of forces into larger units the senior detective officers have as much or in some cases more experience of murder investigation than their colleagues in the capital. We have all the resources we need, but success has been elusive. We must try again and again until this maniac is stopped.

First of all I would like the public to take sensible precautions at night time. Ladies should not walk alone and where possible they should have a male escort. Police patrols will be active in all parts of West Yorkshire. Both the uniformed and detective branch will be making checks and if this causes irritation and inconvenience at times I would ask for tolerance and understanding. Thousands of calls have been received by the police and I hope that we shall continue to receive suggestions however remote they may seem.

Secondly, there will be changes in the investigation team. Detective Chief Superintendent James Hobson will now assume command of the Ripper Squad and he will have authority to pick his team.

He will be assisted by an expert team of specially selected senior officers drawn from different parts of the country. Their function will be to look critically at the police action, and to advise. They are probably the most experienced group of police officers who could be mustered to assist this investigation. They will be supported by a Forensic Scientist and I have asked them to meet in Leeds as soon as possible.

This group will be:

Assistant Chief Constable Andrew Sloan,
National Coordinator of Regional Crime Squads

Deputy Chief Constable Leslie Emment
Thames Valley

Assistant Chief Constable David Gerty
West Midlands

Commander Ronald Harvey
Adviser to the Chief Inspector of Constabulary on Crime

Mr Stuart Kind
Director of the Home Office Central Research Establishment, Aldermaston

Mr Hobson will require command status to work with this group and to control senior officers who will be part of his team. Subject to your approval the Home Office would support his appointment as temporary Assistant Chief Constable and I would ask you to take that course. It would not be an increase in the authorised establishment.

This change in command in no way reflects upon the dedicated officers who have lived with this investigation for a long time. They return to normal duties with my grateful thanks for their loyalty and devotion.

My final appeal is to the press and television. They are a powerful weapon in the investigation. Their help in the (?) city campaign and their link with the public has been invaluable, but I do want to enter a note of caution. We expect criticism, but let it be constructive. Destructive criticism only serves to divert public attention from the main objective. We have tried to cooperate with the press over the whole period of this investigation and very little has been kept from them, but they must appreciate that to reveal every detail can present serious difficulties. For example, a description of the weapon or type of injuries could easily lead to carbon-copy type murders. Some information which has not been publicised is required for elimination purposes or indeed to confront the man responsible. The press and television can rely upon us to reveal as much as we can and I hope we can rely upon their forbearance and understanding.

Someone who did 'strongly suspect' they might know who the Ripper was was Sutcliffe's best friend Trevor Birdsall, who had become suspicious of him following the murder of Jacqueline Hill. He had been out in Sutcliffe's Rover and thought that this could be the 'squarish' car that the police were looking to trace. He had also recently seen Olive Smelt giving an interview on television about the attack on her back in 1975 and he thought that Sutcliffe could have been responsible for that attack too. He had read that the police believed that the Ripper was a 'Geordie', but he still had his suspicions and so rang the freephone number to hear the recording of the 'Sunderland' tape to see if he could tell whether or not it was Sutcliffe putting on a fake accent.

He was certain that the voice wasn't Sutcliffe, but discussed the matter with his girlfriend, Gloria Conroy, (with whom he was living following the break-up of his marriage) and she told him to tell the police of his suspicions anyway – especially as there was now a large reward on offer.

So on 25 November, Birdsall sent an anonymous letter to the police, but wrote down the wrong house number:

> *To whom it may concern,*
> *I am writing to inform you that I have every good reason to believe I now [sic] the man you are looking for in the 'RIPPER CASE'.*
> *It is an incident which happened with the last 5 years. I cannot give any date or place or any details without myself been [sic] known to the ripper or you if this is the man.*
> *It is only until recently that something came to my notice, and now a lot of things fit into place.*

I can only tell you one or two things which fit for example, this man has had dealings with prostitutes and always had a thing about them. Also he is a long distance lorry driver, collecting engineering items etc. I am quite sure if you check up on dates etc., you may find something.

His name and address is

    PETER SUTCLIFFE
    5, GARDEN LANE   CLARKS TRANS.
    HEATON, BRADFORD   SHIPLEY

The letter was marked 'Priority No 1'. An index card was created on the basis of the letter and a policewoman found Sutcliffe already had three existing cards in the records.

The Byford Report found that 'for some inexplicable reason', the papers remained in a filing tray in the Major Incident Room until Sutcliffe's arrest the following January.

The day after Birdsall had sent the anonymous letter, he told his girlfriend what he had done but she didn't think that it was enough so, at 22.10 on the evening of 26 November, the couple visited the main police station, The Tyrls, Bradford.

They were seen by Policewoman Nicholson at the inquiry desk and they told her that they had information in connection with the Ripper crimes. As she was already dealing with someone who was also giving information concerning the Ripper case, PC Butler, a new recruit, dealt with Birdsall and Conroy.

PC Butler interviewed them both and noticed that they had been drinking. He then made the following record in his official notebook:

> On Friday the 16 August 1975 Mr Birdsall was out with Mr Sutcliffe in his car, a blue Ford with white roof, at Halifax at approximately between 11.00 pm and 12.00 pm on Boothtown Road, when we stopped when we saw a woman by herself walking down. Mr Sutcliffe got out of the car and followed her and returned 20 minutes later. He seemed to have changed his manner. He then dropped Mr Birdsall home and said that he was going back home.

At no point was Olive Smelt's name mentioned in Birdsall's interview. Following the interview, PC Butler was unsure about what to do, so he sought the assistance of Policewoman Nicholson who wrote out a report for him using the facts in his pocket book, which, after reading, he signed. The report was transmitted to the Major Incident Room at Millgarth Police Station where it was read by PC Summers. Had the name of Olive Smelt been mentioned then it may have been picked up and treated with more enthusiasm.

However, PC Summers recalls the report because immediately prior to being transferred to the Incident Room on 17 November 1980 he had been a tutor constable to PC Butler at Bradford Central Division and felt some responsibility for the Constable's work. He read the report, noting its contents, and states that the name Smelt was in fact mentioned therein.

PC Summers noted that the report had taken four or five days to arrive and also that it had not been seen by any Supervisory Officer; indexed in accordance with Incident Room Procedures or an Action made out. Accordingly, he placed it in the appropriate basket on the table where he was working for it to be indexed by one of the female indexing team on duty. A 'comprehensive search' took place after Sutcliffe was arrested but it was never found.

It was never established how the report arrived at the Leeds Incident Room without having been seen and annotated by a Senior Officer. Following the Jacqueline Hill murder all information, whether verbal (telephone message forms), letters, or reports from any source were directed to, and received by, the Duty Inspector in the Incident Room, who sorted the information into boxes and into the category of priority or non-priority actions.

The Byford Report stated:

> The failure to take advantage of Birdsall's anonymous letter and his visit to the police station was yet again a stark illustration of the progressive decline in the overall efficiency of the Major Incident Room. It resulted in Sutcliffe being at liberty for more than a month when he might conceivably have been in custody.

The 1983 'Report into the Investigation of the Series of Murders and Assaults on Women in the North of England between 1975 and 1980' states:

> ...the matter was duly reported and submitted to a Sergeant, who caused it to be sent to the Incident Room. Evidence exists that the report was received there but so were a great many others of a similar nature.
>
> ... letters were arriving at this time at the rate of 1,000 daily and anonymous letters received a low priority for obvious reasons. The letter was not acted on before Sutcliffe's arrest.
>
> After Sutcliffe was arrested an investigation was mounted to trace the Constable's report of Mr Birdsall's verbal information to the police but, despite checking 20,475 references and 9,577 action forms, no trace of it has been found.

One person who certainly was wasting the police's time was a man named Steven Bainbridge. He was an unemployed 24-year-old, and on 26 November 1980 he was sentenced to three months imprisonment after contacting the *Daily Mirror* and claiming to be the Ripper. He was found guilty of making threats to kill.

On 1 December, following a recommendation of the external 'Advisory Team', an internal reappraisal team consisting of ten officers, including Superintendent Charlesworth and Superintendent Bass, was appointed to review the 'Letters and Tape Inquiry', the operation of the Major Incident Room, police circulations about the Ripper series and several other issues.

Just two days later, having grown frustrated that detectives were ignoring his warnings, Jack Windsor Lewis, one of the linguistic experts brought in by the Ripper team to tell them where author of the 'Sunderland tape' came from, wrote to the *Yorkshire Post* newspaper and blew apart the theory that the tape and letters could be from the killer. The story was quickly picked up by the national press. Still, the police ignored these warnings and stated that they were 99 per cent certain that they came from the killer.

One week later, on 10 December, Stuart Kind – the Director of the Home Office Central Research Establishment and part of the team put in place to assist the new Acting

Assistant Chief Constable Jim Hobson – wrote a document which stated his reasons for also believing that the Ripper was a local man. They were:

1. He uses a car, probably an old type, with worn cross-ply tyres. Hardly the car for a long distance driver.
2. The centre of gravity of the incidents, weighted and unweighted, tends to be near Bradford.
3. Time of offence correlates well with day length but the late 'fliers' tend to be in Leeds and Bradford.
4. Very good local knowledge.
5. The good description given by the victim Moore does not mention a marked accent, so X probably has a local accent.
6. A five-pound note was issued in Manningham or Shipley (Jordan case in Manchester).

Hypothesis 1
X lives in or near Bradford, possibly in the Manningham or Shipley area.

Hypothesis 2
X selects target towns which are different from the previous two incidents.

Hypothesis 3
X goes out and if unsuccessful in finding a victim in the target town, he looks for one on the way home. It follows that…

Hypothesis 4
The next incident is unlikely to be in Leeds and, on the principle of maximum variety, it is likely to be in Huddersfield or Manchester or, in default, Bradford.

Hypothesis 5
Consideration should be given, should a woman be found in any of these locations suffering from head wounds, to maximum police coverage in Bradford, particularly in the Manningham/Shipley area. Obviously, for maximum likelihood of success, a Manchester incident would give most opportunity for the deployment of police effort.

Leslie Emment, also a part of the team put in place to support Acting Assistant Chief Constable Jim Hobson, wrote an interim report detailing their findings so far. He and the rest of the team had been asked 'To look critically at the past and present conduct of the investigation and comment upon the course of future enquiries.' The report stated:

> We would wish to express at the outset, our admiration for the enormous commitment the West Yorkshire Metropolitan Police has made and sustained over the considerable period of this enquiry, and preface any

comments we make with the clear acknowledgement that we speak with the benefit of hindsight. We are extremely conscious of the pressures which have been, and continue to be, exerted upon individuals and the organisation as a whole. A protracted murder investigation of this kind is, in our experience, unique in the history of the Police Service in this country and for those reasons we believe that the enquiry is of national significance for the Police Service.

At the time of taking up our task, significant changes were in the process of being made in the conduct of the investigation. Mr James Hobson had, some few days earlier, been appointed to head the West Yorkshire Metropolitan Police enquiry and other senior management changes were being implemented. In addition, a 'Review Team' had been appointed. We understand that the Review Team is working to the Officer in Charge of the enquiry, Mr Hobson, and that to date, no specific terms of reference have been documented. This is a factor to which we shall return later in this report. It can thus be fairly said that we entered upon a changing scene which created a climate in which we were able to comment upon matters on a day to day basis by our close contact with Mr Hobson and his senior staff.

During this early formative period, we perceived the need to establish priorities for immediate action. These were discussed as they arose with Mr Hobson and a distillation of these common views were made known to you at a meeting on the 9 December 1980. These may be briefly summarised as follows:

1. Resources and effort to be primarily directed to the Hill murder which had occurred in the 17 November 1980, on the simple basis that as it was still fresh, it gave the best chance of success.
2. To streamline Incident Room procedures which had been inundated with 'Actions' following the recent Hill murder and press and public interest generated by that murder, local events and our own involvement in the enquiry.
3. To increase the staffing levels in both the administrative and operational function to meet these demands, including deployment of additional Regional Crime Squad personnel.
4. To review ground cover policing methods with the aim of preventing/ detecting further similar offences.
5. To plan in detail, the police response to another murder or assault in this series. Not only as regards the physical steps to be taken, such as routine matters of staffing and premises, but more importantly its command and control, integration with the current enquiry, and its effect upon the Major Incident Room.

Having ensured that these immediate steps were in hand, it was apparent that the more medium term problem hinged upon the correct course the enquiry was to follow in future. We recognise the enormous difficulty on this task and are convinced that to enable the Force to make sound judgements, it is necessary to grasp the complexities of the enquiry and in particular to understand:-

1. What has or has not been done?
2. What evidence can be deduced from the overall enquiry to give a weighting to the welter of varying descriptions of suspect persons and vehicles remaining unidentified?

It seems to us, with some over simplification, that these two factors must be answered as quickly as possible and certainly before these important policy decisions are taken. We are of course aware that both these aspects are being actively pursued.

Although you and your Senior Officers are aware of the enormity of the problems faced, we would wish to point out that in our opinion the rest of the Police Service has little concept of the sheer logistical problems involved in the enquiry. We make this point to emphasise the pressing need to evaluate what has been done and what lines of enquiry are now in progress and flowing from this, the importance of the work of the Review Team who are to undertake this task.

Having discussed the proposed time scale of the Review Team's work with Mr Hobson we suspect that its workload may increase significantly. We believe that within its brief, the team should also suggest possible fresh lines of enquiry which may become apparent in their reappraisal. We of course accept that such policy decisions rest with the Investigating Officer but, in view of the sheer volume of information to be sifted, we believe that the Review Team can be of valuable assistance to the Investigating Officer in this respect. To this end we would recommend that the Review Team's workload is carefully monitored so that additional resources can be made available to it if it becomes necessary.

We are aware that the scope of the inquiry has already been reviewed by Chief Superintendent Domaille and his Team which reported some twelve months ago and also of the work done by Commander Nevill. Although we have looked at both these reports and discussed them with Mr Hobson we must say that we remain unclear of the action taken in respect of each report.

The 'letters and tape' aspect is fundamental to any review of the enquiry. During our consideration of this aspect, it became clear that while there was a divergence of views, the majority of officers outside the West Yorkshire Metropolitan Police who are related to the enquiry viz Greater Manchester, Lancashire, Northumbria and Durham, have reservations as to the authenticity of this 'evidence'. Having considered the factors ourselves, we find some difficulty in understanding why the West Yorkshire Police have attached such weight to the letters and tape being authentic. We are aware that one of the priority tasks of the Review Team is to examine this aspect closely. While awaiting their report we believe that the emphasis which has hitherto been placed on the authenticity of the letters and the tape which has led the public and the Police Service at large to believe that the murderer has a North East accent, should be shifted to allow for the possibility of an elaborate hoax. We recommend that the aim of the enquiry should now be to foster an opinion both within and outside the Police Service that the killer does not necessarily originate from the North East of England.

There are additionally a number of other matters which we have raised with Mr Hobson which to date we have not been able to satisfactorily resolve as they require further work. We itemise these recommendations for record purposes:

1. A review with Greater Manchester Police of the £5 note enquiry and its implication for current lines of enquiry.
2. To consider when key witnesses and live victims were last re-interviewed.
3. To establish what photofits or similar impressions have been made and to establish which have been released to the public.
4. To review the current position regarding fingerprint evidence in its widest form with particular reference to Commander Nevill's report.
5. To establish the action taken on Commander Nevill's report.
6. To establish the action taken following the review report by Chief Superintendent Domaille.
7. To clarify how the 'large schedule' and the Special Notice of September 1979 was prepared and published, with particular reference to the differing information contained therein.
8. To consider the appointment of a police officer, preferably a senior Scenes of Crime Officer, to be responsible to the Investigating Officer for all forensic aspects of the enquiry.
9. To review all other assaults on women during the relevant period to establish the grounds upon which some have apparently been excluded from the 'Ripper' series, with possible consequences for the overall enquiry. Such enquiry to include surrounding forces.
10. To review ground cover operations with particular reference to:- (a) Police response to attacks upon women, (b) Command and control functions in response to an incident, (c) Priorities in relation to routes between Nurses Homes and other places where women reside and their places of work in an attempt to identify 'attack areas'.
11. We believe that serious consideration should be given to an instruction calling for the careful examination of all property coming into the possession of the police by an experienced Detective Officer who has the 'Ripper' enquiry in the forefront of his mind.
12. The Review Team, in looking at existing projects, must consider fresh avenues of enquiry based upon the totality of the evidence already in

the system. For example, we have indicated a number of facts which could point to the wanted man living/working in the Bradford area. There will obviously be other inferences which can be drawn from the system which will have to be evaluated.

13. Following our detailed discussions with Professor Gee, while we are conscious that his written report is awaited, we have indicated to Mr Hobson, factors related to the weapon used on the Leach and Whitaker murders and other factors within the system which could point to a person loosely connected with 'farming'.
14. After further consideration of the £5 note aspect of the enquiry with Chief Superintendent Ridgeway of the Greater Manchester Police, to clarify the connection between the £5 note, the Jordan murder and Shipley, we would ask the Investigating Officer to consider the deployment of a small team of high calibre Detective Officers to pursue either or both the two aspects mentioned in 12 and 13 above.

Viewing the changes which are already implemented, and particularly the work of the Review Team, we envisage that some time will elapse before the further information we have discussed becomes available. We therefore propose to leave the Force, beyond occasional visits, until some time perhaps in the middle of January 1981, when the reports of the Review Team and other work now in hand will be available to the Investigating Officer, who may then, through you, wish to consult us further concerning the enquiry. We will be available to the Investigating Officer in the intervening period and would certainly hope to be kept appraised of the situation in the interim. Should these offences remain undetected we believe that at a subsequent meeting, hopefully by the end of January 1981, some positive decisions can be taken as to the course the enquiry should follow and thereafter it would be our intention to submit to you a further and more detailed report to comply with our terms of reference.

We are aware that in certain instances there is a less formal documentation of decision making processes than we feel is desirable. These aspects are being actively pursued by Chief Superintendent Howard but we stress the need to record and document all decisions taken.

Superintendent Charlesworth then wrote an appraisal report in which he identified the criteria which had been established to assess whether or not to include a murder or attack in the Ripper series:

a) Blows to the head with a hammer of diameter 1.2-1.1 inches (plus or minus 5 per cent)
b) Attack on the body with some other stabbing/mutilating instrument
c) Displacement of the brasserie to give access to breasts
d) Lowering of knickers/tights to pubic hair level (in many instances vulva remains covered by crotch of garment precluding penetration).

e) Movement of the body after the initial attack, before the infliction of further injuries – frequently to the trunk.
f) The reluctance of the assailant to stab through clothing.
g) Assailant's return to the body to inflict further injuries or secrete it.

The Byford Report found that:

> It is now apparent that these very restrictive criteria were in fact used on attacks which occurred after the murder of Millward in Manchester ... in two ... cases in particular the victims were able to provide good descriptions of the assailant, including that he had a mandarin or 'Jason King' moustache, and in one case, a goatee beard.
> In the Rooney case, of course ... the victim said that she had seen her assailant sitting in a Sunbeam Rapier motor car before the attack.
> Also excluded, because they did not match the criteria, were the murder of Walls and the attack on Bandara. Although both of these cases involved head injuries, they introduced the apparently novel element of strangulation so that there was perhaps slightly more justification for believing that they had a separate author.
> What is now very clearly established is that had senior detectives of the West Yorkshire Police assembled the photofit impressions from the surviving victims of all hammer assaults, or assaults involving serious head injuries on unaccompanied women, they would have been left with an inescapable conclusion that the man involved was dark haired with a beard and moustache.
> They would also have learned from Olive Smelt, Tracy Browne and Marilyn Moore, all of whom had spoken to him, that he had a local accent and was certainly not noticeably a 'Geordie'.

On 12 December the Home Secretary, William Whitelaw, decided that he would visit the Major Incident Room in Leeds and the West Yorkshire Police HQ in Wakefield to see how the investigation was going.

Just before Christmas, Peter and Sonia Sutcliffe then put their home at 6 Garden Lane, Heaton, Bradford, up for sale, and it's believed the asking price was £37,000. The reason for this, according to Sutcliffe's brother Mick, was that they had been burgled and 'about £3,000 worth of jewellery and cash was taken'. They had decided to buy a country cottage so Sonia could concentrate on her pottery work.

Meanwhile, Trevor Birdsall had heard nothing back from the police following his tip-offs and assumed that they had been acted on and that the police had found nothing to link Sutcliffe to the crimes so, on 28 December, he and his girlfriend Gloria joined Sutcliffe in a local pub for a lunchtime drink to celebrate the festive season. Sonia had stayed at home preparing a special meal for Sutcliffe's family as was their tradition, when they would also exchange presents. On the way home from the pub, Gloria Conroy told Trevor Birdsall that she had felt a churning in her stomach when they had met Sutcliffe and it was with good reason. He was about to go looking for another victim.

Chapter 37

Arrest

At 22.50 on Friday 2 January 1981, Peter Sutcliffe was arrested in his car with a prostitute called Olivia Reivers in the driveway of Light Trades House in Melbourne Avenue, Sheffield, South Yorkshire.

Sutcliffe had left his home in Heaton, Bradford, just after 16.00 and told Sonia that he was going to collect the key of his sister's car which had broken down. However, instead of driving to Bingley, he drove to a scrapyard at Cooper Bridge, Mirfield, on the outskirts of Leeds. While there he stole two registration plates from a Skoda, one which had fallen off the vehicle and one which he pulled off.

At 21.00 that evening he called Sonia from a service station and told her that his car kept breaking down and so didn't know what time he would be home. In fact, he had been fixing the stolen registration plates over his with some black electrical tape and he then began cruising around the Havelock Square red-light district of Sheffield.

The first woman he set his eyes on was 19-year-old Denise Hall, who he had spotted walking along in the area. He wound down his window and asked her if she was 'doing business', but she turned him down and later said that it was because she was frightened by the look in his eye.

About an hour later, at the junction of Broomhall Street and Wharncliffe Road, Sutcliffe was back and this time asked the same question to 24-year-old Olivia St Elmo Reivers. Olivia had left school at 15 and worked in various shops as a sales girl. She moved from Birmingham in 1973 and settled in Sheffield, where she gave birth to her two children, Louise in 1975 and Deroy in 1980. She had been a sex worker for four years and had only had one punter that night before bumping into Sutcliffe. She recalled:

> I don't know why Denise was suspicious, but she turned him down. Obviously something must have warned her off. You might think you can judge people's character by looking at them, but I can't look at a person and decide what sort they are. We were all worried about the Ripper but no one knew what he looked like, we wouldn't have known him if we saw him. Anyway, you can't afford to turn down the chance of ten pounds in this game … I was walking on the pavement when it stopped. The driver asked me if I was doing business and I said I was. I told him it was £10 in the car with a rubber. He said that was OK.

She then got in the Rover and they drove around half-a-mile to Melbourne Avenue and parked towards the back on the driveway of the Light Trades House. Reivers recalled:

He stopped his car and turned out the lights. I said to him: 'Would you like to pay first, please?' He gave me a £10 note and I took a rubber out and had it in my hand putting the money in the packet. He asked: 'Do you mind if I talk to you a bit?' I said: 'No'. He said that he had had an argument with his wife. He did not say what about or what the result of the argument had been. He asked me my name and I said 'Sharon'. He said his name was 'Dave'. He then took off his car-coat and put it on the back seat. He said: 'Would you like to get in the back?' I said: 'No, it's alright'.

Reivers then removed her knickers and Sutcliffe leaned across her with his fly unzipped, and she touched his penis. He then lowered himself on to her and for the next ten minutes tried to have sex, but could not get an erection. She said to him: 'I don't think we'll be able to do it', and he replied: 'It looks like it.' She later recalled:

> he was a bit nervous ... It was then that I began to sense something was wrong. Drunks who don't measure up to it get angry with themselves, but this was the first guy I'd come across who couldn't manage it when he was stone cold sober. Then I noticed he became tense, frightened like, though I don't know what of. For some reason, which I still can't explain, I began to get nervous myself. He was showing no signs of wanting to drive off and I began thinking that he never intended to have sex with me in the first place. I was trying to work out why he had paid me ten pounds.

The conversation then moved back to Sutcliffe telling her that he was not 'able to go with' his wife and just then the car was lit up by the headlights from another car that parked bumper-to-bumper with his Rover. It was the police and, in all probability, they had just saved Olivia Reivers' life. Sutcliffe had nowhere to go.

Sergeant Robert Ring and Probationary Constable Robert Hydes began their nightshift at nearby Hammerton Road Police Station at 22.00 that evening. Sergeant Ring had decided that as Hydes had not yet dealt with prostitutes and their punters, they would set off for the red-light district to give him some experience.

At around 22.30 they drove past Melbourne Avenue and spotted Sutcliffe's Rover parked up the driveway of the Light Trades House, and Sergeant Ring knew there was only likely to be one explanation as to why it was parked there.

Robert Hydes approached the Rover first and as he did so, Sutcliffe told Reivers: 'Leave it to me. You're my girlfriend.' After winding down the window, Constable Hydes asked him what he was doing there, and Sutcliffe replied that he was just talking to his girlfriend. He also told the policeman that his name was 'Peter Williams'.

As this was happening, Sergeant Ring walked to the back of the vehicle and noted the registration plate before returning to the police car and radioing for a check on the plate with the National Police Computer in Hendon. He immediately recognised Olivia Reivers as a local prostitute. As Sergeant Ring was awaiting the results, Constable Hydes returned to the police vehicle and said that he was very sceptical of the information he had been given.

By chance, anti-vice officers Police Sergeant Armitage and Constable Tune were in the control room when the call was received and they immediately identified Olivia Reivers as a convicted prostitute who was the subject of a suspended sentence.

As Sutcliffe was now alone with Reivers, he asked her if she could make a run for it, but she told him that there was no point as she was well-known to the police anyway.

The check of the car registration plate came back as belonging to a Skoda that was owned by a Mr Aslam Khan, so the officers got out and went back to the Rover. Sergeant Ring's police report stated:

> He said that she's my girlfriend and I asked what her name was. He said, 'I don't know, I have not known her that long.' I said, 'Who are you trying to kid? I haven't fallen off the Christmas tree.' To which Sutcliffe replied, 'I'm not suggesting you have'.

As Sergeant Ring leaned into the car and removed the keys from the ignition, he told Sutcliffe that he knew the registration plates were from a different car and so was the tax disc. Sutcliffe, aware that he was about to be arrested, was anxious that the matter be sorted there and then. Sergeant Ring later told the press: '...he produced documents and gave some reason for being in possession of the licence plates. He was anxious we should not arrest him.' He then arrested both Sutcliffe and Reivers on the suspicion of theft before both officers escorted Reivers to their patrol car.

Sutcliffe now knew that he was in deep trouble. Quickly and quietly he grabbed the ball pein hammer and knife that he had been concealing from under his seat, stepped out of his car and walked quietly over to a dark area behind the building. The officers asked him where he was going and Sutcliffe replied that he was 'bursting for a pee'.

Out of sight of the officers, Sutcliffe found an oil storage tank behind the building and took the knife and hammer out of his jacket pocket before dropping them softly onto some leaves. He then covered them over by kicking more leaves on top of them. Sergeant Ring recalled:

> Sutcliffe was coming from this direction. I said, 'What are you doing there?', He said, 'I've fallen off that fucking wall.' I said, 'What were you doing there?' he said, 'I wanted to piss.' I told him to go at the side of the building if he wanted to, but he said he wouldn't bother.

He was then also put into the back of the patrol car while the officers secured his Rover.

As soon as they arrived at Hammerton Road Police Station, Sutcliffe asked if he could now go to the toilet and, as the officers had no reason to suspect that he was anything other than just a punter, he was allowed to do so. It was here that Sutcliffe was able to get rid of a second knife, one that he had concealed in his jacket and was only accessible through a small hole in the pocket. He was able to reach up and hide it in the toilet cistern. It is not clear why he didn't get rid of this knife behind the building at the same time as he hid the other knife and the ball pein hammer. For whatever reason, he decided not to dispose of the piece of rope that was also in his jacket – the same piece of rope that he had strangled Marguerite Walls to death with and had attempted to murder Uphadya Bandara with.

Sergeant Ring, Sutcliffe and Olivia Reivers were then seen by Sergeant Armitage and Constable Tune, who were eager to learn more about the circumstances surrounding the arrest. After a brief chat, Armitage and Tune decided to pay a visit to where Sutcliffe had been arrested.

When they arrived, the first thing that struck them as odd was the fact that Sutcliffe's Rover was facing the road, as usually punters who parked there faced the opposite way for more privacy. We now know that Sutcliffe did this so that he could make a quick getaway.

They looked at the car more closely and it became obvious to them that the registration plates had been taped over the original ones, which were still attached to the car, with some black adhesive tape.

While this was going on, back at the station Sutcliffe felt that there was still a chance to get himself out of this mess. After all, he was only likely to face a charge of theft of the number plates if he could get his story straight. He told the officers his real name and address and then he admitted to the theft of the registration plates, hoping to get out of the station as quickly as possible and back to the scene of his arrest so that he could pick up his knife and hammer before anyone had a chance to discover them.

He told the interviewing officers, DC Bedford and DC Harvey, that he had stolen the registration plates because he was due in court on a drink-driving charge in less than two weeks and that 'The insurance had just run out, and I knew I were about to lose my licence in court, so it weren't worth renewing it.'

He was terrified that Sonia would find out that he had been arrested with a prostitute, so when he was asked for his phone number by the officers he gave them a false one, hoping that they wouldn't check. He was then led to his cell. But the police did check, and when they got through they succeeded only in waking up an Asian family. The police knew that something wasn't quite right.

The officers then rang their counterparts at the Divisional Police Headquarters in Dewsbury, which covered the area from which the registration plates had been stolen, and told them about the theft. The officers at Dewsbury said that they would send some officers to collect Sutcliffe and his car when the morning shift arrived at 06.00.

They then telephoned the Ripper Incident Room at Millgarth Police Station in Leeds. This was because following the poor response from the police (and the press criticism) after the murder of Jacqueline Hill, Chief Constable Ronald Gregory had directed that all men found with a prostitute in suspicious circumstances should be brought to the attention of the Ripper Squad.

Sergeant Ring spoke to Detective Sergeant Bennett and gave him all the details surrounding Sutcliffe's arrest and then asked if the Ripper Inquiry were interested in him. DS Bennett said that he would check the files and call him back.

DS Bennett was able to find that Sutcliffe did have an index card and that it showed that he had been interviewed regarding the £5 note inquiry and also as a result of the 'Cross Area Sighting'. There was also a note saying that his handwriting did not match that of the letters sent from Sunderland and that he had a shoe size of 8½. It also mentioned that he had a gap in the centre of his upper teeth.

DS Bennett wasn't convinced that the reason given for him being eliminated from the inquiry (his handwriting) was particularly strong and so he decided to check for any other papers relating to him that may have been in the system. He was able to find a handwritten statement by Sutcliffe in which he said that he was a long-distance lorry driver (a possible occupation of the Ripper) and that he had denied ever going with a prostitute.

He then checked to see what alibis Sutcliffe had been given for some of the murders and saw that it was mainly his wife who had put him in the clear. The records also showed that some of the interviewing officers were unable to completely eliminate Sutcliffe.

DS Bennett read the reports in full and decided that Sutcliffe was a suspect worthy of re-interviewing regarding the Ripper murders and that he should be kept in police custody. He then telephoned Hammerton Road Police Station and this time he spoke to the other arresting officer, Constable Hydes, and told him that Sutcliffe should not be released.

Three officers from West Yorkshire Police drove down to Sheffield to pick up Sutcliffe and his Rover. They left Hammerton Road Police Station at 08.20 and arrived back at Dewsbury Police Station at 08.55. Throughout the entire journey Sutcliffe hardly said a word.

Just four minutes later, Sutcliffe was being logged in by the desk Sergeant and for the first time he was asked to turn out his pockets, where it was discovered that he had some money that hadn't been picked up by their counterparts in Sheffield. His car was searched next and it was here that the police found three screwdrivers in the glove compartment, including red and blue handled ones.

He was then taken and interviewed, where he freely spoke about his life in general and admitted that he was a lorry driver from Bradford and that he had made regular trips up to Sunderland with his job. He also told the officers that he had previously been interviewed as part of the £5 note inquiry and as a result of the 'Cross Area Sightings'.

Now that the officers had Sutcliffe's correct details, they telephoned Sonia to tell her that they had arrested her husband in regard to the theft of car registration plates. They made no mention of the fact that he had been with a prostitute when arrested, or that they were questioning him in regard to the Yorkshire Ripper attacks.

At the same time they also called the Ripper Incident Room and told them that they ought to take another look at Sutcliffe and to send someone to interview him as they believed he bore a striking resemblance to some of the photofits, had the same hair and facial hair, and also wore the same size shoe as found at three of the attack scenes.

Detective Sergeant Desmond O'Boyle and Detective Constable Rod Hill from the Ripper Squad arrived two hours later, having familiarised themselves with Sutcliffe's files. Shortly after, they interviewed Sutcliffe and discussed his background. Sutcliffe was cooperative throughout and never asked for a solicitor.

Questioning then moved on to Sutcliffe's movements on the evening he was arrested. He said he had left home at around 16.00 to look for spare parts for his Mini (which he had actually already sold) and his Rover. He said that while walking around the scrapyard he saw one of the registration plates laying on the floor and the other he decided to pull off a Skoda. He then explained that he had decided to steal them because he was due in court in a couple of weeks on a drink-driving charge and fully expected to lose his licence. As such, his insurance had expired a couple of weeks before and he saw no point in renewing it.

DS O'Boyle then asked Sutcliffe whether he and his wife had 'normal sex', to which Sutcliffe replied that they did and that 'the last time was about four days ago'. He was then asked if they had a good relationship and he replied: 'We forget about rows when we go to bed.'

He was cooperative throughout the interview, but his demeanour changed when he was asked to provide a blood sample and then, oddly, he asked: 'What if it's the same as the one you're wanting?'

DS O'Boyle found this an odd question and asked Sutcliffe directly if he was the Ripper. Sutcliffe replied that he wasn't, but then asked DS O'Boyle to let him know the result as soon as he had it.

Despite these odd comments, by 17.30 DS O'Boyle felt that Sutcliffe was highly unlikely to be the Ripper and was about to recommend that he be released; when Chief Superintendent John Clark, who was in charge at Dewsbury Police Station, got wind of this however, he remained to be convinced of Sutcliffe's innocence and told DS O'Boyle to call the Ripper Incident Room at Millgarth Police Station and express his 'displeasure' that no one ranked higher than a DS had been sent to interview Sutcliffe.

Detective Inspector John Boyle had just come on to shift in the Ripper Incident Room and, as the highest ranked officer there, was in charge. He agreed with Chief Superintendent Clark that Sutcliffe shouldn't be released yet and told DS O'Boyle to continue to question Sutcliffe to get a better understanding of his background.

DS O'Boyle then re-interviewed Sutcliffe and asked him to explain how he had come to be in Sheffield on the night he was arrested. Bizarrely, Sutcliffe came up with a story in which he stated that after he left the scrapyard with the registration plates he had just stolen, he gave three men a lift to Rotherham and Sheffield and that, 'To my surprise, they offered me £10 to take them.'

He said that as he found himself in Sheffield, he put the false plates on his Rover and then, while he was driving, a woman flagged him down and he stopped because he thought she might be in some sort of trouble. She then asked him if he 'wanted business'.

Sutcliffe recalled:

> I was surprised I did not know she was a prostitute. I thought about things and realised I had £10 burning a hole in my pocket, and I thought I might as well use it. The first girl had disappeared, so I drove on and saw another girl and stopped. She asked me if I wanted business. She got into the car and told me where to drive. I paid her £10. I did not want sex – I just wanted to talk about my problems at home. I did not want sex at all.

Questioning then moved on to the amount of times that his cars had been spotted in the red-light areas of Bradford, Leeds and Manchester, and Sutcliffe stuck to his story of never having been in Manchester – but then offered quite a bizarre possibility. He said that on the day his car was spotted in Manchester, it had actually broken down and he had left it in the car park at Bradford Central Library and that 'someone must have used it to go to Manchester and put it back on that spot'.

He was asked to explain why someone would fix his broken car, drive to Manchester and then bring the car back and put it back on the exact same spot, but Sutcliffe was unable to offer any explanation.

He was then asked to explain his whereabouts on the evening of Jacqueline Hill's murder; he stated that he was certain he was at home all evening with his wife. DS O'Boyle told Sutcliffe he would speak to Sonia the following morning and check out the story. Sutcliffe seemed alarmed by this and pleaded with the detective not to tell her that he had been arrested with a prostitute, but DS O'Boyle told him: 'You got yourself into this. As far as I'm concerned, I think you are a regular punter.' Sutcliffe answered: 'I am not. I've never been with another woman.' DS O'Boyle then said: 'Your car has been seen in the red-light districts of Leeds and Manchester and last night you were caught in a car with a prostitute in Sheffield and you paid her £10. I don't believe these are coincidences.' Sutcliffe then stated: 'It is true – I am not a punter.'

When the interviews had finished for the day, Sutcliffe was locked back in his cell for the night and at 22.00, back in Sheffield, Sergeant Ring came back on duty at Hammerton Road Police Station. He was told by the duty Inspector that Sutcliffe was still in custody, had been taken to Dewsbury and was being questioned by detectives from the Ripper Squad.

Sergeant Ring was trying to think of anything Sutcliffe might have said or done that could help the detectives questioning him, and then remembered Sutcliffe had snuck off to find somewhere to urinate and so decided to go back to the scene and search the area.

He got back to the scene of the arrest at 23.05 and recalled in his statement: 'At the corner of the building and near an oil storage tank among a pile of leaves, I saw an Engineer's ball pein hammer and on closer examination saw the shiny blade of a wooden-handled knife, partially covered by the hammer shaft.'

He immediately radioed back to Hammerton Road and informed them of his discovery and they called the Ripper Major Incident Room. DC David Green of the Scenes of Crimes Department then arrived and photographed the instruments before taking possession of them.

It wasn't until around 01.00 that DI Boyle deemed the new information important enough to telephone Detective Superintendent Dick Holland at his home near Huddersfield and said in a rather excited voice: 'I think we've got him.'

Detective Superintendent Holland told DI Boyle that he wanted an officer stationed outside Sutcliffe's cell in case he tried to commit suicide, and that a briefing would take place at 09.00 at Bradford police headquarters.

DI Boyle then drove straight to Sheffield to join DS O'Boyle and as soon as he arrived he ordered a thorough search of the area where the knife and hammer had been found and ordered Olivia Reivers to be re-interviewed.

At 11.15 on 4 January, following the briefing at Bradford police headquarters, Detective Superintendent Dick Holland, DS O'Boyle, DCI George Smith and DC Jenny Crawford-Brown went to Sutcliffe's home address armed with a search warrant and were met at the door by Sonia. They did a thorough search of the house and garage. Detective Superintendent Dick Holland recalled:

> The first thing I saw was a wooden block with kitchen knives in. The type of block with slots in. It was obvious that the second largest knife of the

set was the one I had covered in clear polythene in my hand – the one that had been found behind the oil tank in Sheffield.

This is the knife that was used in the murder of Helen Rytka.

Sutcliffe's wellington boots, which should have been found on a previous search, were this time discovered and they were found to be the ones worn at the scene of the murders of Emily Jackson and Patricia Atkinson. Then came the search of Sutcliffe's garage, where the police discovered a number of tools, including the yellow-handled screwdriver which he had used to murder Jacqueline Hill in Leeds, and the hacksaw he had used to try to decapitate Jean Jordan in Manchester.

Detectives then went back to the station and took Sonia in for questioning. She was interviewed almost immediately and the police were keen to get an idea of the relationship between her and her husband; they asked her about her husband's movements over the previous two months. She was shown the knife that had been found alongside the ball pein hammer at the scene of Sutcliffe's arrest and confirmed that it was one from a set in their kitchen, and that she had bought the set before she got married. Her interviews lasted until around 20.00 that night, with a brief break in the afternoon.

Meanwhile, back at Dewsbury, Sutcliffe had had breakfast and was taken to be interviewed by DI Boyle and DS Peter Smith, who had been specifically tasked by Detective Superintendent Dick Holland to interview Sutcliffe due to his extensive knowledge of the Ripper murders.

The morning interviews were of a general nature and there was no mention of the Yorkshire Ripper attacks, even though by now the detectives were almost certain they had their man. Instead, they asked questions intended to close down any avenue of escape Sutcliffe may come up with. Sutcliffe was still being cooperative and again did not ask for a solicitor.

When the detectives felt that they had done a good enough job in shutting down any possible escape route for Sutcliffe, the interviews held that afternoon concentrated on the dates of some of the Ripper attacks and in particular 5 November 1980 – the attack on Theresa Sykes.

His work records showed that he had left work at 17.03 that evening and Sutcliffe said that he had gone for a quick drink and that he was certain he was home by 20.00. He was certain he was at home by then because otherwise he would have remembered seeing the bonfires.

Unknown to him, and for the very first time, his wife Sonia gave a different account. She had stated that she clearly remembered him walking through the door not at 20.00 – but at 22.00. Theresa had been attacked at 20.00, which gave Sutcliffe more than enough time to clean himself up and make his way home.

Sonia later told reporters about her questioning:

> I sat in a room for five hours while five policemen fired questions at me. It was a terrible ordeal. They went through my life with a fine toothcomb. I knew nothing.
>
> Of course, the first question in people's mind is did I suspect anything. Well, the police are satisfied that I didn't, and I can honestly say I knew

nothing. The way I see it I'm going to have criticism whatever I do. I know you can't hide yourself away forever. So now I've got to get on with my life. I just can't do nothing.

Sutcliffe was then asked where he had been on the night of Jacqueline Hill's murder – 17 November, and he replied that he had been at home with his wife.

DI Boyle: Every time you have been seen, you always seem to have the same alibi – that you were at home with your wife. I find that rather strange. How can you be sure that's where you were?

Sutcliffe: I'm always at home every night when I'm not on an overnight stay.

DI Boyle switched the focus of the interview to the night of Sutcliffe's arrest in Sheffield and, for the first time, Sutcliffe's composure began to slip. In an interview held between 12.30–13.30, Peter Sutcliffe finally confessed to being the Yorkshire Ripper:

DI Boyle: I understand you were interviewed yesterday by DS O'Boyle about your movements during last Friday afternoon and evening up until the time you were arrested at Sheffield.

Sutcliffe: Yes, I've told him what happened.

DI Boyle: I am not concerned with the allegation of theft of car number plates. I want to speak to you about a more serious matter, concerning your reason for going to Sheffield that night.

Sutcliffe: I've told him all about that night.

DI Boyle: I've spoken to Sergeant O'Boyle and I am not satisfied with your account of that night.

Sutcliffe: What do you mean?

DI Boyle: Why did you go to Sheffield that night?

Sutcliffe: I gave three people a lift to Rotherham and Sheffield from Bradford. They stopped me on the M606 and offered me £10 to take them home, so I did.

DI Boyle: I don't believe that. I believe you went to Sheffield on Friday night with the sole purpose of picking up a prostitute.

Sutcliffe: That's not true. It was only after I got to Sheffield and had declined an offer to go with a prostitute that I decided to use the money I got from the hitch-hikers and go with one.

DI Boyle: When you were arrested in Sheffield you had a prostitute in your car which had false plates on it. I believe you put them on to conceal the identity of your vehicle in the event of it being seen in a prostitute area.

Sutcliffe: No, that's not true. To be honest with you, I've been so depressed that I put them on because I was thinking of committing a crime with the car.

DI Boyle: I believe the crime you were going to commit was to harm a prostitute.

Sutcliffe: No, that's not true.

DI Boyle: Do you recall that before you were put in a police car at Sheffield you left your car and went to the side of a house?

Sutcliffe: Yes, I went to urinate against the wall.

DI Boyle: I think you went for another purpose.

There was no response from Sutcliffe.

DI Boyle: Do you understand what I am saying? I think you are in trouble, serious trouble.

Sutcliffe: I think you have been leading up to it.

DI Boyle: Leading up to what?

Sutcliffe: The Yorkshire Ripper.

DI Boyle: What about the Yorkshire Ripper?

Sutcliffe: Well, it's me.

DI Boyle: Peter, before you say anything further I must tell you you are not obliged to say anything unless you wish to do so but what you say may be put in writing and given in evidence. Do you understand?

Sutcliffe: Yes, I understand.

DI Boyle: If you wish, you may have a solicitor present on your behalf?

Sutcliffe: No, I don't need one. I just want to tell you what I've done. I'm glad it's all over. I would have killed that girl in Sheffield if I hadn't been caught, but I'd like to tell my wife myself. I don't want her to hear about it from anyone else. It's her I'm thinking about, and my family. I'm not bothered about myself.

DI Boyle: You didn't go to the side of the house to urinate, did you?

Sutcliffe: No, I knew what you were leading up to. You've found the hammer and the knife, haven't you?

DI Boyle: Yes we have, where did you put them?

Sutcliffe: When they took the girl to the Panda car I nipped out and put them near the house in the corner. I was panicking, I was hoping to get bail from there and get a taxi back to pick them up. Then I would have been in the clear.

DI Boyle: Tell me, if you are the so-called Ripper, how many women have you killed?

Sutcliffe: Eleven, but I haven't done that one at Preston. I've been to Preston but I haven't done that one.

DI Boyle: Are you the author of the letters and the tape-recording posted from Sunderland to the police and the press from a man admitting to be the Ripper?

Sutcliffe: No, I am not. While ever that was going on I felt safe. I'm not a Geordie. I was born at Shipley.

DI Boyle: Have you any idea who sent the letters and the tape?

Sutcliffe: No, it's no one connected with me. I've no idea who sent them.

DI Boyle: How did this all start?

Sutcliffe: With Wilma McCann. I didn't mean to kill her at first, but she was mocking me. After that it just grew and grew until I became a beast.

Later on, in an interview at 14.50, Sutcliffe was asked:

DI Boyle: Do you know the names of your victims?

Sutcliffe: Yes, I know them all.

DI Boyle: Do you keep any press cuttings of them or make any records?

Sutcliffe: No, they are all in my brain reminding me of the beast I am.

DI Boyle: You say you have killed eleven women. Just take your time and think about how many there are.

Sutcliffe: It's twelve, not eleven. Just thinking about them all reminds me what a monster I am. I know I would have gone on and on but now I'm glad I've been caught, and I just want to unload the burden.

He then went on to give a very calculated description of some of the attacks and murders that he had committed. He gave the detectives information that had not been released to the public and that only the Ripper would know, such as the attempt to decapitate Jean Jordan and the stuffing of horsehair from an old settee down the throat of Yvonne Pearson. He also told the detectives where he had discarded some of the weapons he had used and drew a picture of the walling hammer he had used in the murder of Yvonne Pearson.

Sutcliffe's confession took a total of fifteen hours and forty-five minutes to dictate but it only gave details of twelve murders and two attempted murders – not the full twenty attacks with which he was eventually charged, and certainly not the thirty-two attacks it is now believed he carried out.

Chief Constable Ronald Gregory got wind of Sutcliffe's confession and hastily arranged a press conference for 21.00 that evening. As such, Olivia Reivers and Denise Hall were taken into protective custody to give them time to digest the news and to keep them away from the press. They were first taken to Hammerton Road Police Station and then at 03.00 on to the Hallam Tower Hotel.

The following is the press conference held by the West Yorkshire Police at 21.00 on Sunday, 4 January 1981, announcing the arrest of a suspect in the Yorkshire Ripper case. This press conference should not have been held, because at this point Sutcliffe had been arrested, but not charged with any offence relating to the attacks and murders. Any comment from senior officers to the press could well have prejudiced a future trial. It was held by Chief Constable Ronald Gregory, Acting Assistant Chief Constable Jim Hobson and Assistant Chief Constable George Oldfield.

It began with the Chief Constable of West Yorkshire, Ronald Gregory, announcing:

> On Friday evening last, a man was detained in Sheffield by the Sheffield police in connection with a matter which was identified as theft of number plates of a motor car and the number plates had been stolen from the West Yorkshire area.
>
> He was brought to West Yorkshire as a result of discussions between the South Yorkshire police and the West Yorkshire police; further inquiries were made and this man is now detained here in West Yorkshire and he is being questioned in relation to the Yorkshire Ripper murders.
>
> It is anticipated that he will appear before the court in Dewsbury tomorrow. I cannot say where he is at the moment because a lot of inquiries have to be made. Mr Oldfield and Mr Hobson and other senior investigating officers have to make a number of inquiries tonight but I can tell you we are absolutely delighted with developments at this stage, absolutely delighted.

Chief Constable Ronald Gregory then began taking questions from the gathered press:

> **Press:** Can you give us any details at all about the man?
>
> **Gregory:** No, not at this stage because a man is being interviewed at this very moment in time. But indications are that there will be a charge later tomorrow.
>
> **Press:** Can you tell us whether he has a Geordie accent?
>
> **Gregory:** I cannot tell you that because I've not heard him speak.
>
> **Press:** Can you give us any details of the arrest Mr Gregory? The circumstances of it, if not actual details?
>
> **Gregory:** All I can say is that he was detained in Sheffield. He was with a lady ... he was detained in relation to an incident in Sheffield and he was detained, let me tell you, by a sergeant – two outstanding police officers – a Sergeant Ring of the South Yorkshire Police, Robert Ring, and a Constable

Robert John Hydes of the South Yorkshire Police. They're uniformed officers who have my heartfelt thanks, who made this original detection and as a result of questioning later on by West Yorkshire Police we have reached the present stage but it is just the initial stages and I thought you should know now before we go any further.

Press: Are you scaling down the operation with the general hunt for the Yorkshire Ripper from this moment on?

Gregory: Right.

Press: Do you know yet, sir, what he'll be charged with in the morning? Will it be the motoring offence probably?

Gregory: I can't tell you what the charge will be at this moment but it may be a serious charge.

Press: Can you say whether the two officers were on foot or in a vehicle?

Gregory: The South Yorkshire officers? I think they were on an anti-vice patrol.

Press: Would that imply foot, or vehicle?

Gregory: Vehicle.

Press: Can you say what time?

Gregory: About 11 o'clock on Friday evening.

Press: PM ?

Gregory: Yes, pm

Press: Can you tell us where it was?

Gregory: In Sheffield. I am sorry I am not certain of the area.

Press: Was it near a motorway?

Gregory: Near the centre of Sheffield.

Press: Can you say if there was any violence of any sort?

Gregory: None at all.

Press: Can you tell us whether it was a red light district?

Gregory: I cannot tell you that, I don't know.

Press: What has happened to the lady who was there? You mentioned a lady?

Gregory: She has not come to any harm.

Press: Is she helping with your inquiries?

Gregory: She is, yes.

Press: Does that mean she is under arrest?

Gregory: No, she's not under arrest.

Press: Was it a woman he was with?

Gregory: He was with a lady, yes.

Press: Was she an acquaintance of long standing?

Gregory: No.

Press: Was this car being sought because there had been some sort of incident earlier?

Gregory: No.

Press: Would the officers first stop him because of the question of number plates or because of the lady?

Gregory: They came upon him in a certain position and they looked at the car, checked on the number plates and found they were false.

Press: Would it be fair to say it was an indelicate position?

Gregory: I can't say whether it was number 4-64, or what, I don't know what the position was at all.

Press: At that stage was the lady injured in any way?

Gregory: None at all.

Press: Was he injured?

Gregory: Not at all, no.

Press: Were they in a state of undress?

Gregory: I don't think so, I can't say, I don't know. I have not seen you see, all the statements have not come through yet.

Press: But the car was at a standstill, it wasn't flagged down?

Gregory: No, it was at a standstill.

Press: Can you tell us what car Mr Gregory?

Gregory: It was a Rover motor car.

Press: Was that the old style or the new style?

Gregory: ...bearing false plates. I don't know.

Press: What colour was it?

Gregory: Dark colour VHS.

Press: Can you, getting down to the really important things, are you able to tell us the man's ... without giving his name?

Gregory: His name will be disclosed tomorrow.

Press: What about his age?

Gregory: His age will be disclosed tomorrow, he's about 30 odd and he comes from Bradford.

Press: Is he married?

Gregory: I think he is a married man.

Press: Had he got a North East accent?

Gregory: I don't know about that, I don't know yet. I've not spoken to him, he's a married man.

Press: Is he a family man?

Gregory: I don't know.

Press: As far as you know Sir is he or has he been observed ... to be living with his wife?

Gregory: It's too early to go into too much detail and if I could I would tell you but he's helping police with their inquiries at this very moment in time.

Press: Do we have an occupation for him, Sir?

Gregory: I don't know his occupation, No.

Sgt. Robert Ring and PC Hydes were at home looking forward to some time off. Chief Constable, James Brownlow called Sgt Ring at home. After a short conversation, he turned to his wife and told her: 'It looks as if I may have caught the Ripper!'

PC Hydes heard the news in much the same way. South Yorkshire operations room phoned him with instructions to ring his Chief Constable, James Brownlow, at his home.

Sgt Ring later recalled to the *Police Gazette*:

> It still hasn't sunk in. We'd started duty at 10 pm and I went out with Bob Hydes who was posted to a car beat. He was driving, and when he got out to issue a fixed penalty ticket, I took over to get the police car off the double yellow lines.
>
> Then we went to Melborne Avenue where a lot of local ladies take their clients. We saw this Rover and I told Bob to check the driver while I checked the car. The PNC showed that the number was allocated to a Skoda, so we re-checked it. In the meantime, the driver had been giving Bob details which he found unsatisfactory. I told Bob to arrest him and the woman with him for theft, and to caution them. We took him back to Hammerton Road Police Station.
>
> Whenever we get possible suspects through age, circumstances, description, we tell the Ripper Squad, and at that stage he was just another good suspect.
>
> I was hoping to be off from Sunday until Wednesday, but I didn't mind coming back for duty for this.

PC Hydes recalled:

> I'd only just passed the driving course and New Year's night was the first time I'd been driving on my own. After parade on Friday night, Sgt Ring said he'd come out with me.
>
> After we'd arrested him, and contacted the Ripper Squad, I suppose I thought there might be a chance that we had got the right man, but a lot of bobbies must have thought that about a lot of suspects.

Meanwhile, at South Yorkshire police headquarters in Sheffield, PC Hydes and Sgt Ring attended a special 'parade' for the press. Both policemen said they were 'delighted, although it is of course too early to say any more'. Sgt Ring told the gathered press that it was 'just straight forward coppering'.

Chief Constable James Brownlow later defended his decision to allow the press access to his officers:

> Following the arresting officers being identified by statements made to the press and intense press activity being concentrated in the Sheffield area, I allowed the two officers to be photographed and interviewed but in controlled circumstances so there would be no prejudice to the course of justice.
>
> My principal objective was to prevent as far as possible inaccurate rumour and speculation which would be contrary to everyone's interest. I believe the objective was achieved.

At 22.30 that evening, Sutcliffe's request to be the one to tell his wife about his confession was granted.

> **Sonia:** What on Earth is going on Peter?
>
> **Sutcliffe:** It's all those women. I've killed all those women.
>
> **Sonia:** What on Earth did you do that for, Peter? Even a sparrow has a right to live.

They were given ten minutes together; bizarrely, Sonia was more concerned about whether he had slept with the women, than how – and more importantly why – he had attacked and murdered these women in such a brutal fashion. He assured her he'd only had sex with one, Helen Rytka, and even then he hadn't really wanted to. This was an odd conversation, but then they were an odd couple. Sonia was then given a bed for the night in the accommodation block next door.

Meanwhile, in the Major Incident Room, detectives were again searching the index for information on Sutcliffe and they had a look again at the 'Cross Area Sightings' and discovered, for the first time, that Sutcliffe's Rover had been noted on seven separate occasions in the red-light area of Bradford.

Chapter 38

Interviews

At 07.45 the following morning, 5 January, Sonia was allowed to telephone her mother and her sister to warn them of what had happened before they read about it in the newspapers – but she was too late. Her sister, Marianne, had reporters on her door who had already told her. Sonia and her sister kept reverting to Czech during their conversation and the police, who were monitoring the phone call, kept threatening to terminate the call if she wouldn't speak in English.

Two hours later, Sutcliffe began to conclude his voluntary statement that had started the previous day. DI Boyle, DS O'Boyle and DS Smith were present this time.

DS O'Boyle produced the hammer and the knife found at the scene of his arrest and reminded Sutcliffe of the caution.

>**DS O'Boyle:** Have you seen these before?
>
>**Sutcliffe:** Yes, they're mine. Those are the ones that I left at the house in Sheffield.

DS O'Boyle then produced a blue and pink cord.

>**DS O'Boyle:** This was found in your possession. I believe you may have used this in an attack on a woman.
>
>**Sutcliffe:** Yes, I used it on that girl at Headingley not so long ago. She was walking slow like a prostitute. I followed her down the narrow road. I hit her on the head with a hammer. I didn't have any tools on me to finish her, so I used that rope to strangle her, but I was overcome with remorse so I didn't finish her off. I apologised to her and left her there.
>
>**DS O'Boyle:** There was a student called Bandara attacked in Chapel Lane on Wednesday 24 September last year.
>
>**Sutcliffe:** That's the one I'm talking about…
>
>**DS O'Boyle:** A similar incident to that happened on 20 August 1980 when a woman called Marguerite Walls was found murdered having been attacked and strangled in a similar fashion at Pudsey. Did you do that?
>
>**Sutcliffe:** No, that wasn't me. You have a mystery on your hands with that one. I've only used the rope once on that girl at Headingley.

DS O'Boyle: Do you recall me asking you where you were last Bonfire Night? I've made some enquiries and I now believe you attacked a girl called Teresa Sykes at Huddersfield that night, about 8 pm.

Sutcliffe: Yes, that's right, I did. I saw her walking along the road and followed her down this footpath and hit her a couple of times and knocked her down. But someone started shouting and I ran away and hid in a garden.

DS O'Boyle: Is there anything else you want to tell me?

Sutcliffe: All this really started in 1974. I was done out of £10 by a prostitute in Manningham. She went to get it changed at a garage next to the Belle Vue pub and didn't come back. This poisoned my mind against prostitutes.

The interviewing officers were being put under enormous pressure to get Sutcliffe charged and into court by Chief Constable Ronald Gregory, and DS O'Boyle recalled: 'Mr Gregory was saying, "You have to get this man into court, I want him in court now." It was said that they couldn't cope with the crowds and that if we didn't hurry up there could be all sorts of grief.'

If the interviewing officers had more time to question Sutcliffe, would they have been able to get more confessions out of him? We'll never know, but what we do know is that they had to leave out references and details of the attacks on women who had survived.

As they were getting ready to charge Sutcliffe with the murder of the most recent victim, Jacqueline Hill, it suddenly dawned on the officers that Sutcliffe had not been searched. This should have been done as soon as he arrived at Dewsbury.

Slowly, Sutcliffe began to remove his clothes. DS O'Boyle searched his coat first and discovered that the insides of the pockets had been cut out and it was presumed that this had been done so he could hide his weapons deep within the bottom of the coat lining. When he reached into the lining, DS O'Boyle was surprised to find a pair of underpants. Sutcliffe admitted that they were his and then, as he continued to undress, the reason for them being in his coat became obvious.

As he removed his trousers it became obvious that Sutcliffe was wearing a V-neck sweater, with his legs placed inside the long sleeves and the body of the sweater had been pulled up over his backside so that the V-neck at the front exposed his genitals. Confused, DS O'Boyle asked Sutcliffe why he was wearing a sweater in such a way and Sutcliffe stated that they were 'leg warmers'.

When he took the sweater off, it was examined closely and it was found that the area where Sutcliffe's knees would be had been reinforced with extra padding and it was believed this had been done to protect him as he knelt over his victims and stabbed them or when he knelt on his victim's chest as he strangled them, as had happened in the case of Marguerite Walls.

Exposing his genital area also made it much easier for him to masturbate at the scenes. The garment spoke volumes about his sexual motives and his state of mind during his attacks.

Amazingly, none of the detectives present informed a Senior Investigating Officer of what Sutcliffe had been found to be wearing and none of them documented the find.

Interviews

This piece of information would have proved extremely useful for the prosecution at the later trial to prove that the attacks were sexual in motive, and was only made public knowledge in 2003 in Michael Bilton's book *Wicked Beyond Belief*.

DS Smith later recalled:

> DS O'Boyle then took from Sutcliffe the clothes he was wearing for forensic examination and then he was supplied with a change of clothing. At 4.41 pm the same day I was present in the Detective Sergeants Office at Dewsbury Police Station with DS O'Boyle when DI Boyle formally cautioned and charged the accused Sutcliffe with the murder of Jacqueline Hill. He replied: 'Well, I'm terribly sorry about this tragic loss to her family and friends and I would do anything to alter what has happened. I am glad that I have been apprehended because I was totally out of my mind when I committed this and others acts.' He was also charged with the offence of theft of vehicle registration plates. He made no reply.

Sutcliffe appeared at Dewsbury Magistrates' Court at 16.53. There were close to 2,000 people outside, baying for his blood with chants of 'Die, die, fucking die, you bastard', and others holding placards with 'Hang the Ripper!' printed on them. As the police van approached, people were punching the van and throwing stones and coins at it. Sonia Sutcliffe later described the public's reaction as 'a bit over the top'.

Sonia, flanked by detectives, was the first to get out of the van, followed by her father.

More than 100 journalists were waiting in the packed courtroom when Sutcliffe arrived. No members of the public were allowed in the courtroom but Sonia and her father Bohdan were there as her husband was ushered into the dock by three officers.

The Court Clerk, Dean Gardener, asked: 'Are you Peter William Sutcliffe, of 6 Garden Lane, Heaton, Bradford?' After he confirmed that he was, the Court Clerk continued:

> You are accused that between 16 November and 19 November 1980 you did murder Jacqueline Hill against the peace of our sovereign Lady the Queen. Further, you are charged that at Mirfield, between 13 November and 2 January, you stole two motor vehicle registration plates to the total value of 50p, the property of Cyril Bamforth.

At that point Sonia, who was sitting immediately in front of the dock, turned around and touched Sutcliffe's hand and spoke briefly to him.

The County prosecuting solicitor, Maurice Shaffner, stated that Sutcliffe was not legally represented. Sutcliffe was advised to get legal representation before his next court appearance by the Magistrate, Mr John Walter. Sutcliffe added that he didn't want reporting restrictions lifted.

He was remanded into custody for eight days at Armley Prison in Leeds and when they left the court DS O'Boyle and DI Boyle drove him around Bradford so that he could show them where he had either hidden or thrown away some of the weapons he had used, including the claw hammer he had used to kill Patricia Atkinson. At 17.30 he was taken in a Police car and pointed out the car spares premises at Mirfield from which he had stolen the Skoda number plates the preceding Friday. Sutcliffe then took the officers to the Hartshead Moor Service Station on the M62 in an effort to recover the sharpened Philips screwdriver. However, on arrival there he recognised that he had confused it with the Woolley Edge Service Area on the M1. Sutcliffe was not taken there at this point.

They then went to Bingley Road in Cottingley, close to Sharpe's Printers Limited, where Sutcliffe had said he'd thrown away the claw hammer over a low wall. This was the one he had bought in a hardware shop in Clayton, Bradford, and used to kill Patricia Atkinson and possibly Jayne MacDonald. The police found nothing, but later investigations revealed that in the winter of 1978 or 1979 an elderly groundsman who worked for the printers had found a claw hammer on Bingley Road nearby. He kept it and the police took possession of it on 8 January.

Sutcliffe was then taken home for the last time by DC Alan Foster and DC Martin Pennock, where he pointed out various items of clothing that he had worn during the attacks. By then, Sonia was home too, along with several senior detectives, including Detective Superintendent Dick Holland and Detective Chief Superintendent Jack Ridgeway. Ridgeway later recalled that the house 'was the most sterile place I have ever been in, very inhuman'.

Oddly, as police were examining clothing in his bedroom, Sonia walked upstairs and said her husband could not go off to jail before he had eaten a piece of Christmas cake and had a glass of warm milk.

He was taken back to Dewsbury Police Station where Dr Fraser-Newman took hair samples and fingernail scrapings. He was then taken to Armley Prison and was put into a room by himself in the hospital wing. The room had a shower and Sutcliffe underwent twenty-four-hour-a-day supervision. He was escorted on each outing from the ward and a logbook was kept by prison officers in which they noted anything about the prisoner they thought relevant, including any sign of illness.

When his works' lorry was searched by officers, they found a card taped to the window which read:

IN THIS TRUCK IS A MAN
WHOSE LATENT GENIUS IF
UNLEASHED WOULD ROCK THE
NATION, WHOSE DYNAMIC ENERGY
WOULD OVERPOWER THOSE
AROUND HIM. BETTER LET
HIM SLEEP?

The open field next to Sutcliffe's house on 6 Garden Lane was also thoroughly searched for evidence by police, as Sutcliffe had told them he had burned pieces of bloodstained clothing in a drum there.

The following day, due to a leak in the police department, Peter Sutcliffe was named publicly as the Yorkshire Ripper by some of the newspapers.

Interviews

The story was big news and one man who was happy to speak to the press was Sutcliffe's boss, Thomas Clark. He told the gathered journalists that Sutcliffe was:

> a quiet and sensitive model worker. He was the perfect employee. His only fault was that he was sometimes late for work. If you told him off he would cry rather than have a go back. His eyes would well with tears. He was a really quiet, conscientious and sensitive lad. But to know him socially was impossible.

Another person who was happy to speak to the press was Sonia's mother, Maria. She told the *Daily Express*:

> We just can't believe it was Pete. He is so loving, so generous, so thoughtful. He would do anything for anyone if he could. He would give you a lift in his car, fix your car for you. Nothing was too much trouble for him. There is not a kinder man living under the sun.
>
> Sonia and Pete were so very happy. They lived with us for three years before they bought their house in Garden Lane. We loaned them some money for the purchase and Sonia said it was their castle. It was the home she had dreamed of. They worked so hard to make the house the way they wanted and they repaid all the money, a few thousand pounds, they had borrowed from us.
>
> We just can't believe what they are saying about Peter. I will not believe it even if it comes from his own lips. He couldn't have been capable of committing those terrible things for so many years without giving some secret away, without letting something slip.
>
> Whoever did these things must have a split personality and couldn't possibly live a normal life with such things on their conscience. He was concerned for Sonia and myself. He frequently drove me to hospital, where I work as a nurse, in his car. He said he was worried about me going to work alone at night when it was so dark.
>
> Sonia did not like him being away on his driving job and he worried about her. He told her never to walk out alone at night and to always lock the doors and windows in the house, just in case.
>
> They have been married for six years and they knew each other for six years before that. Sometimes I would say to Sonia that I was worried about Pete going off with another woman. He is a very good looking man and the women went for him, but Sonia said she trusted him completely. She told me, 'Don't worry mum, Pete will never look at another woman.'
>
> I don't believe that he ever did. He loves Sonia so much, they lived through each other. She has spoken to us on the telephone and she is completely shattered. The whole thing is like a bad dream, we can't take it in. She has told us that she will stand by him and she does not believe these things.

Sutcliffe's brother, Mick, also told the newspaper: 'He has been a bit of a tearaway in his time, but since he got married five years ago he's calmed down a lot and I can't believe he'd be guilty of this.' He also told of the death of their mother:

> We were all deeply affected by her death but Peter took it worst. He was very close to his mother and being the eldest boy he was a bit of a favourite. Me and him didn't get on all that well with Dad – we were always scrapping. But Peter was never really in any serious trouble.
>
> ...
>
> The police have had me in several times for questioning about the Ripper murders because I've got form for grievous bodily harm, actual bodily harm and a bit of burglary. But I didn't know they suspected Peter.

Sutcliffe's cousin, Edward Coonan, added: 'Peter was the last person in the world I would have suspected. He always came across as a kind, softly spoken man.'

John Sutcliffe, Peter's father, gave his exclusive interview to the *Daily Mail*. He told how his world fell apart at 08.40 on Monday 5 January when a friend passed him a newspaper carrying the story of the Ripper's arrest. The story contained the name 'Peter Sutcliffe' and the friend joked: 'Is it your brother?' John Sutcliffe replied that he had a son called Peter and then saw the address printed and told his friend, 'Oh my God, it is him!' In a state of shock, he was helped into the manager's office and then driven to his daughter Maureen's home in Bingley.

> Even then I clutched at any hope that a mistake had been made, that the man with the police was not my son. It was absolutely impossible. It could not be the man I knew and loved. One of the foremost thoughts in my mind was for his wife Sonia. What would she be going through? It was all so unreal – my mind was just a whirl. How can you define what goes on at a time like that? It's just impossible.

He said that when he reached Maureen's home she was out taking her young daughter to the dentist. In the house, however, was his younger daughter, Jane. She had been carried to the house in a state of near-collapse having found out the news at work. A doctor was called and she had to be sedated.

He said that they had all recently enjoyed a Sunday Christmas dinner at the house in Garden Lane. Peter and Sonia had invited him, Peter's brothers Carl and Mick, his sisters Jane and Maureen, Jane's boyfriend Eddie, and Maureen's two children.

> It was a lovely, warm, family occasion. As usual, Peter was his attentive self, helping Sonia to prepare the meal, clear the table between courses and then wash and dry the dishes. He wanted to make sure everyone had a good time. He is that kind of boy.
>
> It was a marvellous day. It was everything that Christmas Sunday could possibly be for a happy family. Pete was always great company and on that

day he was in good form, although he drank very little. He loved to joke and have long conversations with the family.

Sonia made a special Continental-type main dish and we had a few drinks and a coffee afterwards. I had a pleasant hour's sleep afterwards while the family watched TV and the kids played on the carpet...

Pete to me was always a model son. He laughed a lot. He was in no way a serious, brooding type of man. Never at any time in his life can I remember any incident taking place which was completely contrary to his usual good nature.

On the Christmas Sunday night, we were leaving about 10.30 pm in two taxis. Pete walked down the driveway of his house with us, helping the children. He kissed the girls and gave me a very warm handshake and wished all of us a Happy New Year. He stood on the curb waving as the taxis pulled away. His wife Sonia was framed in the doorway also waving to us. That was the last I saw of him...

My son was always so placid, so even-tempered. He was a model son, a perfect husband. He always liked a laugh and a joke, never smoked and drank only moderately. A friend of mine who works for the same company as Peter came to me the other day and said: 'That lad of yours, Pete, is a fine hard-working young man and a hell of a nice one.' That's why the whole thing is so unbelievable. I know this is the kind of thing the public would expect a father to say, but if you knew him, you would say the same thing. The whole thing is incredible.

The *Daily Express* then wrote a small article on the effect of Sutcliffe's arrest on the red-light areas in the north of the country. It quoted landlords and detectives, and shockingly stated:

There was a near-carnival atmosphere in the red-light districts of Northern cities last night. 'Almost like the old days,' said publicans on both sides of the Pennines. 'We've not seen so many girls about for ages.' In Manchester's Moss Side, Bradford's Lumb Lane and the Chapeltown area of Leeds, smiling streetwalkers plied their trade in greater numbers than for three or four years. 'It almost reminds you of the January sales,' chuckled a vice squad officer from West Yorkshire police. 'You could say business is booming!'

Meanwhile, in Armley prison, a note in Sutcliffe's logbook read: 'He has need to talk at times and boasts about near-misses with police, e.g. having blood all over his hands and being chased by police. Says does not go out intending to kill but gets compulsions to.'

On 7 January the police felt it was necessary to hold a press conference in order to clarify certain pieces of information which had appeared in the press and media. Nothing was said by the police at that press conference which might impede or prejudice the trial of Sutcliffe. It stated:

Between 5 July 1975 and 17 November 1980, a number of women were either murdered or severely assaulted in various parts of Yorkshire and Lancashire. Detailed examination of the victims by a Home Office Pathologist clearly indicated that the pattern of head injuries present in each case could be attributed to the same or very similar weapons. These offences were grouped together and have been investigated both separately and jointly in what has become known as the 'Yorkshire Ripper Enquiry'.

In all there was a total of 13 murders – 10 in the West Yorkshire area, 2 in Manchester and 1 at Preston in Lancashire. A massive investigation took place and was conducted over the whole of the period by very experienced West Yorkshire detectives...

About midnight on Friday 3 January 1981, two officers, a sergeant and a constable of the South Yorkshire Police, were carrying out normal checks in the so called 'red light' district of Sheffield when they had occasion to question a man who was in a car with a prostitute in a secluded situation. It was discovered that the number plates displayed on the vehicle did not relate to that vehicle. The man was taken into custody when it was discovered that the number plates had been stolen from premises in the West Yorkshire Police Area. The man was handed over to the West Yorkshire Police at Dewsbury in connection with the number plates offence and because he had been found in the company of a prostitute he was later interviewed by detectives from the 'Ripper' enquiry team. The man was eventually identified as Peter William Sutcliffe, 34 years, of 6 Garden Lane, Bradford.

For some time there was nothing to connect Sutcliffe with any of the 'Ripper' offences but when the area in which he had been arrested was later searched, a hammer and a knife were found. This was put to him and he thereupon admitted the responsibility for a number of murders.

Sutcliffe has now made a voluntary statement in which he has admitted a responsibility for 12 of the murders referred to earlier, the only exception being the murder of Joan Mary Harrison which took place at Preston, Lancashire in November 1975. Sutcliffe has been re-questioned by the head of the Lancashire CID but still denies being responsible for that offence.

Peter William Sutcliffe is a married man; there are no children of the union; he is a long distance lorry driver and is a native of Shipley in West Yorkshire. He has no trace of a 'Geordie' accent and denies being the author of either the three letters or the tape recorded message ... He appeared before the Dewsbury Magistrates on the 5 January 1981 charged with the theft of the car number plates and with the murder of Jacqueline Hill at Leeds on the 17 November 1980. He was remanded in custody to Leeds Prison. Arrangements have been made with Sutcliffe's Solicitor that in accordance with the present arrangements he will not appear in Court on each subsequent remand date.

While the investigation now appears to have been successfully concluded there is still a great amount of work to be done and enquiries to be completed before it will be possible to bring this man to trial.

Sutcliffe was visited that afternoon by Sonia. It was noted in his logbook that: 'He said very little, but she never stopped talking.' Sonia then went to stay with her parents in Tanton Crescent.

On 8 January, having been thinking about the events surrounding Sutcliffe's arrest and subsequent time at Hammerton Road Police Station in Sheffield, Sergeant Ring remembered that Sutcliffe had gone to the toilet when he first arrived at the station. He told Detective Inspector Slack and the two of them went to the toilets and found the wooden-handled knife that Sutcliffe had placed in the lavatory.

Sutcliffe was then brought to Dewsbury Police Station to be questioned about it and he admitted that he had concealed the knife in the lavatory cistern, but that he had never used it on any of his victims.

Peter Sutcliffe was then taken back to Armley Prison, where he was visited by Sonia, and his Solicitor, Mr Kerry McGill. Mr John Leach, a Prison Officer, was present during the visit and Sutcliffe told his wife that he was guilty of all the charges and had given the police details. Leach later recalled:

> Mrs Sutcliffe used to run the business in that she used to take the lead very much. She had three pieces of paper with itemised things which she could run through quickly because of the limited times of visits. I think they were just personal matters between Sutcliffe and his wife. They got talking and Sutcliffe said at one stage 'I wouldn't feel any sort of animosity towards you if you decided to make a life of your own because I am going to do a long time in prison, 30 years or more, unless I can convince people in here I am mad and maybe then ten years in the loony bin'.

This was noted down in his logbook.

Denise Hall, the prostitute who had turned Sutcliffe down before he picked up Olivia Reivers, was charged with prostitution. She had been back on the streets and was arrested shortly after turning down a punter in his car. She was bailed to appear in court on 16 February. She told the *Daily Star*: 'I think I have been treated very unfairly, and other people think so, too. I spent all that time helping police and I never complained once. Now they are doing me. It doesn't seem right.'

The following day Sonia visited Sutcliffe again, and Prison Officer John Leach wrote in his logbook: 'A little less frantic than previous visit from his wife but she completely overwhelms and dominates him and the situation.'

On 13 January it was reported that police in Sweden who were investigating the murders of two sex workers in 1980 wanted to interview Sutcliffe. According to a police spokesman in Gothenburg, Interpol had been asked to approach the British police as a matter of urgency. One woman was killed in Gothenburg in August, and the other in Malmo in September.

The next entry in Sutcliffe's logbook (which was later used at his trial) was on 16 January. It stated: 'Something said by wife during visit. She kept asking why he had not informed her of his compulsive thoughts, so he could get medical advice. He told her to leave it to the medical people to find out.'

Two days later, the logbook stated: 'Appears quieter than of late. Reading a lot. Begins talking over experiences. Says it seems as if it was his purpose to do what he did.'

At 10.05 on 18 January, Sutcliffe was interviewed in the presence of his solicitor at Armley Prison by DS Peter Smith and DI Boyle. He was cautioned and reminded of a previous interview with regard to a Phillips screwdriver which he had thrown away, and they asked him if he could show them where he had thrown it. Sutcliffe said that he would. This was the screwdriver used to kill Josephine Whitaker and Barbara Leach that he had ground down into a bradawl.

Accompanied by his solicitor and some Prison Officers, they drove in a prison van at his direction to the Woolley Edge Service Station, off the M1 Motorway (Southbound). There he pointed to an embankment at the side of the lorry park and said: 'That's where I threw it. I was in my lorry.' It was eventually found after an extensive search by Police Officers from the Western Area Task Force.

DI Boyle asked him when he had thrown the screwdriver and he said: 'Sometime last summer.' Sutcliffe was taken back to Armley Prison where, at 11.05, in the presence of his Solicitor, Sutcliffe was interviewed by DI Boyle and DS Smith in the Visitors' Room, where he was again cautioned:

DI Boyle: Was it your own screwdriver or the firm's?

Sutcliffe: It was mine, an old one, I've had it in the garage for a long time.

DI Boyle: Can you describe it?

Sutcliffe: It had a wooden handle with the varnish worn off.

DI Boyle: Have you adapted it in any way?

Sutcliffe: I think I used it as a hole puncher for riveting. I sharpened it up with a grindstone.

DI Boyle: Would that alter the initial shape of the head?

Sutcliffe: Yes, it did, it was no good as it was for that job.

DI Boyle: What shape did it finish up?

Sutcliffe: It ended up sharp at the end.

DI Boyle: What stone did you sharpen it on?

Sutcliffe: Either on the floor in the garage at home or with a Black & Decker carborundum, it altered it from a star shape to like a bradawl.

DI Boyle: Did you use it for work as well?

Sutcliffe: No, I didn't use it for work.

DI Boyle: What was it doing in your cab?

Sutcliffe: I just took it to throw away, that's all. It looked a horrible looking thing...

At 09.50 on 22 January, Sutcliffe was interviewed in Armley Prison by DS Smith and DI Boyle, in the presence of Sutcliffe's solicitor. This was Sutcliffe's first attempts at trying to show the police that he had 'mental' problems. Sutcliffe was told that there were 'a few points which need to be cleared up', before being cautioned.

DI Boyle: You have said you attacked Anna Rogulskyj in Keighley in July 1975 with a hammer. Was that the first?

Sutcliffe: Yes, I'm sure it was.

DI Boyle: Where did you hit her?

Sutcliffe: On the head.

DI Boyle: What were your intentions when you hit her?

Sutcliffe: I think I intended to kill her but as it turned out I didn't.

DI Boyle: How did you come to have a hammer with you at that time?

Sutcliffe: Because I had this idea in mind before that. I think this had developed over a period of time.

DI Boyle: What do you mean?

Sutcliffe: I think it may have started back in 1965/66 when I had an accident on my motorbike. I was with a gang of mates and went up to (the) pub at Eldwick. There was some trouble with a bus load of people from Bradford who were having a party at the pub. We realised we were outnumbered and we rode away. The bikes had been attacked as well, some being knocked over and some had the tyres let down…

DI Boyle: What happened?

Sutcliffe: I ran into a telegraph pole just round a right hand bend about half a mile from the pub going towards Bingley, just above Edward Beck Bottom. I went into this telegraph pole with my head. I was wearing a crash helmet.

DI Boyle: Were you injured?

Sutcliffe: The day after I had a badly bruised head and forehead and face.

DI Boyle: Did you receive any medical treatment at the time or later?

Sutcliffe: At the time I was carried into the nearest house and cleaned up. I've no idea if a doctor saw me then.

DI Boyle: Was an ambulance called?

Sutcliffe: Someone took me home in a vehicle, I can't remember much about it…

DI Boyle: How did the accident affect you?

Sutcliffe: I was left with severe bouts of morbid depression. I used to be subject to hallucinations.

DI Boyle: What kind?

Sutcliffe: Just seeing things that are not there and getting strange noises in my head, humming and buzzing.

DI Boyle: When did they start?

Sutcliffe: I can trace them back to shortly after the accident.

DI Boyle: What effect did this have on you?

Sutcliffe: I used to think I was hearing things and occasionally I'd start conversing with myself.

DI Boyle: In what way?

Sutcliffe: It used to be when I had these sort of attacks. I knew what I was doing but I had this inner conflict.

DI Boyle: About what?

Sutcliffe: My mind was in a haze and I didn't know what was right or wrong. I didn't know whether I was acting rationally or not.

DI Boyle: How often did this occur?

Sutcliffe: Sometimes on average I might get two a month, and other times I might think I was alright, and a few times I thought I was okay and then it would come back, the periods were not regular and there was no pattern to them.

DI Boyle: Did anything trigger these bouts off?

Sutcliffe: I think it was probably linked to the bouts of depression I had and it was possibly then that I had the attacks of buzzing and humming.

DI Boyle: How did these attacks of depression relate to your attacks on prostitutes?

Sutcliffe: I now remember that the incident with a prostitute in Manningham Lane who I gave the £10 to was in 1969 sometime, not as I have previously told you in '74. I remember I had my Morris Minor when I picked her up in Manningham Lane.

DI Boyle: Was it in your mind at that time to cause her any harm?

Sutcliffe: No, I think it was connected with problems with Sonia.

DI Boyle: What do you mean?

Sutcliffe: At that time I was working at the Water Board. I'd been there I think for about a year, she'd started seeing an Italian ice-cream man ... he used to pick her up from the Tech and take her out at night.

DI Boyle: How did you feel about that?

Sutcliffe: I was depressed and upset because I wasn't in a position to do much about it as I worked on shifts and I was on call. I was deeply upset about it.

DI Boyle: Were you jealous?

Sutcliffe: I suppose a bit but I didn't know if anything had happened and I didn't want to lose her. I couldn't concentrate at work, there was one occasion when I went to work I'd been told the night before by my brother ... that he'd seen Sonia and this man ... out together in his Triumph Spitfire car, I'd been there all day with an assistant ... he didn't understand fully the mechanics of the job but I left my post to go and sort out this domestic trouble.

DI Boyle: What happened as a result?

Sutcliffe: I was demoted and got a steady number at the Waterworks base at Gilstead.

DI Boyle: Is this why you picked up the prostitute?

Sutcliffe: I think it had a direct bearing on it. I was wanting to level the score and I thought by just picking her up I wouldn't have reason to judge Sonia going with this man.

DI Boyle: When you picked up the prostitute did you intend having intercourse with her?

Sutcliffe: I thought so at the time, but I changed my mind before I got to the stage where we had to do it.

DI Boyle: You said earlier when first interviewed, that you were duped out of a ten-pound note. What effect did this have on your attitude towards prostitutes?

Sutcliffe: It left me feeling bitter towards them especially when there was a sequel to this with the same person a few weeks later in the Old Crown pub in Bradford.

DI Boyle: What happened?

Sutcliffe: I approached her and said I hadn't forgotten, and she could still give me it back. She flatly refused and started joking about it in a loud voice to someone else who was with her. After this I left the pub feeling humiliated and outraged and embarrassed and I felt a hatred for her and her kind...

DI Boyle: Did this incident lead to an attack on a prostitute in Bradford about this time? We have received information from Trevor Birdsall that you, while out in a car with him, left the vehicle and subsequently attacked a prostitute.

Sutcliffe: That's right.

DI Boyle: What happened?

Sutcliffe: I got out of the car and asked her the time and I hit her.

DI Boyle: What with?

Sutcliffe: A sock with something in it, I can't remember what.

DI Boyle: Why did you do it?

Sutcliffe: I got depressed and was having this trouble with violent headaches and was associating all my troubles and blamed the prostitutes for my problems.

DI Boyle: Were you seen by the police about this incident?

Sutcliffe: Yes.

DI Boyle: What happened?

Sutcliffe: The police visited my parents' home in Bingley, he said he'd traced me through the car, he asked me if I'd hit her with a weapon and I told him I'd used my hand. He said it was possible I had used my hand and gave me a lecture and said the woman was willing not to press any charges.

DI Boyle: Did you hear anything more about the incident?

Sutcliffe: No.

DI Boyle: What was your intention when you attacked this prostitute?

Sutcliffe: I was out of my mind with the obsession about finding this prostitute and I'd been out with Trevor looking out for this particular one and it was getting late. I just gave vent to my anger to the first one I saw...

DI Boyle: Was the first one you killed Wilma McCann in Leeds?

Sutcliffe: Yes.

DI Boyle: What time was it when you picked her up?

Sutcliffe: Maybe 10.00 pm, I'm not sure.

DI Boyle: Where were you going when you saw McCann?

Sutcliffe: To the red-light area.

DI Boyle: What do you call the red-light area?

Sutcliffe: Round the Chapeltown area.

DI Boyle: Where did you actually see McCann?

Sutcliffe: I'd gone under the underpass and taken the A58 Wetherby turn-off and followed this round to the left which continued left on a downhill slope. She was at the bottom of a road where it straightened out, on the left side walking on the grass. She was obviously hoping to get a lift, she said, 'Thanks for stopping', and was cheerful and friendly so I set off and carried on driving and instead of carrying on round to the right she suggested I carried straight on. She remarked something about it being a nice car.

DI Boyle: What were your intentions when you picked her up?

Sutcliffe: I just stopped on impulse to give her a lift as I'd just come round the bend.

DI Boyle: Go on.

Sutcliffe: I'd gone there for the purpose of picking up a prostitute with the intention to kill her. I realised shortly after she had got into the car that she was a prostitute because she asked me if I wanted business, and the evil chain of events went on from there.

DI Boyle: Are the events related in your statement true in relation to McCann?

Sutcliffe: Yes, most of them are but some points need straightening out. I may have given the impression by what I've said to her and what she replied that the intent was to have sex, but this is not the case. This kind of talk was just a preamble leading up to the true purpose of my killing her. It was my idea to get her to go up a distance up the field. To accomplish this, I had to put up with all kinds of language and abuse because she couldn't see the point. I had the tackle with me in my pocket and, in fact, I didn't go back to the car and return it.

DI Boyle: What tackle?

Sutcliffe: A hammer and a kitchen knife. I hit her with the hammer, she still made loud noises and I hit her with it again and the noises still didn't stop. I then took the knife out of my pocket and stabbed her about four times as I've previously described.

DI Boyle: Why did you pull her clothes up and expose her body?

Sutcliffe: So that when they're found they will look as cheap as they are.

DI Boyle: Is there any special significance about the way you have inflicted the injuries or the area in which they have been inflicted?

Sutcliffe: No, because there's been no one particular area. In any case, the main areas are the lungs, the heart and the throat which I thought were areas where it would kill them quicker...

DI Boyle: Was the next one you killed Emily Jackson?

Sutcliffe: Yes.

DI Boyle: Is your account in your voluntary statement of how you killed Emily Jackson correct?

Sutcliffe: Yes, as far as revenge is concerned but not so far as sexual gratification is concerned...

DI Boyle: When you pushed the piece of wood against her vagina, had you opened her legs first?

Sutcliffe: No, but thinking back I may have positioned her to show her as disgusting as she was...

DI Boyle: Was the next one you killed Irene Richardson?

Sutcliffe: Yes.

DI Boyle: Where exactly did you pick her up?

Sutcliffe: On that same estate near where I picked Jackson up, it was near Cowper Street, outside the big club on the corner with the steps leading up.

DI Boyle: How far did you drive to the place you killed her?

Sutcliffe: About a mile and a half to two miles.

DI Boyle: In talking about Richardson, you mentioned some toilets a number of times. Are you sure they were toilets?

Sutcliffe: I'm going by what she seemed to think. There was a building in a field, and it looked like toilets.

DI Boyle: Did you park close to this building?

Sutcliffe: Yes, there's a long approach road to it. I parked on the opposite side of the building from the road.

DI Boyle: You talked about a Stanley knife. Is that what you slashed her with?

Sutcliffe: Yes, I think that's what I had with me at the time.

DI Boyle: Did you use anything else on her?

Sutcliffe: I only remember using a hammer and a Stanley knife.

DI Boyle: Did you move her body at all?

Sutcliffe: If I moved the body at all it was only a couple of feet, it was all at the back of the building.

DI Boyle: Why did you place her boots over her legs before you left her?

Sutcliffe: For two reasons, one because I could hear voices from I don't know where, and a car had just driven into an entrance just behind the building, that was to the block of flats I found out later where Jimmy Savile lived. Secondly, I was surprised to see how luminous she appeared in the dark.

DI Boyle: With regard to Richardson, this was more than a year after you killed Jackson. Why was it so long?

Interviews

Sutcliffe: The main reason really is my state of mind, it seemed okay apart from having a personal battle in my own mind which was in absolute turmoil about whether the right thing was to kill people or not. The next time it happened was like every other time, after some kind of a brainstorm.

DI Boyle: What do you mean by brainstorm?

Sutcliffe: If I ever got into like a morbid depressive state by being over worried by one thing and another, this is when it would lead to a state of hallucination but the only outlets for everything was to brood and blame everything on prostitutes.

DI Boyle: Was the next one you killed Patricia Atkinson at Bradford?

Sutcliffe: Yes…

DI Boyle: You had seen her giving another fellow a hard time. What made you pick her up?

Sutcliffe: I stopped, it was obviously why I picked her up, no decent woman would have been using language like that at the top of her voice.

DI Boyle: Tell us again what you did as you went into her flat.

Sutcliffe: I hung my coat on the door.

DI Boyle: What did you hang it on? There's no hook.

Sutcliffe: I just recall going in and hanging it up. If it wasn't the door, it was on the bed or somewhere near the door because the hammer was in the jacket pocket.

DI Boyle: Which jacket?

Sutcliffe: The brown car coat the police have got. The reason I took the coat off was so she wouldn't see the hammer.

DI Boyle: After you'd hit her on the floor, how did you get her on the bed?

Sutcliffe: I just picked her up under the arms and hoisted her up.

DI Boyle: Did you stand on the bed to do this?

Sutcliffe: No.

He was then shown a claw hammer.

DI Boyle: This was found near where you say you threw a hammer away, could this be the one you used on Atkinson?

Sutcliffe: Yes, that is the very same one.

DI Boyle: Is that the claw hammer you say you purchased from a hardware shop at Clayton?

Sutcliffe: Yes.

DI Boyle: Did you use this hammer on any other killing?

Sutcliffe: I can't say for sure.

DI Boyle: Why did you hit her with the claw end of the hammer?

Sutcliffe: Because I don't think I had any other weapon with me.

DI Boyle: What sort of injuries did that cause?

Sutcliffe: The claw of the hammer caused similar injuries to a knife like a gash or something...

Sutcliffe was shown an old screwdriver with a pointed end.

DI Boyle: This was recovered from the place you indicated at Woolley Edge Service Station. Is this the implement you referred to?

Sutcliffe: Yes.

DI Boyle: In which incident did you use this?

Sutcliffe: In the incident involving Barbara Leach in Bradford and Josephine Whitaker at Halifax.

DI Boyle: You refer to it in your statement as originally having been a Phillips screwdriver. Are you sure about that?

Sutcliffe: Yes, I am, it was a giant Phillips screwdriver having been badly worn and been converted into a bradawl.

DI Boyle: Have you modified or altered any other tools to use them as weapons on attacks on women?

Sutcliffe: I've not modified any tool for that purpose.

He was then shown a ball pein hammer.

DI Boyle: This ball pein hammer was found apparently secreted behind timber in a garage at your home. Has this been used to attack a woman?

Sutcliffe: It may have been because I kept them together, I don't choose one, I just pick one up...

When DS Smith asked Sutcliffe about the knife found in the lavatory cistern at the Sheffield Police Station, Sutcliffe said: 'I threw it in there. I went there straight away as soon as I got to the police station. I dropped it in the top of the water cistern so it wouldn't be found in my possession.'

Sutcliffe also told DS Smith that when he was questioned by police prior to his arrest, 'Sonia automatically gave me an alibi on the occasions I was questioned. These occasions were weeks, sometimes months after the event. My wife would agree that we were at home, as we were practically all of the time.'

Sutcliffe told DS Smith about his cars being spotted in the red-light areas of Leeds, Bradford and Manchester. None of the sightings coincided with any of the killings. The police put it to him that on these occasions he was 'touring round these areas seeking to do a prostitute harm.' Sutcliffe said: 'It is quite obvious there were occasions when I did not see any prostitutes. After a certain length of time if I didn't see any prostitutes I would go home. It was my intention to get rid of the prostitutes at any cost.'

It was around this time that one of the detectives working on the case, Detective Sergeant Edward Dodsworth, tried to sell details of the Ripper investigation to the press. The 35-year-old telephoned freelance journalist Malcolm Hoddy and suggested to him that the information he had was worth £1,000. Instead of publishing the information, Malcolm Hoddy contacted the police, and a sting operation was set up.

Hoddy, wearing a concealed microphone, met DS Dodsworth in a local pub where police officers in a car outside heard the detective name two well-known figures who had been questioned by the 'Ripper Squad'. He also named a well-known actor who had given information about a man he suspected. As Dodsworth left the pub, he was arrested by the waiting officers.

At court on 27 May, DS Dodsworth, who said he had offered the information because he was hard-up for money and living beyond his means, was fined £750 and ordered to pay £400 costs.

On 26 January DS Smith and DI Boyle interviewed Sutcliffe in the hospital at Leeds Prison in the presence of his solicitor, Kerry McGill, in a continuation from the previous interview.

DI Boyle: Did you kill Jayne MacDonald?

Sutcliffe: Yes.

DI Boyle: When you dragged her to the yard after the initial attack was she face down all the time?

Sutcliffe: I think she was.

DI Boyle: You say you stabbed her in the back and the chest. Which came first?

Sutcliffe: I think the chest first, but I don't remember clearly stabbing her in the back, I just thought I did.

DI Boyle: Did you stab her before starting to drag her?

Sutcliffe: I don't think so, no.

DI Boyle: Did you put something into one of the wounds after you stabbed her?

Sutcliffe: No.

DI Boyle: Did you attack Maureen Long at Bradford?

Sutcliffe: Yes.

DI Boyle: Has it been your habit to try to get money back you have paid to prostitutes?

Sutcliffe: No, I think in most cases I have acted before it got to that stage...

DI Boyle: Did you kill Yvonne Pearson at Bradford?

Sutcliffe: I did.

DI Boyle: Is the version of that incident in your statement correct?

Sutcliffe: Yes.

DI Boyle: Before you covered her up, did you place something between her legs?

Sutcliffe: No, I don't think so.

DI Boyle: You describe the instrument on that occasion as a walling hammer. What do you mean by a walling hammer?

Sutcliffe: It's like a lump hammer, a long oblong block on a nine-inch shaft...

DI Boyle: What happened to that hammer?

Sutcliffe: I honestly couldn't say, I thought it was in the garage.

DI Boyle: Did you kill Elena Rytka at Huddersfield?

Sutcliffe: Yes.

DI Boyle: Is the version about the killing of Rytka in your statement correct?

Sutcliffe: Not exactly, as I confused certain aspects of this with the killing of Richardson in Leeds.

DI Boyle: What happened with Rytka?

Sutcliffe: From the outset the one purpose I had in mind was to kill her at the first opportunity, but things were made difficult from the moment I parked the car because Helen unfastened her trousers and seemed prepared to start straight away. It was very awkward for me to find a way of getting her out of the car. We were there five minutes or more while I was trying to decide which method to use to kill her. Meanwhile, against my wishes she was in the process of arousing me sexually. I found I did not want to go through with this, so I got out of the car on the pretext of wanting to urinate.

DI Boyle: Did she have a Durex ready for use?

Sutcliffe: Not to my knowledge.

DI Boyle: What do you mean about trying to arouse you sexually?

Sutcliffe: This she had done to my distaste by manipulating my penis with her hands.

Interviews

DI Boyle: Carry on.

Sutcliffe: I didn't urinate, but I managed to persuade her to get out as well as we'd be better off in the back of the car. As she was attempting to get in I realised this was my chance, so I hit her from behind on the head with the hammer. Unfortunately, during the downward swing the hammer caught the top edge of the door frame and gave her a very light tap on her head. She apparently thought I had struck her with my left hand, and she said, 'There no need for that, you don't even have to pay.' I expected her to immediately shout for help as there were a couple of taxis in view about a distance of forty yards or so.

DI Boyle: How do you know they were taxis?

Sutcliffe: I was sure they were taxis because one of them appeared to have a taxi sign on the roof.

DI Boyle: Was the taxi sign lit?

Sutcliffe: Yes.

DI Boyle: Were the taxi lights on?

Sutcliffe: The side lights were on.

DI Boyle: Carry on.

Sutcliffe: She was obviously very scared. I then pushed her forward onto the ground and she stumbled and fell somewhere in front of the car just out of sight of the taxi drivers. I jumped on top of her and covered her mouth with my hand, it seemed like an eternity, and she was struggling. I told her if she kept quiet, she would be alright. As she had got me aroused less than a minute previously, I had no alternative than to go ahead with the act of sex as the only means thereby of persuading her to keep quiet as I had already dropped the hammer several yards away. After what seemed like several more minutes I got up and saw that the cars had gone so I started to grope around looking for the hammer. I found it and as I was turning towards her, she tried to run past between me and the car, this is when I hit her a heavy blow to the head.

DI Boyle: Where was the blow?

Sutcliffe: I think it was to the back of her head. I then dragged her back in front of the car and may have hit her again before I dragged her back. I began gathering her belongings and throwing them over a wall.

DI Boyle: Had you taken her jeans and pants off before having intercourse?

Sutcliffe: She'd pulled them down and I pulled them off her ankles and threw them over a wall with her shoes and her bag.

DI Boyle: Carry on.

Sutcliffe: She was obviously still alive then. I took the knife from the front of the car and stabbed her several times in the heart and the lungs.

DI Boyle: What kind of knife?

Sutcliffe: I think it was a kitchen knife.

DI Boyle: Where is it now?

Sutcliffe: I think it was later retrieved by the police from my home.

DI Boyle: What happened then?

Sutcliffe: After this I pulled her to a place a few yards away where I thought she wouldn't be found so quickly. When I got there, I covered her with a sheet of asbestos or corrugated metal.

DI Boyle: Is your account of how you concealed the body and what you were wearing on that occasion as you describe in your statement correct?

Sutcliffe: It's as correct as far as I can remember it to be.

DI Boyle: When you picked Rytka up which way did you travel to the wood yard?

Sutcliffe: Downhill and turned left along a bottom road which I think was below the wood yard and turned sharp right into a cul-de-sac in the wood yard.

DI Boyle: Did you take any money or any other articles from Rytka when you left her?

Sutcliffe: No...

DI Boyle: Did you attack a girl called Uphadya Bandara at Headingly, Leeds on the evening of 24 September 1980?

Sutcliffe: Yes...

DI Boyle: What were your intentions when you attacked Bandara?

Sutcliffe: I think my intentions were to kill her. At this point I want to say that in myself I didn't want to kill any of them, it was just something that had to be done.

DI Boyle: How long had you been in the vicinity before you attacked her?

Sutcliffe: About five minutes or so.

DI Boyle: Did you ask anyone for directions at any time that evening?

Sutcliffe: No.

DI Boyle: What were you wearing at that time?

Sutcliffe: I think I had that brown car coat on, I'm not sure what shoes I had on, it may have been some black boots.

DI Boyle: Which hammer did you use on her?

Sutcliffe: I'm not sure, I can't remember which one.

DI Boyle: Did you put her handbag in or on a dustbin?

Sutcliffe: I can't remember whether I lifted the lid up or not.

DI Boyle: Was it your intention to hide the body behind the dustbin?

Sutcliffe: To move her out of sight of the road, yes...

DI Boyle: Has the ball pein hammer we recovered from Sheffield actually been used for attacks on women?

Sutcliffe: I think it's been used before but I'm not sure when.

DI Boyle: What about the kitchen knife found at Sheffield with the hammer?

Sutcliffe: That's not been used before.

DI Boyle: Were there some other occasions when other people were sat in your car waiting while you went off and attacked women?

Sutcliffe: No, only those two occasions with Birdsall.

DI Boyle: Other people, David and Ronnie Barker, tell us that you have been with them visiting red light districts in Leeds, Bradford, Halifax, York and Manchester. What was your purpose in all these visits?

Sutcliffe: Just simply we went out for a few drinks which was rarely.

DI Boyle: One of these other people claims to have record of some occasions when you were out together. Three of those occasions coincide with dates of offences you have admitted. The first is 14 of August 1975 when you are said to be out drinking with a group of people in Bingley. Do you recall that?

Sutcliffe: No.

DI Boyle: Another was on the 25 of June, the very night you say you killed Jayne MacDonald in Leeds. On that night had you been drinking in pubs and clubs in Bradford with some friends before you went to Leeds?

Sutcliffe: I'm not sure of these days, I don't remember anything but these killings. I doubt it as I only used to go out on odd nights...

DI Boyle: Apart from drinking, what did you do on these nights out with your friends?

Sutcliffe: We usually had a game of snooker.

DI Boyle: They say you were out looking at and chatting up prostitutes. Is that true?

Sutcliffe: I had done this on occasions but not for that purpose, only to pass comment on them or remark if I saw one.

DI Boyle: Did anything happen when you were out with these friends which led you to go on later and attack women?

Sutcliffe: No.

DI Boyle: On previous occasions you were interviewed by the police regarding your movements on certain murder dates. You accounted for your movements and gave your wife as alibi. It is now obvious that your wife was not in a position to alibi you for the dates in question.

Sutcliffe: On the occasions when I was asked for an alibi and named my wife as someone who could verify this I must stress that these occasions were usually weeks, sometimes months after the particular event and in this case I was able to satisfy the police because my wife would automatically agree that we would have been home as we were practically all the time anyway.

There was then a break for refreshments before the interview resumed at 15.45 – and Sutcliffe admitted to the murder of Marguerite Walls and the attack on Marcella Claxton.

DI Boyle: I wish to put another matter to you and that is the murder of Marguerite Walls at Pudsey on the evening of 20 August 1980. This woman was attacked from behind and killed in circumstances which appear identical to the attack on Bandara which you have already admitted, and I believe you are responsible for killing Walls.

Sutcliffe: Yes, this is true, I did.

DI Boyle: Will you tell us what happened?

Sutcliffe: I was on my way to Leeds with a view of killing a prostitute when I saw that this woman was walking towards me at a distance of about sixty yards. She disappeared around a corner on my left, so I slowed down and turned into this particular road. I was already in some kind of a rage, and it was just unfortunate for her that she was where she was at the time 'cos I parked the car and got out and followed her along the road. Having caught up with her over a distance of three or four hundred yards, I let her have it with a hammer. I hit her on the head. It seems as though there was a voice inside my head saying 'kill, kill, kill' and as I hit her, I shouted, 'You filthy prostitute.' There was nobody else about but as she was on the pavement I dragged her inside a gateway quite a few yards in what appeared to be someone's garden. Round about this time somebody walked past the entrance. I don't know whether they had seen me or not because they appeared to look in. I didn't have a knife on me this time, but I had a length of cord which I strangled her with. I removed her clothes and

I was going to leave her in an obvious position for people to see but round about this time the road outside started to be quite busy with pedestrians going back and forth. I changed my mind and covered her up with some straw instead.

DI Boyle: Where did you finally place her body?

Sutcliffe: In the far corner of the garden near a wall. I was very upset again after this time; I knew I couldn't do anything to prevent myself carrying on killing. The inner torment was unimaginable because as strange as it may seem I never wanted to kill anybody at all, I just had to get rid of all the prostitutes whether I liked it or not.

DI Boyle: Was it the same ligature used on Walls as you did on Bandara later?

Sutcliffe: Yes, I think it was most likely the same piece of rope.

DI Boyle: Are you sure?

Sutcliffe: It may possibly have been a different piece.

DI Boyle: Why didn't you tell us about this killing before?

Sutcliffe: Because when I was questioned initially, I knew I was in such deep water through killing through the method I normally use that this would possibly open completely new lines of enquiry into other murders which could have been committed and which I knew I hadn't done. I thought that maybe it would be better to sort this out at a later date when I had cleared up all the other matters and having denied it first it would have made matters worse at the time if I had changed my mind again. Nothing I would have said could have been taken seriously. This is why I'm making a true account of everything and every detail.

DI Boyle: Why did you change your method of killing?

Sutcliffe: Because the press and the media had attached a stigma to me, I had been known for some time as the Yorkshire Ripper which to my mind didn't ring true at all. It was just my way of killing them but actually I found that the method of strangulation was even more horrible and took longer.

DI Boyle: Even so you repeated this method on Bandara.

Sutcliffe: This is when I decided I couldn't kill people like this. I couldn't bear to go through with it again as there was something deep inside preventing me.

DI Boyle: Which hammer did you use on Walls?

Sutcliffe: I think it was the one with the piece of wood missing from the handle that you recovered from Sheffield, or the one you found in the garage.

DI Boyle: What were you wearing when you killed Walls?

Sutcliffe: The same brown car coat and some brown cord trousers and black boots that you've taken from the house.

He was then asked about another matter, and replied:

Sutcliffe: No, but there's another one I've remembered, a woman in Leeds who I attacked in Soldiers' Field, who I intended to kill.

DI Boyle: When was this?

Sutcliffe: I think it was 1976. I'm a bit vague on it.

DI Boyle: Tell me what happened.

Sutcliffe: I picked her up in the Chapeltown area, she asked me if I was the police. I said 'No, do I really look like a policeman?' She decided to get into the car and suggested where we go. We ended up in what I knew later as Soldiers' Field. We got out of the car at my suggestion, and she took off her trousers while leaning against a tree and she sat down on the grass and suggested we started the ball rolling. Straight after she said this, I hit her with the hammer. Again, I don't know what it was this time but I just couldn't go through with it, I could not bring myself to hit her again for some reason or another and I just let her walk away, possibly to tell the nearest policeman or passer-by what had happened. I went back to the car in a stupefied state of mind. I just had a feeling of morbid depression. I didn't care whether she told anybody or not and I drove back home.

DI Boyle: How many times did you hit her?

Sutcliffe: Only once I think.

DI Boyle: Did you hit her on the front or back of the head?

Sutcliffe: Possibly from the back.

DI Boyle: On 9 May 1976, a woman, Marcella Claxton, was attacked in Soldiers' Field, Leeds in circumstances similar to what you describe. We have evidence she was struck more than once on the head and received some severe head injuries. Does this incident fit in with your recollection?

Sutcliffe: Yes, that's the one but I only recall hitting her once, as she got up and walked away, but owing to my state of mind I'm not sure whether I hit her more than once.

DI Boyle: What vehicle were you using on that occasion?

Sutcliffe: My white Corsair.

DI Boyle: Have you any recollection of the clothing you were wearing?

Sutcliffe: No, none at all.

Interviews

Sutcliffe was further interviewed regarding other matters, following which DI Boyle said to him:

> **DI Boyle:** I asked you earlier if you were the author of the letters and tape sent to Mr Oldfield and the media purporting to be the Yorkshire Ripper. Do you still say you have no knowledge of these?
>
> **Sutcliffe:** Yes, I've no knowledge and it is not part of my attitude as I'm not proud of doing any of the murders and I did not want to do them as I've already said.

Two days later, on 28 January 1981, an entry in Sutcliffe's prison logbook stated: 'Talkative, but only about crimes and any possible trial outcome. Has no intention of disclosing anything about himself when not involved in crimes. Now says he was possessed when he committed offences.'

This was Sutcliffe trying to convince everyone that he had committed the murders and attacks because of some kind of mental illness. He began to tell anyone who would listen that he had heard the voice of God talking to him one day in 1966 when he was a gravedigger and that it was this voice that was telling him to kill prostitutes.

The next known entry was on 10 February, where the logbook stated:

> Talkative tonight, especially about prisoners on D-Wing calling and shouting to each other from windows and an extremely noisy cockroach outside. Quite cheerful talking about trying to rid country of prostitutes and the merits of our police force. Very talkative. Spoke about when gravedigger and used to hear voices which he was convinced came from the grave. One occasion heard voice from Polish tomb. Eyes open very wide and seemed to gleam – obviously when he reached points of conversation interesting to him.

Sutcliffe was again interviewed by DS Smith and DI Boyle at Leeds Prison in the presence of his solicitor, Mr. McGill. The time was 15.30.

> **DI Boyle:** I have a number of lengths of rope which have been recovered variously from your home and garage. I want you to assist me in identifying them.

He was then shown a piece of rope recovered from a garage at his former home of 44 Tanton Crescent.

> **DI Boyle:** Do you recognise that?
>
> **Sutcliffe:** Never seen it before.

Rope in a noose, recovered from Sutcliffe's lorry:

> **Sutcliffe:** I don't think I recognise that one, but I use ropes all the time to pull engines out.

Rope with length of twine attached:

> **Sutcliffe:** That's a piece of lifting rope, I had two or three in the garage and the twine would stop it slipping.

Length of rope knotted at each end recovered from his garage:

> **Sutcliffe:** Yes, I've seen that one before, that's one of mine, I've held the car boot down with it and used it to carry an engine.

Rope recovered from his bedroom:

> **Sutcliffe:** I can't recognise that one.

Rope recovered from his garage:

> **Sutcliffe:** That's a lifting piece for lifting engines out.

Rope also recovered from the garage:

> **Sutcliffe:** That's another piece I've used for lifting engines.

He was shown a piece of pink and blue cord found in his possession when arrested in Sheffield:

> **DI Boyle:** Do you recognise this?
>
> **Sutcliffe:** That's a piece of rope I used for the Bandara and Walls incident. I think I used the same rope on both but I'm not hundred per cent sure.
>
> **DI Boyle:** Have you used any of the other pieces of rope I've shown you as ligatures to attack women?
>
> **Sutcliffe:** No.
>
> **DI Boyle:** Have you used any pieces of rope or wire as ligatures and thrown them away?
>
> **Sutcliffe:** I'm certainly not aware of having thrown any away.

He was shown a knife with a black wooden handle which they had recovered from the Sunbeam Rapier he used to own:

> **DI Boyle:** Has that knife been used by you on any attacks on women?
>
> **Sutcliffe:** I think that's certainly the same size as the one I used on MacDonald, but I can't be certain.
>
> **DI Boyle:** Did you put that knife in the Rapier?

Sutcliffe: I'm not certain but it looks like the knife I used when I fitted the carpets in the car.

DI Boyle: Can you remember when you fitted the carpets in the car?

Sutcliffe: Maybe two or three months after I got the car because I remember water getting in and making the old carpet wet and mouldy.

He was then shown a ball pein hammer:

DI Boyle: This hammer was found on some waste land adjoining your home about three months ago. Is it one of yours?

Sutcliffe: No, I've never seen it before. It's got a funny shaped shaft.

He was shown a handbag and a black Sim Luxe cigarette lighter:

DI Boyle: These were found on a tip at Bingley about eighteen months ago… together with some bloodstained overalls. Have you seen these before?

Sutcliffe: No.

DI Boyle: Do you ever wear rings on your fingers?

Sutcliffe: Only if I get dressed up to go out somewhere special.

DI Boyle: What rings do you possess?

Sutcliffe: Two gold rings, one with a red stone in it.

DI Boyle: Where are they now?

Sutcliffe: They're at home on the chest of drawers.

DI Boyle: In your statement relating to the murder of Jean Jordan at Manchester, you stated you were wearing a pair of old casual grey trousers and a pair of soft slip-on shoes dark brown colour. Are those shoes still in existence?

Sutcliffe: Yes. The police have taken them away from my house. I pointed them out, they were in a wardrobe in the bedroom.

DI Boyle: With regard to your statement regarding the Richardson murder, can you tell me how far the couple you saw sitting on a bench were away from the point you attacked Richardson?

Sutcliffe: I saw them when I was driving away down the road, they could have been about 50 yards away.

DI Boyle: You say in your statement regarding Richardson that you went to Leeds after closing time, can you be more precise about the time?

Sutcliffe: No, but she said she was going to the club, so I presume the pubs were shut.

DI Boyle: Do you ever wear a cap or a hat?

Sutcliffe: Occasionally.

DI Boyle: What kind?

Sutcliffe: A soft one like an Army type hat.

DI Boyle: A brown knitted hat has been found in your Rover and a green hat in the Mini. Are they yours?

Sutcliffe: Yes, they're mine.

DI Boyle: Between June 1978 and November 1979 there are reported sightings of your red Corsair PHE 366G, black Sunbeam Rapier NKU 888H, and brown Rover FHY 400K, on a large number of occasions predominantly in the prostitute areas of Bradford and on a few occasions in the prostitute areas of Leeds and on one occasion in Manchester, at times which indicate to us that you were not journeying home from your employment, and there are a number of occasions when your vehicles were sighted in these areas at different times on the same dates. These sightings do not coincide with any of the murder dates, and I put it to you that on these occasions you were touring around these prostitute areas seeking to do a prostitute harm.

Sutcliffe: Well, it's quite obvious there were occasions when I didn't see any prostitutes and that would warrant return trips over the same route. After a certain length of time if I didn't see any I would go back home.

DI Boyle: What was your intention on these visits?

Sutcliffe: It was my intention to get rid of prostitutes at any cost.

On 20 February 1981, at Dewsbury Magistrates' Court, Sutcliffe was committed for trial accused of thirteen murders (Wilma McCann, Emily Jackson, Irene Richardson, Patricia Atkinson, Jayne McDonald, Jean Jordan, Yvonne Pearson, Helen Rytka, Vera Millward, Josephine Whitaker, Barbara Leach, Marguerite Walls and Jacqueline Hill) and seven attempted murders (Anna Rogulskyj, Olive Smelt, Marcella Claxton, Maureen Long, Marilyn Moore, Uphadya Bandara and Teresa Sykes), and the case was transferred to Leeds Crown Court. The prosecution requested, and the magistrates agreed, to the withdrawal of one charge of the theft of number plates worth 50p.

No charges were ever brought for the attacks on Gloria Wood, Tracy Browne, Rosemary Stead, Maureen Hogan, Debra Schlesinger, Carol Wilkinson, the students, Ann Rooney, Yvonne Mysliwiec or Mo Lea.

Epilogue

Having been charged, Peter Sutcliffe decided that he didn't much fancy spending the rest of his life in a prison cell. He quickly came up with a plan – that he was acting under the guidance of God to eliminate prostitutes and that was why he had murdered, or attempted to murder, those women with whom he was charged. He would stick to this story for the rest of his life. So convincing was he to some, that he managed to persuade various psychologists that he was telling the truth.

This was to be his defence when his trial began at the Old Bailey in London on Tuesday 5 May 1981, where he pleaded guilty to the manslaughter of thirteen women on the grounds of diminished responsibility, and guilty to the attempted murder on seven further women. The fact that his trial began just four months after his arrest shows how desperate the police were, by accepting the plea of manslaughter, to get Sutcliffe convicted and imprisoned and hope that the public would not question their investigation too thoroughly. Normally, a case of multiple homicide would take anywhere from eighteen months to two years to come to trial, allowing both prosecution and defence counsel to fully prepare.

As it was, the trial was to last less than three weeks and it became more a case of the psychologists who had believed Sutcliffe's story of obeying God's instructions being on trial, rather than Sutcliffe himself.

At 16.15 on Friday 22 May 1981 Peter William Sutcliffe was found guilty of thirteen counts of murder and seven counts of attempted murder by a majority of ten to two.

Bibliography

Beattie, John, *The Yorkshire Ripper Story* Quartet/Daily Star, London
Bilton, Michael, *Wicked Beyond Belief* Harper Press, London
Bowen, David, *Body of Evidence* Constable, London
Burn, Gordon, *Somebody's Husband, Somebody's Son* Faber and Faber, London
Clark, Chris and Tate, Alan, *Yorkshire Ripper The Secret Murders* John Blake, London
Clarkson, Mark *The Beast of Bingley* Self published
Cobb, Richard Charles, *On The Trail of the Yorkshire Ripper*, Pen & Sword Books, Barnsley
Cross, Roger, *The Yorkshire Ripper* Harper Collins, London
Hellawell, Keith, *The Outsider* Harper Collins, London
Kinsley, Peter & Smyth, Frank, *I'm Jack* Pan Books, London
Jones, Barbara, *Voices From an Evil God* Blake, London
Lee, Carol Ann, *Somebody's Mother, Somebody's Daughter* Michael O'Mara Books Limited, London
Lea, Mo, *Facing the Yorkshire Ripper* Pen & Sword Books, Barnsley
Perrie, Robin & James, Alfie *I'm the Yorkshire Ripper (Conversations with a killer)* Mirror Books, London
Yallop, David *Deliver Us From Evil* Corgi Books, London

Files accessed at the National Archives: BN 119/4, DPP2/7405, DPP2/7428-36, DPP2/39-44, HO 287/2844, HO 287/2925, HO 287/3228, HO 287/3275, RF 6-9-1 & RF 6-9-2.

Coming in Part 2 – The Trial, Imprisonment and Death of The Yorkshire Ripper

In *The Trial, Imprisonment and Death of the Yorkshire Ripper*, the way in which Peter Sutcliffe changed his defence after being charged with thirteen murders and seven attempted murders is shown in full – and how he was caught out.

The trial at the Old Bailey in London is explored in full, with transcripts showing how the prosecution counsel were able to demonstrate that Sutcliffe had possibly lied to the psychologists, rendering their diagnosis of paranoid schizophrenia null and void.

Having then been found guilty of thirteen counts of murder and seven counts of attempted murder, you will follow Sutcliffe through the various prisons and mental health hospitals that he stayed in until his death. The mental conditions he claimed to suffer from, as well as the various attacks he suffered in incarceration, are fully explored.

The murderer of Joan Harrison, so long believed to be a victim of the Yorkshire Ripper, is also exposed, as is man with the Sunderland accent who sent the letters and tape to the detectives and press claiming responsibility for the murders and attacks that Sutcliffe was carrying out – John Humble.